UNDERSTANDING CRIME STATISTICS

In *Understanding Crime Statistics*, James P. Lynch and Lynn A. Addington draw on the work of leading experts on U.S. crime statistics to provide much-needed research on appropriate use of these statistics. Specifically, the contributors explore issues surrounding divergence in the Uniform Crime Reports (UCR) and the National Crime Victimization Survey (NCVS), which have been the two major indicators of the level and of the change in level of crime in the United States for the past 30 years. This book examines recent changes in the UCR and the NCVS and assesses the effect these have had on divergence. By focusing on divergence, the authors encourage readers to think about how these data systems filter the reality of crime. *Understanding Crime Statistics* builds on this discussion of divergence to explain how the two data systems can be used as they were intended – in complementary rather than competitive ways.

James P. Lynch is coauthor (with Albert D. Biderman) of *Understanding Crime Incidence Statistics: Why the UCR Diverges from the NCS* and (with Rita J. Simon) of *Immigration the World Over: Statutes, Policies, and Practices*. He has published in many journals, including *Criminology, Journal of Quantitative Criminology*, and *Justice Quarterly*.

Lynn A. Addington's recent work has appeared in the *Journal of Quantitative Criminology* and *Homicide Studies* and has been supported by grants from the American Education Research Association (National Center for Education Statistics – National Science Foundation), the American Statistical Association, the Bureau of Justice Statistics, and the National Institute of Justice.

D0874947

CAMBRIDGE STUDIES IN CRIMINOLOGY

Edited by

Alfred Blumstein, *H. John Heinz School of Public Policy and Management,*
   Carnegie Mellon University

David Farrington, *Institute of Criminology*

Other books in the series:

(*continued after the Index*)

Understanding Crime Statistics

Revisiting the Divergence of the NCVS and UCR

Edited by

James P. Lynch
John Jay College of Criminal Justice

Lynn A. Addington
American University

CAMBRIDGE
UNIVERSITY PRESS

CAMBRIDGE UNIVERSITY PRESS
Cambridge, New York, Melbourne, Madrid, Cape Town, Singapore, São Paulo

Cambridge University Press
32 Avenue of the Americas, New York, NY 10013-2473, USA

www.cambridge.org
Information on this title: www.cambridge.org/9780521862042

First published 2007

Printed in the United States of America

A catalog record for this publication is available from the British Library.

Library of Congress Cataloging in Publication Data

Understanding crime statistics : revisiting the divergence of the NCVS and
UCR / edited by James P. Lynch, Lynn A. Addington.
     p.   cm. – (Cambridge studies in criminology)
Includes bibliographical references and index.
ISBN-13: 978-0-521-86204-2 (hardback)
ISBN-10: 0-521-86204-3 (hardback)
ISBN-13: 978-0-521-68041-7 (pbk.)
ISBN-10: 0-521-68041-7 (pbk.)
1. Criminal statistics – United States – Evaluation.   I. Lynch, James P.
(James Patrick), 1949–   II. Addington, Lynn A., 1967–   III. Title.   IV. Series.
HV6787.U52   2007
364.97301'5195 – dc22   2006016380

ISBN-13   978-0-521-86204-2 hardback
ISBN-10   0-521-86204-3 hardback

ISBN-13   978-0-521-68041-7 paperback
ISBN-10   0-521-68041-7 paperback

Contents

SOURCES OF DIVERGENCE IN THE UCR

CONCLUSION

Acknowledgments

This book would not have been possible without the active encouragement and support of Alfred Blumstein. For more than 30 years, Al has appreciated the importance of crime statistics for building data-driven policy in the area of crime and justice and has worked to ensure that these data are both available to researchers and of high quality.

The idea for this book arose from a 2004 conference, "Understanding Crime Statistics: Revisiting the Divergence of the NCVS and the UCR," which was sponsored by the National Consortium of Violence Research (NCOVR). In addition to NCOVR, American University provided space and logistical support for the meeting. We appreciate the contributions from both of these organizations to this important work. Most of the authors in this volume presented the first draft of their papers at this conference. These preliminary studies benefited from insightful comments by other conference attendees, specifically David Cantor, Laura Dugan, Janet Lauritsen, William J. Sabol, and Brian Wiersema. Most of all, we are thankful to the contributors to this volume for the quality of their initial work and for their perseverance through the editorial process.

Finally, we would like to acknowledge the extensive influence of Albert Biderman and his contribution to this collection of scholarship and to crime statistics more generally. Al passed away in 2003, but he left us with an extensive catalog of research spanning decades as well as a rich resource in his book *Understanding Crime Incidence Statistics: Why the UCR Diverges from the NCS*. These resources provided us with a strong foundation upon which to build this volume. His unique and forward-thinking ideas more than anyone else's have shaped – and continue to shape – crime statistics in the United States. We hope that current and future generations of criminologists and crime statisticians do not squander Al's legacy.

Contributor Biographies

Lynn A. Addington is an assistant professor of justice, law, and society at American University in Washington, D.C. She holds a Ph.D. in criminal justice from the University at Albany, State University of New York, and a J.D. from the University of Pennsylvania Law School. Her research interests include the nature of violent crime and its impact on adolescent victims, measurement of crime, and utilization of national crime statistics. Her recent work concerning measurement of crime has appeared in outlets such as the *Journal of Quantitative Criminology* and *Homicide Studies.*

Cynthia Barnett-Ryan is a survey statistician with the Crime Analysis, Research, and Development Unit of the Federal Bureau of Investigation's Uniform Crime Reporting (UCR) Program. She has been a part of the FBI UCR Program since 1997. In her capacity as a survey statistician, she is responsible for conducting criminal justice research and analysis on behalf of the FBI. Barnett-Ryan's research interests include UCR issues and their impact on crime statistics, as well as rural crime, regional effects on crime, hate crime, and the National Incident-Based Reporting System. She is a graduate of West Virginia University with a master's degree in applied social research and a bachelor's degree in anthropology from Washington University, St. Louis, Missouri.

Shannan M. Catalano received her doctorate in criminology and criminal justice from the University of Missouri–St. Louis in 2004. Since 2003, she has worked as a statistician in the Victimization Statistics Unit at the Bureau of Justice Statistics in Washington, D.C. She is the

Although the general principle of complementarity is widely accepted, criminologists and social statisticians have yet to identify specifically which components of the crime problem are best addressed by each system and under what circumstances. Addressing this issue requires both an intimate understanding of the procedural differences between the two data series as well as an appreciation for how the differences and changes in these procedures can affect each system's description of the crime problem. This volume, *Understanding Crime Statistics: Revisiting the Divergence of the NCVS and UCR*, moves to that level of detail. Its main purposes are to bring thoughtful consideration to the appropriate use of crime statistics by exploring the issues surrounding divergence in the UCR and NCVS and to suggest how these systems can be used in complementary ways. Ultimately we seek to provide needed insights as to how recent changes in both indicators contribute to divergence as well as guidance regarding which data series is best suited to address particular research problems. Before launching into this enterprise, we use this introduction to explain the utility of studying divergence and the need to revisit divergence now. We also clarify two common misunderstandings concerning crime statistics that often inhibit researchers' ability to visualize the NCVS and the UCR as complementing each other.

WHY STUDY DIVERGENCE?

Studying divergence (or convergence) between the UCR and the NCVS serves as an important heuristic device for understanding the complementarity of the two data systems. Other organizing principles such as the customary parallel descriptions of the two series cannot provide the focus needed to study complementarity. Parallel descriptions of the UCR and NCVS, especially those that are thorough, often leave the reader swimming in a sea of details and lacking any capacity to assess the importance of the design and characteristics of each data set. Divergence provides an organizing framework that enables a thoughtful and practical evaluation of the UCR and NCVS. In the context of divergence, detailed information describing differences in definitions and procedures becomes meaningful. Specific changes or differences in the series become important in proportion to their contribution to

user disinterest and the defensiveness and poverty of statistical agencies perpetuates ignorance of the social organization of statistical systems necessary to use these data appropriately and in a complementary
fashion. We hope our book will enlighten readers about the important
aspects of these statistical systems that affect the data they produce.

OVERVIEW OF THE VOLUME

Understanding Crime Statistics addresses the general ignorance of the
NCVS and UCR that impedes understanding these systems and using
their data appropriately. To begin the volume, the first two chapters
provide detailed, but focused, information on these two systems that
identifies those aspects of the social organization of both series that
are likely to have a major effect on the divergence of the resulting
trends. Using the information from these chapters as a foundation,
our book turns to crime- specific and issue-specific discussions. These
chapters examine specific aspects of the social organization of the UCR
and NCVS systems and assess empirically whether particular factors
contribute to divergence. Finally, our book concludes with a discussion
of the lessons learned and suggestions for how to utilize the UCR and
NCVS in complementary ways. The following provides a more detailed
summary of the chapters included in this volume.

In Chapter 2, Callie Rennison and Michael Rand provide a description of the purpose and design of the NCVS. The NCVS gathers information on the incidence of criminal victimization for households and
household members aged 12 and older from a nationally representative sample of households. Specific types of victimization counted in
the NCVS include completed and attempted rapes and sexual assaults,
robberies, aggravated and simple assaults, burglaries, thefts, and car
thefts. This chapter concerns not only the current design but also the
substantial redesign of the crime survey that occurred in 1992.

In Chapter 3, Cynthia Barnett-Ryan provides an overview of the
UCR. The Uniform Crime Reporting System is administered by the
Federal Bureau of Investigation and collects crime data from state
and local police departments. The UCR includes information on murder, forcible rape, robbery, aggravated assault, burglary, theft, motor
vehicle theft, and arson. In addition to crimes known to police, the

UCR also collects arrest information. Under its traditional "summary system," the UCR collected aggregate-level data from agencies and used specific classification and counting rules to facilitate accurate counting of crime events. This chapter describes those rules and procedures, some of which are discussed in subsequent chapters as sources of divergence. This summary system is in the process of changing to an incident-based system, the NIBRS. This chapter addresses both the traditional way in which the UCR collected crime statistics as well as the changes instituted with NIBRS.

The volume then turns to the issue of investigating divergence and assessing what is currently known about it. David McDowall and Colin Loftin, in Chapter 4, introduce the topic of divergence (and convergence) and consider the definitions and measures of divergence. Literature in this area is summarized with an eye to evaluate critically the definitions proposed by previous researchers and to examine how these definitions have been used to evaluate divergence in the UCR and NCVS. The chapter focuses on four of these definitions that range from more to less demanding requirements for finding divergence. Under the strictest or most demanding definitions, the data systems show little evidence that they converge. Under broader criteria, support for convergence (and against divergence) is stronger. The authors also explore an important complicating factor that divergence itself may have changed over time.

The next two sections of the volume concern specific sources of divergence, first with a view to sources from the NCVS and then with a focus on the UCR. In Chapter 5, Shannan Catalano focuses on how changes from the 1992 massive redesign of the NCVS may have affected divergence between the NCVS and UCR. Specifically, this chapter focuses on the effect of particular aspects of the redesign (new instrument, increased use of computer-assisted telephone interviewing) as well as other changes in the crime survey over time (reduction in sample size, declining response rates). The chapter addresses how these changes in the NCVS could contribute to divergence in the two series with regard to estimates of violent crimes such as aggravated assault and robbery.

Mike Planty examines in Chapter 6 the effect of series victimization reporting in the NCVS on divergence. Some individuals experience criminal victimization repeatedly. These high-volume victims pose a problem for crime surveys because respondents cannot always distinguish these victimizations as discrete events. Surveys have developed different procedures to identify and count this special case of victimization. The NCVS employs a "series victimization" procedure when an individual reports six or more victimizations that are similar in nature. The number of events is counted, but detailed information is collected only on the most recent incident. Series victimizations are excluded from annual estimates published by BJS. It is likely this decision rule has had an effect on divergence between the NCVS and UCR because certain crimes like domestic assaults that have increased as a proportion of all violence over time include a disproportionate number of series victimizations. Planty's chapter examines this issue, considering in particular how reasonable methods of including series victimizations in annual estimates might affect divergence as well as "overlap." The term overlap is used to refer to the instances when the UCR rate estimates for violence exceed those rates of the NCVS violent crime reported to the police.

In Chapter 7, Jacqueline Cohen and James Lynch consider another source of divergence that may arise from the eligible respondents to the NCVS compared with the general population served by police agencies. The chapter examines whether the NCVS's household sampling frame has resulted in the underrepresentation of marginal populations and an undercounting of behavior such as violent crime victimization that is prevalent in these populations. This chapter identifies the problem by comparing data from the National Hospital Ambulatory Care Survey (NHAMCS) with the NCVS. The NHAMCS employs a sample of emergency rooms rather than housing units sample as is done in the NCVS and other Census-administered surveys. Large differences between the NCVS and NHAMCS are found in the rate of emergency room visits due to violent victimization. In addition to the underrepresentation of marginal populations, the chapter examines other possible explanations for this disparity such as the degeneration of the NCVS's housing unit frame as well as differences in definitions and procedures in the two surveys.

The next section focuses on sources of divergence in the UCR. In Chapter 8, Lynn Addington examines how changes in the UCR may help us to understand the extent to which sources of definitional differences contribute to divergence between UCR and NCVS. Two in particular are the inclusion of commercial victims of crime (burglaries, robberies, thefts, and motor vehicle theft) in the UCR but not in the NCVS and the inclusion of victims under age 12 in the UCR but not in the NCVS. In addition, the UCR uses a "Hierarchy Rule" that is not used in the NCVS. It is generally assumed that all three of these factors contribute to divergence. Until this point, it was unclear to what degree. The chapter uses the incident-level data in NIBRS to estimate how much the inclusion these two victim groups and the Hierarchy Rule contribute to UCR crime trends and divergence with the NCVS. This chapter also describes caveats of using the NIBRS data, which is relatively new and does not have full participation from law enforcement agencies nationwide.

Richard Rosenfeld addresses changes in the police industry and their contribution to divergence in Chapter 9. Specifically, the chapter focuses on how changes in police recording of aggravated assaults have contributed to recent convergence in the UCR and NCVS. Widespread speculation exists that police agencies have broadened the scope of aggravated assaults over the past two decades and upgraded events, especially in the domestic violence category, from simple to aggravated assaults. These changes are believed to be less likely to have affected assaults committed with a firearm or other weapon than those without weapons. It is expected that little change should be observed over time in the relationship between the weapon-related offenses in the two series and that convergence should be limited to time trends in the nonweapon events. Rosenfeld examines national-level trends in weapon and nonweapon UCR and NCVS assaults since 1980 and finds evidence for both of these expectations.

In Chapter 10, Michael Maltz deals with the issue of missing data and its possible effect on divergence of the two data series. Missing data is a substantial issue in the UCR. To the extent that the contours of the missing data problem have changed over time, this could affect the convergence and divergence of the UCR and the NCVS trends. To explore this possibility, Maltz relies on a new analytic tool based on annotated UCR data to identify patterns of missing data and sheds new light on the divergence issue. His chapter focuses on missing data in the aggregate counts of crimes known to police and the arrest data collected by the UCR. The chapter also addresses ways in which imputing UCR data may contribute to divergence between the two series.

The volume concludes with a discussion of why the NCVS and UCR trends diverge and what this divergence means for the use and development of these data series. Specific attention is given to how the differences in the two systems can be used in a complementary way to provide a more accurate and enlightening picture of the crime problem. The concluding chapter includes suggestions for how to increase use of existing data in a complementary way as well as initial proposals for more systematic change that would enhance complementarity.

OVERVIEW OF THE TWO NATIONAL MEASURES OF U.S. CRIME

CHAPTER TWO

Introduction to the National Crime Victimization Survey

Callie Marie Rennison and Michael Rand

If we knew more about the character of both offenders and victims, the nature of their relationships and the circumstances that create a high probability of crime conduct, it seems likely that crime prevention and control programs could be made much more effective.

> The President's Commission on Law Enforcement and
> the Administration of Justice, 1967a

For more than 30 years, the National Crime Victimization Survey (NCVS) and its predecessor the National Crime Survey (NCS) have provided detailed information about the nature and extent of personal and property victimization in the United States. Much of our current understanding about crime, such as the most vulnerable segments of the population, the proportion of crime involving weapons, the types of injuries sustained in violent crimes, and the extent of reporting to police, is derived from the NCS and NCVS. The NCVS also serves as a model for victimization surveys implemented throughout the world because it incorporates many innovative methodological protocols that enhance its ability to produce reliable estimates of the nature and extent of criminal victimization. These methodological techniques combined with the large sample size and the extensive details collected by the survey on crime events are all reasons that the current NCVS remains the "most comprehensive and systematic survey of victims in the United States" (Mosher et al., 2002, p. 137).

The views expressed in this chapter are attributable to the authors and do not necessarily reflect those of the U.S. Department of Justice or the Bureau of Justice Statistics.

The NCVS and the Uniform Crime Reporting System (UCR) comprise the two ongoing national measures of crime in the United States. As noted in the introduction to this volume, both programs are essential because neither measure is capable of providing all the information about the extent and nature of crime. To appreciate fully the relationship between the NCVS and the UCR, especially with regard to the divergence in crime estimates, requires an understanding of the origins and methodology of each system. Barnett-Ryan in Chapter 3 of this volume provides a detailed review of the background and methodology of the UCR. The current chapter summarizes the history and origins of the crime survey and describes the methodology used in the NCS and NCVS. This chapter is divided into four sections. The first summarizes the origins of the NCS and NCVS. The second reviews the methodology of NCS, which is the original crime survey. The third describes the significant changes made to the crime survey since its inception in 1972. The chapter concludes with a summary of the methodology used in the current NCVS.

THE ORIGINS OF THE NCS AND NCVS

In 1965, responding to rapidly rising crime and unrest in urban areas, President Lyndon Johnson convened the President's Commission on Law Enforcement and the Administration of Justice to examine the causes and characteristics of crime in the United States and to recommend policies and programs to address this crime (President's Commission on Law Enforcement and the Administration of Justice, 1967a). As one of its concerns, the Commission found a lack of requisite information from which to develop policy recommendations. At the time, the only source of crime data available was the UCR.

Although official crime data served many useful purposes, four main limitations prevented it from addressing the needs of the Commission. First, official crime records reflected only crimes known to law enforcement agencies and not the "dark figure of crime" – those offenses not reported to police (Biderman and Reiss, 1967). Because of this omission, the Commission "found it very difficult to make accurate measurements of crime trends . . . " (President's Commission on Law Enforcement and the Administration of Justice, 1967b, p. 40).

Sellin (1931) noted a second and related limitation of official crime data, arguing that crime data reflect law enforcement activity and not necessarily actual trends in crime. Another problem was that official statistics were open to possible manipulation and misrepresentation that could threaten their validity (Beattie, 1941; Mosher et al., 2002). Finally, official statistics lacked important information about the criminal incident, including details about the characteristics of the victims, the offenders, and the offenses (Dodge and Turner, 1971). The Commission believed these details were necessary to develop useful policy recommendations.

Given the limits of official crime data, the Commission decided a new source of crime statistics was needed and promoted the creation of the first national survey of crime victimization (President's Commission on Law Enforcement and the Administration of Justice, 1967a). Such a survey could compensate for the UCR's limitations. A victimization survey could specifically ask about crimes not reported to police as well as gather greater details concerning crime incidents and victims. Survey data also would not be affected by changes in law enforcement policies or be open to manipulation. Before undertaking such a victimization survey, however, many questions had to be addressed. Particular concerns centered on whether a victimization survey could identify enough crimes to provide reliable estimates with samples of reasonable size and cost. To assess the feasibility of using sample surveys to collect national crime victimization data, the Commission launched three pilot studies (Mosher et al., 2002).

The Commission's initial pilot study was conducted in 1966 in Washington, D.C. The study consisted of a probability sample of households in three police districts in which 511 individuals were interviewed regarding their victimization experiences. A second pilot study was conducted in three cities: Boston, Chicago, and Washington, D.C. This study sought to estimate criminal victimization of businesses and organizations in high crime areas as well as to measure household victimizations in Boston and Chicago. The third study was the first to employ a national sample. The National Opinion Research Center (NORC) conducted this survey and interviewed one respondent from each of 10,000 sampled households regarding their victimization experiences.

These pilot studies found that significantly more crime was measured through victimization surveys than in official police records (Dodge and Turner, 1971). These pilot studies also demonstrated that self-report victimization surveys were a reasonable method of identifying criminal victimizations not reported to the police. Ultimately these studies supported regularly collecting national victimization data (President's Commission on Law Enforcement and the Administration of Justice, 1967b). Implementing a national victimization survey was done with the original goals of providing (1) an independent calibration for the UCR,[1] (2) an ongoing measure of victim risk, (3) an indicator of the crime problem independent from those generated by police activity, and (4) an indicator of society's definitions of crime (U.S. Department of Commerce, 1968, p. 53). A national victimization survey also was believed to serve five main purposes: (1) to shift the focus of the criminal justice system to the victim and away from the offender, (2) to be an index of changes in police reporting, (3) to provide a basis for the study of granting of compensation to crime victims, (4) to determine involvement by the victim, and (5) to measure public confidence in police efficiency.

To gather this victimization data on an ongoing basis, the Commission recommended that a national criminal justice statistics center be established (President's Commission on Law Enforcement and the Administration of Justice, 1967b). In 1968, the Law Enforcement Assistance Administration (LEAA) was created and charged with implementing a national victimization survey.[2] In cooperation with the Bureau of the Census, LEAA conducted a series of studies to resolve methodological issues associated with implementing a national victimization survey.[3] Among the issues examined were the use of a single

---

[1] Although this use of the survey was popular among criminologists and government officials, some of the researchers most intimately involved with the development of the method (and specifically Albert Biderman) believed that this was an unwise and impossible task.

[2] The NCS was housed in the National Criminal Justice Information and Statistics Service, an agency within the LEAA. LEAA was the predecessor to the Office of Justice Programs, which houses the Bureau of Justice Statistics, the current sponsor of the NCVS.

[3] Readers interested in a complete overview of these methodological issues are directed to Lehnen and Skogan (1981, 1984).

household respondent as opposed to interviews with each household member, the respondent's ability to recall events, the length of reference periods, the minimum age of respondent, and the appropriate question cues and wording. In examining these methodological issues, a tension existed between the scientific desire to maximize data accuracy and the practical need to minimize costs of the survey and provide annual estimates of victimization (Biderman, 1967; Cantor and Lynch, 2000; Dodge, 1970; Dodge and Turner, 1971; Murphy and Dodge, 1970).[4]

Based on recommendations from the Commission and the findings from the methodological studies, the NCS was created and first implemented in 1972 (Hubble, 1995; Martin, 1982). The NCS originally was composed of four interrelated victimization surveys: a national household sample referred to as the Crime Panel, a Central City household sample, and a national and Central City sample of commercial establishments (the Commercial Victimization Surveys; Penick and Owens, 1976). Only the Crime Panel survived beyond 1976 and became what is commonly referred to today as the National Crime Survey (Biderman and Lynch, 1991). Because the rest of this chapter is devoted to examining this particular survey in greater detail, the three discontinued surveys are briefly summarized in the paragraphs that follow.

The Central City household surveys were designed to estimate the level and change of victimization for a selected set of crimes committed against residents of major cities across the country (LEAA, 1976c). The surveys were designed to obtain benchmark estimates of crime in the cities. This information could then be updated in subsequent enumerations for that city. For example, eight "impact" cities that received funding from LEAA were surveyed in 1972 and again in 1975 (Lehnen and Skogan, 1981).[5] Approximately 12,000 households per city were interviewed using procedures that were similar but substantially different from those in the Crime Panel. The goal of the surveys was to evaluate the impact of LEAA funding to these cities. The Central City

---

4   Indeed, as discussed later in this chapter, the need to minimize costs is a recurrent theme throughout the history of the crime survey and with the NCVS today (e.g., Lauritsen, 2005).

5   These eight cities were Atlanta, Baltimore, Cleveland, Dallas, Denver, Newark, Portland (Oregon), and St. Louis.

survey also was fielded in the nation's five largest cities in 1973 and 1975 (Lehnen and Skogan, 1981).[6] Thirteen additional cities received the Central City survey once in 1974 (Lehnen and Skogan, 1981).[7] The Central City surveys were discontinued after 1975. External reviews of the crime survey recommended that the Central City surveys be consolidated with the national sample (NAS 1976, p. 4). This recommendation was not implemented largely because of the high cost of the Central City surveys (LEAA, c. 1977–1978).

The national Commercial Victimization Survey (CVS) was first fielded using a sample of 15,000 businesses in July 1972 (LEAA, 1976a). The Central Cities Commercial Victimization Surveys were conducted concurrently with the Central City household surveys using samples of between 1,000 and 5,000 businesses in each city. Both surveys collected data on robbery and burglary victimization of commercial establishments. Both CVSs were discontinued in September 1977 on the basis of findings by external reviews that the sample was undersized, the survey was of limited utility as fielded, and the survey failed to collect information beyond that already gathered by the police (Lehnen and Skogan, 1981; Penick and Owens, 1976).

As mentioned earlier, the national household survey or the Crime Panel was the only one of the original four surveys to continue after 1976. The remainder of this chapter describes the methodology of the national household sample component and its successor, the NCVS. All further references to the NCS refer to the national household sample.

THE NATIONAL CRIME SURVEY

LEAA contracted the Census Bureau to design and implement the NCS. The national household sample component of the National Crime Survey was first fielded in July 1972 (Hubble, 1995). The NCS was designed to provide annual estimates of the extent and characteristics of personal and household crimes in the United States as well as estimate year-to-year changes in crime rates. This section

[6] These five cities were Chicago, Detroit, Los Angeles, New York, and Philadelphia.
[7] These 13 cities were Boston, Buffalo, Cincinnati, Houston, Miami, Milwaukee, Minneapolis, New Orleans, Oakland, Pittsburgh, San Diego, San Francisco, and Washington D.C.

reviews the sample, data collection techniques, and survey protocols used by the NCS. The NCS is reviewed in detail because it provides the foundation for the current NCVS and also provides a means of assessing the changes made to the survey, especially the massive redesign in 1992.

Sample Design and Size

The NCS initially used a sample of about 72,000 housing units and group quarters in the United States. The sampling frame included only principal living quarters including "dormitories, rooming houses, and religious group dwellings" and specifically excluded individuals who were "crewmembers of merchant vessels, Armed Forces personnel living in military barracks, and institutional persons, such as correctional facility inmates" (LEAA, 1976a, p. 145). The NCS sample was selected using a stratified, multistage cluster design (Hubble, 1995; Lehnen and Reiss, 1978). This design was selected as an efficient and cost-saving method to collect data (Lehnen and Reiss, 1978). Data collection in a large stratified sample is less expensive than in a similarly sized simple random sample because the sample cases are concentrated in fewer geographic areas (Alreck and Settle, 1995; Cochran, 1977; Groves et al., 2004). Therefore, fewer interviewers are required. The consequences of this economy are larger sample design effects and differential chances for selection of sampling units.[8]

To obtain the NCS sample, addresses were selected by sampling from 1,930 primary sampling units (PSUs) across the United States (LEAA, 1976a). NCS PSUs comprised counties, groups of counties, or large metropolitan areas in the United States. Once identified, the PSUs were grouped into 376 strata from which a sample of PSUs was obtained. Large PSUs were included in the sample automatically, and each was assigned its own stratum. These 156 PSUs were called self-representing because all were selected into the sample. The remaining 220 PSUs were non-self-representing because only a subset of these was selected to represent all of the remaining PSUs. Non-self-representing

---

[8] Sample design effects refer to increases in sampling error that come from clustering sample units and departing from a purely random selection. A design effect of 2.0, for example, would mean that the standard errors obtained from the cluster sample were twice as large as would have been obtained from a random sample of the same size.

PSUs were grouped into strata by combining areas that shared certain common characteristics such as "geographic region, population density, population growth rate, proportion of nonwhite population" (LEAA, 1976a, p. 145). From the sampled PSUs, the sample of households was obtained in two stages. These stages were designed to ensure that prior to any weighting adjustments, each sample housing unit had the same overall probability of being selected.

The first stage consisted of selecting a sample of enumeration districts (EDs) from the selected PSUs (Biderman and Lynch, 1991; LEAA, 1976a, p. 145). EDs are established for each decennial census and are geographic areas ranging in size from a city block to several hundred square miles, usually encompassing a population ranging from 750 to 1,500 persons. Enumeration districts were systematically selected proportionate to their population size. In the second stage, each selected ED was divided into clusters or segments of about four contiguous housing units. These clusters were formed from the list of addresses compiled during the most recent census. Procedures allow for the inclusion of housing constructed after each decennial census enumeration.[9]

Once a sample address was selected, it remained in the sample for three years and was interviewed seven times at six-month intervals (Hubble, 1995). Following the seventh interview or enumeration, a new household rotated into the sample. To accomplish this rotating panel design, the sample of households was divided into six rotation groups, each containing six panels of sample units. The panels and rotation groups were staggered so that in any given month, one-sixth of the sample was being interviewed for the first time, one-sixth for the second, and so forth (Lehnen and Reiss, 1978). In 1973, the survey's first full calendar year of data collection, interviews were conducted with 145,000 residents aged 12 and older in 65,000 households every six months.[10]

---

[9] Addresses included in the sampling frame comprised those obtained via the most recent decennial census, addresses for new construction based on building permits, and addresses obtained from Census Bureau employees who canvassed selected areas and identified all housing units.

[10] Lehnen and Reiss (1978, p. 374) pointed out that it was not until January 1, 1977, that a "complete rotation design was reached where each rotation group [was] interviewed once every six months for three years, or seven interviews."

Household addresses remained in the sample during the three years of the interviews. Because the NCS was a survey of households, individuals were not followed, and it was possible the composition of the household changed during that three-year period because of circumstances such as relocation, marriage, divorce, or death. Regardless of these individual changes in household composition, all persons living in the household who were over age 12 were interviewed at each enumeration. It was also possible for whole families to move and be replaced by entirely new households during the interview period. In these instances, interviewing still continued as if the original respondents were present in the household.

Data Collection

NCS Instruments. On the basis of findings from a series of methodological studies, NCS data collection was designed as a two-stage process. In the first stage, respondents were screened to determine whether they believed they were victims of crime during the six-month reference period. In the second stage, detailed information about any event uncovered during the screening process was collected to determine whether the event was a crime within the scope of the survey and to classify the crime by type. Information collection was accomplished using three survey instruments: the Control Card, the Basic Screen Questionnaire, and the Incident Report.[11]

The Control Card served as the administrative record for each sample unit. It was completed during the initial interview at each unit and updated in subsequent interviews. The Control Card obtained basic information about the sample unit including a record of visits, telephone calls, interviews, and noninterview reasons. In addition, it listed the name, age, gender, marital status, education, and relationships of all persons residing in a household. An important role of the Control Card was its brief description of all victimizations reported by household members in each interview. This record served as a quick reference during future interviews to ensure that victimizations previously counted were not reported again and duplicated in NCS estimates.

---

[11] Interested readers are directed to LEAA (1976, pp. 125–144) for copies of the Basic Screen Questionnaire and the Incident Report.

Each household had one person designated the "household respondent." In addition to answering individual questions, the household respondent was asked an additional six screen questions about offenses against the household itself, such as burglary and motor vehicle theft (Skogan, 1981).[12] The household respondent was a household member at least 18 years old who was deemed likely to give accurate answers regarding the household questions. This person was always the first person interviewed in the household during each enumeration. The individual designated as the household respondent might differ across enumerations.[13]

The Basic Screen Questionnaire was used to screen for crimes committed against the household or against an individual household member during the six-month reference period (Biderman, 1981). As discussed earlier, the household respondent answered questions regarding possible victimizations against the household. All household members over age 12, including the household respondent, were asked about their victimization experiences. The Screen Questionnaire accomplished this by using a set of 13 questions that ask whether the respondent experienced any of the types of victimization measured by the survey. The language used in the screening questions avoided legal terms. For example, screen questions related to violence asked: "Did anyone beat you up, attack you or hit you with something, such as a rock or bottle?" and "Were you knifed, shot at, or attacked with some other weapon by anyone at all?" (see figure 2, Skogan, 1981, p. 8). The responses were used solely to screen for offenses and not for creating estimates of victimization. For each incident mentioned in the

[12] Individual respondents occasionally volunteered reports of household incidents not mentioned by the household respondent. In such cases, the interviewer is instructed to fill out an incident report regarding this crime.

[13] The household respondent is not necessarily the same person who was designated the head of household, the reference person, or the principal person. The *reference person* is the person identified by the household respondent as the person aged 18 or older who owned or was purchasing, or rented the living quarters. The reference person is synonymous with the *head of household*. This term is used as a reference point to determine the relationship of all other household members. Also, the head of household's demographics (age, gender, race) are used when presenting characteristics of victims of property crimes. The *principal person* in a husband/wife situation is the wife. The principal person's demographic characteristics are used in assigning a household weight.

Screen Questionnaire, respondents were asked the number of times they were victimized during the reference period. A Crime Incident Report was completed for each incident.

In the NCS, respondents aged 14 and older were asked about their own victimization experiences. Respondents between the ages of 12 and 13 were not asked directly about their personal experiences unless a parent specifically consented to the interview. Instead, a proxy respondent was used (Dodge and Turner, 1971; Martin, 1982). A proxy respondent was a knowledgeable household member who answered questions on the child's behalf. In very unusual situations, knowledgeable individuals who did not reside in the household were permitted to serve as a proxy respondent (Dodge and Turner, 1971; Martin, 1982). Although the NCS had a strong preference for direct interviews of the respondent, proxy interviews were allowed in two other situations. One situation was cases in which respondents were too incapacitated to respond for themselves. The other situation was for individuals who were absent from the household during the entire two-week interviewing period.

The second part of the interview concerned completion of a Crime Incident Report (CIR). A CIR was completed for each incident recorded on the Screen Questionnaire. For example, three CIRs would be completed for a respondent who reported having his or her property taken by force in one incident and two separate incidents of being beaten. The CIR collected detailed information about each victimization including the time, date, and place; information about the offender, including any relationship to the victim; circumstances of the incident such as whether a weapon was used; consequences to the victim, including injury and loss of or damage to property; and whether the incident was reported to police.

The detailed information gathered in the CIR was used to determine whether the incident described was a crime measured by the survey and if it occurred during the appropriate time period. If the incident was classified as a crime, the characteristics of the event determined the type of crime. The determination of whether a crime occurred and what type of crime occurred was not made by the field representative or by the respondent. Rather, these determinations were made during data processing at the Census Bureau on the basis of the entries on the CIR. An algorithm was used that combined incident attributes and allowed each incident to be classified into the appropriate crime type category (LEAA, c. 1974). If the incident did not meet any of the criteria for any crime measured by the NCS, it was not included in survey estimates of crime victimization. The crime classification scheme was hierarchical, meaning that an incident involving more than one crime was classified into the most serious crime category (LEAA, 1976a). The crime hierarchy used by the NCS placed violent victimizations above property victimizations. The resulting hierarchy from most to least serious was as follows: rape, robbery, aggravated assault, simple assault, personal larceny (purse snatching and pocket picking), burglary, motor vehicle theft, and property theft. Although this hierarchy was used to make official estimates with NCS data, the attributes used in this classification were available in the public use files, which allowed researchers to use a different hierarchy.

The NCS utilized a special protocol for victims of repeated crimes both to address the difficulties that these respondents had in remembering details of each separate incident and to minimize the interviewer and respondent burden of completing a large number of incident reports. A protocol called "series victimization" allowed one incident report to cover multiple victimizations if certain criteria were met (LEAA, 1976a). To be considered a series victimization, the respondent must have been victimized at least three times during the six-month reference period, all the incidents must have been similar in nature, and the respondent was unable to recall details of each of the victimizations (Dodge and Balog, 1987; Martin, 1982). For series victimizations, the details of only the most recent incident in the series were recorded in the CIR along with the number of times the person was victimized. In addition, series victimizations indicated only the quarter rather than the exact date of the victimization (LEAA, 1976a, 1976b).

Survey Mode. The NCS was conducted using Paper and Pencil Interviewing (PAPI). PAPI is a data collection mode in which the interviewer questions the respondent in person or on the telephone and records the responses on a paper instrument. In the NCS, PAPI interviews were conducted both in person and by telephone. The initial contact with a sample household each enumeration period was done in person (LEAA, 1976a, 1976b). If interviews with all household members could not be completed during that visit, interviewers could call back by telephone if respondents were agreeable. In addition, subsequent interviews were conducted either in person or on the telephone.

Survey Protocols

Bounding. The NCS utilized a six-month reference period so respondents were asked about criminal victimizations that they or their households experienced during the six months prior to the month of interview. The six-month reference period was selected because research demonstrated that longer recall periods present greater problems for respondents in recalling events they have experienced, whereas shorter recall periods increased the cost of interviewing greatly (Dodge and Turner, 1971; Turner, 1972). The six-month recall period provided the best balance between accuracy and economy (Cantor and Lynch, 2000).

Survey respondents often have difficulty remembering not only salient events but also exactly when those events occurred (Skogan, 1981). "Telescoping" refers to this tendency to identify incorrectly the timing of past events. Research has found that telescoping generally is in the direction of moving events into the more recent past (Skogan, 1981). For example, when asked whether the respondent had been the victim of an assault in the last six months, that respondent might describe an incident that actually occurred eight months before. In an effort to minimize the effect of telescoping, the NCS used a methodological procedure known as "bounding," in which the prior interview and the information gathered from it are used during subsequent interviews to ensure that events from before the reference period and events reported in prior interviews are not counted twice (Lehnen and Reiss, 1978; Neter and Waksberg, 1964). Methodological investigations prior to the launching of the NCS suggested that unbounded data produced victimization rates about 35% higher than estimates from bounded data (Dodge and Turner, 1971). This bounding procedure served as both a cognitive and a mechanical bound. The prior interview served as an event that respondents could use during the recall process to determine whether an event was within or outside of the reference period. In addition in the NCS, if the interviewer noted a possible duplication of events from a prior interview using the Control Card information, the respondent was questioned further to determine whether it was, in fact, a new or the same victimization. If it was the same incident, a new report was not completed.

Bounding had special relevance for the first enumeration of an NCS sample household. Because the first interview was by definition not bounded, the information gathered from respondents during the initial interview served only to establish a boundary for the second interview and was not used in the computation of victimization estimates. Bounding was considered a substantial methodological advance when the survey was designed. Although bounding was expensive, because one-seventh of the interviews conducted were not used to produce estimates, the resulting data were believed to be more accurate estimates of crime victimization. This technique was not perfect because some interviews that contributed to crime estimates were still not bounded.

Four situations account for why an interview outside the incoming rotation would be unbounded.[14] In all these situations, data collected from the unbounded interview would be included in deriving national crime victimization estimates. The two most common arise from respondents "aging into" the sample and from replacement households. One common reason for unbounded interviews is the aging of household members into the sample after the initial interview (Skogan, 1981). Because households were interviewed over a three-year period, it was possible for a household member who was under 12 during the initial interview to become an eligible respondent while the household was in the sample. To illustrate, a child who turned 12 after the household's third interview would be interviewed during the fourth interview. This interview would be unbounded. A second common reason for unbounded interviews occurred when an entire household moved from the sampled housing unit and was replaced by another family. Information from the new family's first interview would

[14] As reported in Lehnen and Reiss (1978), Reiss (1977, p. 8) estimated that only about 4 in 5 household and person interviews are bounded. Specifically, he estimated that between 17% and 19% were unbounded in a given data year.

be unbounded. Less common reasons for unbounded interviews concern missed interviews and the use of proxy respondents. The interview would be unbounded if an individual was not interviewed in one enumeration but was interviewed in the following enumeration. In addition, personal interviews following proxy interviews were not bounded. This issue would be of concern if the proxy respondent missed an incident or recalled information about an incident incorrectly.[15]

Noninterviews. At times, the NCS interviewer was unable to obtain an interview of an individual or of an entire household. Noninterviews were categorized into four basic types: Type A, B, C, and Z (Bushery, 1978; Biderman and Lynch, 1991). *Type A noninterviews* refer to situations in which an entire eligible *household* is not interviewed. Households may not be interviewed for a variety of reasons: no one was at home during the approximately two-week interview period; the household refuses to be interviewed; or the household is not reachable, for example, due to impassable roads. If a household respondent cannot be interviewed, the entire household becomes a Type A noninterview. *Type B noninterviews* occur when an address is vacant or occupied entirely by persons who have usual residences elsewhere. Although these cases are not eligible for interviews during the current enumeration period, they could become eligible at a later time. Additional reasons for Type B interviews are dwellings under construction and dwellings converted to temporary business. *Type C noninterviews* refer to situations in which the sample address is permanently ineligible for interview. For example, a housing unit may have been demolished, a house or trailer moved, the dwelling burned down, the house converted to a permanent business, or the property condemned. A *Type Z noninterview* refers to a *person* who is not interviewed in an otherwise interviewed household. A household respondent can never be a Type Z noninterview. If the household respondent cannot be interviewed, the *household* is coded as a Type A noninterview.

Although the NCS has four types of noninterviews, only Type A and Type Z noninterviews were used in the calculation of response rates

---

[15] For a discussion regarding the influence of proxy interviews, see Murphy and Cowan (1976).

and of most interest to researchers. Type A and Z noninterviews represent households and persons who were eligible for interview but not interviewed. From the survey's outset, keeping noninterviews to a minimum was a priority component of NCS interviewing protocols. Historically, NCS response rates were quite high; in 1973, for example, interviews were completed with 96% of eligible households and 95% of eligible individuals. NCS weighting procedures adjusted for noninterviews (LEAA, 1976a).

Estimation. Once the data were collected, they were used to make annual estimates of the level and change in level of crime. In doing so, the data were weighted to represent the national noninstitutionalized population, specific types of crime were excluded, and different units of count were used. Customarily, weights were simply the inverse of the probability of selection, such that if a sample of 1 in 10 persons were drawn, the weight applied to each case would be 10. In addition to this, the weights used in the NCS include adjustments for nonresponse and for undercoverage. In the case of nonresponse, groups with low response rates received an additional increment to their weight to compensate for the fact that more respondents in that particular group failed to respond. Undercoverage adjustments to the weights were increments added to the weights for groups who were underestimated in the decennial census. Because the Census address list is the sampling frame from which the NCS sample is selected, when it underrepresents certain groups, these will be underestimated in the sample. This increment to the weights attempts to adjust for known undercoverage.

Two classes of crime were excluded from annual estimates – series crime and crimes occurring to eligible victims while they were outside of the United States. Series incidents were excluded because respondents cannot accurately date the multiple incidents in the series. Without a date of occurrence, it is difficult to include series in annual estimates. Events that befall members of the noninstitutionalized population outside of the United States were not part of the crime rate for that year.

Three units of count were available in the survey – victimization incidents, persons or victims, and households. In estimating victimization rates for personal crimes, the number of victimizations weighted with the person weight was divided by the weighted number of persons in the sample. When an incident rate was estimated, the person weight assigned to the victimization was divided by the number of victims in the incident to account for the fact that all of the victims have a chance of reporting the event and to eliminate the effect of any double counting. Household crimes such as burglary and motor vehicle theft employ the household as the unit of count. The number of victimizations reported in the sample was weighted by the household weight and divided by the weighted number of households in the sample. Household weights differ from person weights because there are many fewer households than persons.

Major Changes to the Crime Survey Over Time

Evaluation of the methodology used to conduct victimization surveys did not end when the NCS was fielded in 1972. Over the next two decades, methodological examinations were conducted on virtually every aspect of the survey. Within three years of the first fielding of the NCS, LEAA contracted with the National Academy of Sciences (NAS) to conduct a thorough review of the entire NCS program. One reason for seeking this external review was in response to concerns about the new survey's methodology (Penick and Owens, 1976). In 1976, the NAS published recommendations for improvement of the survey that included the following among its recommendations (Penick and Owens, 1976):

- an extensive improvement of the NCS screener to increase its effectiveness in prompting respondents' memories as well as to minimize its complexity (Biderman and Lynch, 1991);
- additional questions to allow the measurement of constructs important for studying the dynamics of crime victimization such as ecological factors, victim characteristics, lifestyle activities, and protective or preventive measures (Hubble, 1995); and
- significant methodological changes to optimize the field and survey design for the NCS (Penick and Owens, 1976).[16]

---

[16] In addition, the NAS recommendations largely accounted for the discontinuation of the Commercial Victimization Survey and the Central Cities surveys that were previously discussed.

Following publication of the Penick and Owens (1976) NAS report, LEAA conducted an internal evaluation and conference to develop a five-year research plan on national victimization survey statistics. These assessments concluded that a program of research and development was required to redesign the NCS, and the Bureau of Social Science Research (BSSR) received the contract to do the research. Using a consortium of experts, BSSR directed the thorough and complex redesign of the NCS. BSSR submitted recommendation to the Bureau of Justice Statistics (BJS) for the redesign of the survey in 1986, and Census conducted additional testing from 1986 to 1992, before the redesigned survey was introduced in 1992.

The implementation of interim changes in the survey also slowed the redesign process. Between 1972 and 1992, changes were introduced to reduce survey costs and to make the interviews more efficient. The changes adopted before the redesign in 1992 were restricted to those believed to be "non–rate affecting," or changes that would not significantly affect the amount or type of crime measured by the survey. The more significant "rate affecting" changes were not implemented until the redesign. Even after the redesign, the survey still experienced changes. The following section details the most significant changes to the survey in chronological order with special attention to changes that occurred during the redesign.

Changes to the Survey: Pre-1986
Clarifications and Methodological Refinements. As the first ongoing national survey of crime, the NCS broke new ground. Because of its newness and the complexity of many of the survey's concepts, situations arose that required clarifications to survey procedures or changes in the survey instruments. Interested readers are directed to Martin (1982) for a chronicle of six revisions to the original NCS questionnaires between 1972 and 1980. Two of these illustrate the situations that necessitated clarification of interviewer procedures and addition of response categories for more accurate data collection. An example of clarifying survey procedures was the revision made to interviewer instructions dealing with offender weapon use. Original interviewer manuals did not cover whether animals or parts of the body could be considered weapons. Revisions to manuals corrected such omissions by

instructing interviewers that "[n]o animal is to be considered a weapon for the purposes of the NCS" and that parts of the body are never weapons (Martin, 1982). An example of a change to the NCS forms to improve data collection accuracy was the revision to the response categories of the Incident Report question, "How did the person(s) attack you?" This question was asked of respondents who reported being hit, knocked down, or attacked. The 1972 questionnaire had seven response categories, one of which was the broad category of "hit with object held in hand, shot, knifed." In 1978, this category was split into three distinct responses: "shot," "knifed," and "hit with object held in hand" (Martin, 1982).

Cost-Reducing Changes. By the late 1970s, increases in the cost of implementing the survey were outpacing BJS's resources. Beginning in 1980, BJS began implementing a number of changes to reduce the cost of fielding the NCS. These included increasing the percentage of interviews conducted by telephone and reducing the sample size (Mosher et al., 2002). Originally, initial contacts for all seven interviews were conducted by personal visit. In January 1980, the third, fifth, and seventh interviews were converted to telephone interviews. In March 1980, the third, fifth, and seventh interviews were switched back to personal interviews and the second, fourth, and sixth interviews were conducted over the telephone. In June 1984, the first major reduction in the sample size decreased the survey from its original size of 72,000 households to 65,000 households per six-month period.

Changes to the Survey: 1986

Based on recommendations from the redesign consortium, a number of changes were implemented in 1986. These changes focused on the survey's procedures and questionnaires but were restricted to those deemed to be non–rate affecting. The changes implemented in 1986 were collectively referred to as "near-term" redesign changes to differentiate them from the subsequent redesign of the survey. The near-term changes included alterations in the use of proxy interviews, incident form changes, the use of computer-assisted telephone interviewing, and cost-saving changes.

Proxy Interviews. One near-term change altered the protocol for interviewing 12- and 13-year-old respondents. Originally, 12 and 13 year olds were interviewed by a proxy respondent unless a parent gave permission to interview the child. This procedure was initially adopted because of concerns over possibly antagonizing the adult parent respondents in the household and concerns that young respondents would be unable to understand sufficiently the survey's concepts (Taylor, 1989). Subsequent research suggested that these fears were largely unfounded. Parents generally were willing to allow their 12- and 13-year-old children to respond for themselves, and these youths were capable of providing accurate information. Beginning July 1986, 12 and 13 year olds were interviewed directly unless the parent expressly refused permission (Biderman and Lynch, 1991).

Question Changes. Many questions were added to the CIR, which grew from four pages with about 20 questions and subparts to more than 18 pages with 85 questions and subparts. The changes to the CIR were instituted to improve the information collected about the characteristics and consequences of criminal victimization (Hubble, 1995). Examples of new questions included those related to self-protective actions by the victim as well as the consequences of such actions, bystander behavior during the incident, substance abuse by offenders, the victim's long-term contacts with the criminal justice system, and measures of threats prior to actual attacks (Taylor, 1989).

Along with the addition of questions to the CIR, response categories were expanded and revised to gather more precise information regarding the characteristics of the crime. Examples of improved response categories included new items on offender's use of a weapon, details concerning location of the crime, greater information regarding the type of property stolen and the property recovered, and expanded codes for items measuring reasons for reporting and not reporting crimes to police (Taylor, 1989).

Computer-Assisted Telephone Interviewing. Beginning in the mid-1980s, the Census Bureau began testing computer-assisted telephone interviewing (CATI) in a number of household surveys it conducted, including the NCS. CATI interviews were first included in the 1988 estimates

(BJS, 1990). In 1988, about 5% of the 50,000 eligible households were interviewed using CATI. Initial studies suggested that this new interview procedure would have no serious effects on the data collected by the crime survey. Subsequent research demonstrated substantially higher reports of victimization from CATI interviews (Hubble and Wilder, 1995; Rosenthal and Hubble, 1993).

Cost-Saving Changes. During the implementation of near-term changes, modifications continued to be introduced to reduce survey costs. These included additional increases in the number of telephone interviews and elimination of some response coding. In March 1986, the number of telephone interviews further increased. The third and seventh interviews were converted to telephone interviews, leaving only the first and fifth as personal interviews. A second cost-saving change was the elimination of all coding of respondent's occupations. The screen questionnaire asked respondents about their job in the week before the interview, and the incident report asked about the respondent's job at the time of the incident. The responses to these open-ended questions were coded in a clerical operation during data processing. Beginning in July 1986, the questions on the screen questionnaire were not changed, but the coding was curtailed. The questions on the incident report were transformed into an occupation question with 27 precoded categories.

The 1992 Redesign

In 1992, after three years of pretesting using 5% and 10% subsamples of the NCS sample, BJS and the Census Bureau were ready to implement the "long-term" rate affecting changes to the survey based on the work of the redesign consortium (BJS, 1994; Hubble, 1995). The dramatic changes to the NCS implemented at this time are collectively referred to as the "1992 redesign." It was also about this time that BJS changed the survey's name to the National Crime Victimization Survey (Hubble, 1995). As previously mentioned, the pre-redesign survey is typically referred to as the NCS and the post-redesign survey as the NCVS.

The changes implemented in the survey redesign significantly improved its ability to measure victimization in general and certain difficult-to-measure crimes such as rape, sexual assault, and domestic violence in particular. The redesign was implemented using a split-sample design (BJS, 1994; Kindermann et al., 1997). For 18 months, from January 1992 to June 1993, data from half the sample were collected using the NCS methodology, and data from the other half were collected using the redesigned NCVS methodology. The split-sample approach allowed the effect of the redesigned methodology to be evaluated.[17] The first full year of NCVS data based on the redesign was available in 1993.[18] Details of these specific changes to the methodology are outlined in the following sections, which include changes to the survey instruments, changes in protocols regarding measuring certain victimizations, and cost-saving changes. The discussion concludes with a summary of the effect of the redesign on survey estimates.

Crime Screening. One of the most important changes implemented by the redesign was a new crime screening strategy (Taylor and Rand, 1995). As described earlier, the NCS Screen Questionnaire comprised six questions for the household respondent and 13 questions for every household member aged 12 or older to ascertain whether the household or the household members had experienced any criminal victimization during the previous six months. The NCS Screen Questionnaire had remained unchanged since the survey began in 1973.

In 1992, the screen questionnaire was radically reshaped based on models of the response process developed over the previous 15–20 years by psychologists, sociologists, and survey researchers (Strack and Martin, 1987; Sudman et al., 1996, pp. 55–79; Tourengeau, 1984). The NCVS redesign was the first U.S. government survey based on models of this type (e.g., Biderman et al., 1986; Biderman and Moore, 1982). These models are quite similar and include five steps: (1) encoding, (2) comprehension, (3) retrieval, (4) formatting, and (5) editing. The process begins with the encoding of information into memory. Information about an event, like a victimization, cannot be retrieved from memory if it is never stored. When asked a question, the respondent

---

[17] Readers interested in further details about the effect of the redesign on survey estimates are directed to Kindermann et al. (1997) and Rand et al. (1997).

[18] The sample that produced 1993 estimates was about 83% of the full NCVS sample because a portion of the split sample was in place for interviews in January through June.

must interpret the meaning and develop an understanding of what the interviewer is asking. This is comprehension. Information is retrieved from memory through a search process that attempts to match the type of experience asked about during the screening interview with events stored in memory. Once retrieved, the response is formatted and edited. This involves actively deciding on whether the response is formatted in ways consistent with any response alternatives, judging the reasonableness of the answer (e.g., comparing it against some norm), and editing the response to adhere to social desirability or other criteria.

As described elsewhere (Biderman et al., 1986; Cantor and Lynch, 2000), the screening strategy for the NCVS was based on promoting comprehension of the recall task and retrieval of the desired information from memory. To accomplish this, the screener:

- included many more specific cues to the attributes of crime events. This was done to improve comprehension by clearly and specifically conveying the type of events within the scope of the survey. It avoids the use of terms based on categories of events that have legalistic overtones (e.g., "burglary," "robbery," "victimization").
- targeted cues to underreported crimes that do not fit stereotypes, that are easily forgotten, and that are sensitive (e.g., spouse abuse or sexual assault). This was done both to reduce comprehension failures and to overcome editing that might affect the reporting of sensitive crimes (Biderman et al., 1986).
- organized the interview into multiple frames of reference, for example, acts, locales, and relationship to offender, to improve retrieval. Events may be stored in memory according to a variety of attributes and not just the criminal act. By using different frames, one increases the chance of prompting mention of eligible events.
- controlled the pace of the interview. Failures of retrieval may also be due to the respondent prematurely deciding that he or she has not been victimized and aborting any further retrieval (failures of "metamemory"). This problem was abetted by the relatively quick pace of the original screener (average time to administer was approximately eight minutes). The redesigned screener takes longer to administer and has a much slower pace (about twice as long as the original).

In summary, the new screening strategy was designed to increase comprehension and retrieval and to reduce editing of eligible crime events. Comprehension would be improved by widening the concepts around which memory search is initiated. Rather than searching for a narrowly defined group of events, the new cueing strategy attempts to expand definitions so that a wider memory search will occur. Similarly, the larger number of cues and the varied frames of reference were intended to aid retrieval by increasing the possibility that particular memory paths or classification hierarchies are accessed. Because the target event may be stored under a number of attributes (e.g., location, involvement by a particular individual, consequences) and it is unclear how the event may be stored in any particular respondent's memory, the use of a wide range of cues should increase the possibility of retrieving the information. Finally, the use of relatively neutral terms to describe potentially sensitive events and cueing specific events that are traditionally underreported (e.g., violence by someone known to the respondent) serve to communicate that these events are eligible for reporting. This was done both to improve comprehension and to reduce editing.

The following question illustrates how these strategies were implemented in the new "short cue" screening interview.

> People often don't think of incidents committed by someone they know. (Other than any incidents already mentioned,) did you have something stolen from you OR were you attacked or threatened by:
>
> a. Someone at work or school
> b. A neighbor or friend
> c. A relative or family member
> d. Any other person you've met or known? (BJS, 1994; Taylor and Rand, 1995)

New Crimes Included in the Screener. The redesigned crime survey increased the scope of crimes specifically included in the screener to include rape and sexual assault, domestic violence, and vandalism. The NCS was developed in 1972, a time when it was not considered appropriate for the federal government to ask a respondent directly about rape and sexual assault. The concern, as voiced by Turner (1972, p. 2), was that "[a]n inquiry phrased in such indelicate terms would

likely promote public charges of the unbridled insensitivity of government snoopers as well as congressional outrage." As a result, the NCS
did not screen for rape, but estimated these crimes based on information obtained about these offenses in screens focusing on attacks and
attempted attacks (BJS, 1994). By 1992, such direct questions were
no longer deemed too sensitive to ask on a government survey, and
there was increased interest from the research community and policy
makers in obtaining information regarding sexual victimization. The
redesigned survey included screen questions specifically asking about
rape and sexual assault (Taylor and Rand, 1995).[19]

In addition, at the time the NCS was developed, domestic violence
generally was not considered to be a criminal justice problem. The
redesigned survey specifically sought to obtain information on victimizations perpetrated by intimate partners, family members, and
acquaintances. As described in the previous section, the redesigned
questionnaire also screened for offenses committed by persons known
or related to the victim. This change helped to prompt respondents
to report intimate partner and domestic violence that they might not
consider to be a crime.

The NCVS new screening questionnaire also introduced questions
measuring vandalism as a type of property crime (Taylor and Rand,
1995). To minimize the burden these additional questions might
impose on respondents, both in time and in effort required to recall
multiple incidents of vandalism, the questions focused on all vandalism experienced by the household during the six-month reference
period (BJS, 1989).

Other Changes to the Survey Instruments. The redesign added questions
to the screener questionnaire regarding the extent to which respondents engaged in various routine activities such as shopping or using
public transportation. These questions were included to explore the
relationship between lifestyle activities and vulnerability to criminal
victimization (Hubble, 1995; Taylor and Rand, 1995). In addition

---

[19] Sexual assaults were not measured in the NCS. Sexual assaults are defined by the
NCVS as attacks or attempted attacks involving sexual contact between the victim
and offender other than rape or attempted rape.

to the changes in the screener questions, questions were added to the redesigned incident report. These included questions about the offender's perceived gang membership, bystander behavior, and the interaction during the incident between the victim and offender (Taylor and Rand, 1995).

Measurement of Theft. The redesign also changed the way thefts were measured by the survey. The NCS defined theft as either a household or personal crime depending on where the crime took place (Martin, 1982). Property stolen from the vicinity of the home – for example, a bicycle from the backyard – was considered a household crime. If the property was taken from a place away from the home such as at school or work, this victimization was considered to be a personal theft. This dichotomy had implications for how these thefts were weighted; household thefts received household weights, and personal thefts received personal weights (LEAA, 1976a). As a result, this distinction affected national estimates produced by the weighted data. The dichotomy also limited the utility of the data because rates of personal theft could not be combined with rates of household theft to produce an overall theft rate.

The redesign corrected this problem. The NCVS classified all thefts as household crimes unless there was contact between the victim and offender. These "contact thefts" included pocket picking and purse snatching. Classifying thefts as a household crime allows the uniform use of household weights and also avoids the problem of trying to assign ownership of stolen property to individual household members.

Series Victimization Protocol. The redesign also changed the series victimization protocol. Prior to the redesign, series victimization was defined as a victim who experienced at least three incidents that could not be differentiated enough to fill separate incident reports for each incident. This designation invoked a protocol that allowed the completion of a single incident report for the series. Based on research demonstrating that victims could remember the details of more individual incidents, the threshold for implementing the series protocol was raised to six or more similar victimizations (Dodge and Balog, 1987; Hubble, 1995). As before, the series protocol was used as a last resort in those situations in which the respondent was unable to remember details of all the incidents. The redesign also changed how series victimizations were utilized in BJS publications. Historically, BJS excluded series victimizations from both NCS and NCVS annual estimates. Since the redesign, special reports that aggregate data over a number of years include series victimizations, but these are counted as only one victimization for the entire series (e.g., see Hart and Rennison, 2003; Klaus and Rennison, 2002; Rennison, 2001a, 2001b, 2002a, 2002b, 2003; Rennison and Welchans, 2000).

Sample Cut. The implementation of the redesigned survey incurred additional costs. To remain within its budget, BJS implemented an offsetting cut in the overall survey sample. In October 1992, the NCS and NCVS samples were each reduced by 10%, resulting in an overall sample of 58,700 households (NCS and NCVS combined) each six months.

Increased Use of CATI. The 1992 survey redesign also included the large-scale implementation of CATI in the NCVS. Earlier testing found CATI to be a viable interviewing technique for the crime survey. In addition, CATI was believed to produce more accurate estimates because it required interviewers to read every question and eliminated difficulties in following the survey's complex questionnaire skip patterns. In 1992, about 1,500 NCVS households per month (or 15% of the sample) were designated as eligible for CATI. In July 1993, the CATI workload was increased to 3,500 cases per month or about 30% of all NCVS interviews.[20]

The 30% of interviews conducted by CATI were not selected randomly but were restricted to PSUs that have more than one interviewer. This was done so that the Census Bureau would have the capability of conducting in-person interviews in that PSU. If a large proportion of cases in a single interviewer PSU were interviewed by CATI

---

[20] In some cases, the CATI interviewer is unable to complete the interview. Such situations might arise when households moving from the sample address, a household member cannot be reached, or the household refuses the interview. These are called "CATI recycled interviews" because the interview recycles back to the interview field staff for further attempts to reach the respondent (U.S. Census Bureau, 2004).

from a central CATI facility, then there would not be enough cases for the interviewer resident in the PSU to conduct.

Interview-to-Interview Recounting. The redesign also introduced changes to increase accurate recall of crimes. One new protocol concerned victimizations that respondents may have experienced between the end of the survey reference period and the day of the interview. Since the survey's inception, the reference period was the six months prior to the month in which the interview took place (Cantor and Lynch, 2000). For respondents interviewed in January, for example, the reference period was July 1 through December 31 of the previous year. Because the interview period each month can last about 2 weeks, it is possible for a respondent to be victimized after the end of the reference period but before the interview. Historically, these victimizations could only be reported during the subsequent interview. This practice encouraged error such as the respondent forgetting to report the incident or misremembering details about it. As a result, the redesign introduced a protocol called "interview-to-interview recounting." This change allowed the interviewer to complete an incident report for any incident occurring during the reference period or at the end of the reference period in the days prior to the interview. In the case of a postreference period incident, the Census interview staff simply would hold those incident reports until the next interview, at which time the incidents were included with the other information collected.

Impact of the Redesign on Victimization Estimates. In general, the redesign had the anticipated result of increasing the number of crimes counted by the survey. Increases were not uniform across types of crime, however (Kindermann et al., 1997; Rand et al., 1997). The redesigned screener increased estimates of difficult to measure offenses such as rape and domestic violence because of the changes in the screening questions. It also increased estimates of crimes *not* reported to the police to a greater extent than it did crimes reported to the police. One reason for this occurrence is that improved cues for certain questions caused respondents to recall more of the less serious crimes – those that are also less likely to be reported to law enforcement officials (Kindermann et al., 1997). As a result, the percentage of crimes reported to police based on NCVS data is lower than the percentage calculated based on data collected with the NCS survey design. This effect was largest for simple assault, which does not involve the presence of weapons or serious injury (Kindermann et al., 1997).

Because the estimates from the redesigned survey are collected using a different screening strategy, post-redesign data are not comparable to that collected prior to 1992. BJS has published adjusted NCS estimates to extend the time series back to 1973, but this is practicable only at the most aggregated crime levels because such adjustments are based on one year's data and may not be stable if extended to detailed victim, offender, or circumstance data (Rand et al., 1997).

Beyond the 1992 Redesign

Since the 1992 redesign, additional non–rate affecting changes to the NCVS have been made. This section describes these important changes, which are categorized as changes implemented to reduce survey costs and those implemented to provide new directions for the crime survey.

Cost-Saving Changes. The cost-saving changes include changes in survey mode, reduction in sample size, increased use of CATI, and changes in quality control protocols. The telephone interview protocol was changed again in July 1996. Beginning that month, only the first interview at each household is required to be in person. If the household respondent agrees, all following contacts with the household are conducted by telephone. Additional sample cuts were instituted in 1996 (12%) and 2002 (4%). In 2004, the NCVS sample comprised 48,000 households and interviews are obtained with about 42,000 of these households.

Prior to July 2003, the sample PSUs were grouped into three CATI usage categories: (1) maximum-CATI PSUs for which all the segments in the PSU were CATI-eligible; (2) half-CATI PSUs for which half of the segments in the PSU were randomly designated to be CATI-eligible; and (3) non-CATI PSUs for which none of the segments were CATI-eligible. The level of CATI usage for each PSU was established with a concern regarding an optimal workload for the field interviewers. In the half-CATI PSUs, a random sample of about 50% of the segments in each PSU was taken and designated as CATI-eligible. The sample cases in CATI-eligible segments from the half-CATI and maximum-CATI PSUs were interviewed from CATI facilities. The other sample cases were interviewed by the standard NCVS field procedures of telephone using PAPI. Since July 2003, all households became CATI eligible. Regional offices assign CATI if it does not adversely affect an interviewer's workload (BJS, 2003). Foreign-language households are exempt from CATI with the exception of Spanish-speaking households because the Census Bureau employs Spanish-speaking interviewers at their telephone interview centers. Currently about 40% of all households are sent to CATI. About 30% are interviewed using CATI and 10% are recycled back to field interviewers because the CATI interviews could not be completed.

A fourth change to reduce survey costs involved temporary and permanent changes in the survey's quality control protocols. For example, performance rating observations of interviewers were suspended from July 1992 through January 1993. Re-interviews, which are conducted on a sample of households to evaluate the completeness and accuracy of interviews, were suspended for one month in August 1992.

New Directions. Additional changes since 1992 have been implemented based on a need for the survey to address new directions in victimization concerns. These changes concern the addition of particular questions due to the evolving definition of crime, the inclusion of topical supplements, and efforts to release data more quickly (Taylor and Rand, 1995).

Because it is the primary measure of the victimization data of the U.S. population, periodically BJS has been mandated to expand the scope of the survey to address new issues related to crime. Four examples include the following: In January 1999, questions were added to determine the extent to which victims of NCVS measured crimes perceived to be hate crimes. The Crime Victims with Disabilities Awareness Act in 1998 mandated BJS to add questions to identify victims of crimes with developmental disabilities. In 2001, BJS added questions to explore the extent to which people are victimized by computer-related crimes, including viruses. These computer crime questions were replaced with identify theft questions beginning in 2004.

Although the NCS had been used as a vehicle for a few supplements,[21] this practice expanded after the redesign. These supplements collect additional information on crime-related topics beyond that possible with the ongoing survey and often are administered to targeted subsamples of the NCVS sample. The supplements are conducted for many purposes and can be sponsored by other federal agencies. Since 1992, the NCVS has included supplements on school crime, police and public contact, and workplace risk. A supplement related to stalking is planned for 2006.

To allow for an earlier release of the initial NCVS estimates, BJS changed the way it constructs annual estimates in the mid-1990s. Because of the survey's retrospective nature and six-month reference period, 17 months of data are required to compile a complete calendar year of data (BJS, 2000). For example, the estimate for 1993 was based on interviews conducted from February 1993 to June 1994. The interviews in February 1993 asked about crimes occurring in August 1992 through January 1993. For the 1993 estimate, crimes in August through December 1992 were excluded, and those in January 1993 were included. For this reason, the earliest that estimates based on complete data collection or a "data year" are available for release is during the last quarter of the following year (BJS, 2000).

Beginning with its report *Criminal Victimization 1996*, BJS based its annual estimates on interviews occurring during a calendar year rather than on crimes occurring in a calendar year (BJS, 1997). These new estimates were called by BJS "collection year" estimates.[22] Although this method includes some crimes that occurred during the previous year and exclude some crimes occurring during the reference year, BJS estimated that this change had only a small impact on the annual estimates. To illustrate, the overall violent crime rate in 1995 using the data year was 44.5 per 1,000 persons aged 12 and older. Using

---

[21] These supplements included the National Survey of Crime Severity, the Victim Risk Survey, and the School Crime Supplement.

[22] BJS extended this change to its compilation of tables, "Criminal Victimization in the United States, Statistical Tables," beginning with the 1995 edition of this report (BJS, 2000).

the collection year, the rate was 46.6 (Ringel, 1997). This difference, however, would be greater during periods of changing crime rates and less during periods of stable crime rates (Ringel, 1997).

THE CONTEMPORARY NATIONAL CRIME
VICTIMIZATION SURVEY

The contemporary NCVS reflects more than 30 years of improvements in survey methodology as well as evolving emphases on crimes of interest. The survey remains a work in progress as it changes to reflect the current needs of researchers and policy makers. The survey retains many of the core methodologies it possessed at its inception. This section summarizes the methodology of the contemporary NCVS and highlights the aspects retained from the original NCS design previously discussed.

The survey is still conducted for BJS by the Census Bureau using a sample of American households drawn from each decennial census. The NCVS uses the same sampling design as the NCS. Addresses remain in sample for three years and are interviewed seven times at six-month intervals. Interviews are conducted with every household member aged 12 and older. The interview is conducted in two parts. The first consists of a screening interview to identify any crimes experienced during the previous six months, and the second collects detailed information about the incidents.[23]

As described in earlier sections of this chapter, the current survey has changed over the course of its history. The crime screener used today has been improved to capture certain offenses more directly as well as to capture new types of crime. The 2005 NCVS measures sexual assault, vandalism, and identity theft, all of which are crimes not measured by the NCS in 1972. The survey has evolved from using exclusively in-person interviews to one that employs predominantly telephone interviews, with an increasing proportion of these interviews done with CATI.

[23] The NCVS Screen Questionnaire is available at www.ojp.usdoj.gov/bjs/pub/pdf/ ncvs1/pdf. The NCVS Incident Report is available at www.ojp.usdoj.gov/bjs/pub/ pdf/ncvs2.pdf.

The sample size of the survey has decreased dramatically over time. In 2004, the NCVS sample was about 46,000 addresses across the United States. Interviews were completed with about 76,000 residents of 42,000 households each six months. The response rates for 2004 were 92% of eligible households and 89% of eligible respondents in interviewed households. The NCVS response rate remains among the highest of all household surveys conducted by the Census Bureau, but it has grown over time. In 1973, the first full year of NCVS interviewing, the response rate was 96% of eligible households and 95% of eligible respondents. The growth in the nonresponse rate reflects the increasing difficulty of conducting surveys generally. Although still extremely high, the nonresponse rate for some subpopulations could be of concern if this increasing trend continues.

NCVS METHODOLOGY AND DIVERGENCE WITH THE UCR

If crime survey and UCR methodologies had remained constant for the past three decades, the examination of differences over time between the survey estimates and police-based estimates of crime might be a somewhat simpler exercise. One could examine differences between the programs and factor in changes in society to explore the reasons for differences between estimates from the two programs. The changes made to the NCS in its redesign, however, make this examination much more complex.

Subsequent chapters address the ways in which specific changes in the redesign (such as CATI) as well as issues regarding series victimization counting may contribute to divergence. Which changes to the survey over the past three decades may be most significant to the examination of NCVS/UCR divergence? Certainly the redesign, which increased NCVS estimates of violent crime by 50% and estimates of some individual crime types to a greater degree, would be of prime consideration. The series protocol, which increased from three or more to six or more similar incidents in the redesign, may play a role in examining divergence. The growth in the survey nonresponse rate should also be examined to assess whether adjustments have compensated for the higher nonresponse rates of some subpopulations. Some other changes that might draw one's focus are increased telephone interviewing and the related growth of CATI interviewing. With the information provided by this chapter, the reader can evaluate estimates from the two programs in light of their methodologies and the changes over time.

References

Alreck, P. L., & Settle, R. B. (1995). *The survey research handbook: Guidelines and strategies for conducting a survey.* New York: Springer.

Beattie, R. H. (1941). "The sources of criminal statistics." *American Academy of Political and Social Science* 217:19–28.

Biderman, A. D. (1967). "Surveys of population samples for estimating crime incidence." *Annals of the American Academy of Political and Social Science* 374:16–33.

Biderman, A. D. (1981). "Notes on the methodological development of the National Crime Survey." In R. G. Lehnen & W. G. Skogan (Eds.), *The National Crime Survey: Working papers, volume I: Current and historical perspectives* (NCJ-75374). Washington, DC: U.S. Department of Justice.

Biderman, A. D., Cantor, D., Lynch, J. P., & Martin, E. (1986). *Final report of the National Crime Survey redesign.* Washington, DC: Bureau of Social Science Research.

Biderman, A. D., & Lynch, J. P. (1991). *Understanding crime incidence statistics: Why the UCR diverges from the NCS.* New York: Springer-Verlag.

Biderman, A. D., & Moore, J. (1982). *Report on the workshop on cognitive issues in surveys of retrospective surveys.* Washington, DC: Bureau of Social Science Research and U.S. Census Bureau.

Biderman, A. D., & Reiss, A. J., Jr. (1967). "On exploring the 'dark figure' of crime." *Annals of the American Academy of Political and Social Science* 374:1–15.

Bureau of Justice Statistics. (1989). *National Crime Victimization Survey (NCVS) redesign: Questions and answers* (NCJ-15117). Washington, DC: U.S. Department of Justice.

Bureau of Justice Statistics. (1990). *Criminal victimization in the United States 1988* (NCJ-122024). Washington, DC: U.S. Department of Justice.

Bureau of Justice Statistics. (1994). *Technical background on the redesigned National Crime Victimization Survey* (NCJ-151172). Washington, DC: U.S. Department of Justice.

Bureau of Justice Statistics. (1997). *Criminal victimization 1996, changes 1995–96 with trends 1993–96* (NCJ-165812). Washington, DC: U.S. Department of Justice.

Bureau of Justice Statistics. (2000). *Criminal victimization in the United States 1995* (NCJ-171129). Washington, DC: U.S. Department of Justice.

Bureau of Justice Statistics. (2003). *Criminal victimization in the United States 2003 statistical tables.* Washington, DC: U.S. Department of Justice. Retrieved July 11, 2006 from http://www.ojp.usdoj.gov/bjs/pub/pdf/cvus/cvus03mt.pdf.

Bushery, J. M. (1978). "NCS noninterview rates by time-in-sample." Unpublished memorandum, U.S. Department of Commerce, Bureau of the Census, Washington, DC.

Cantor, D., & Lynch, J. P. (2000). "Self report surveys as measures of crime and criminal victimization." In D. Duffee (Ed.), *Criminal justice 2000: Measurement and analysis of crime and justice* (Vol. 4). Washington, DC: U.S. Department of Justice. Pp. 85–138.

Cochran, W. G. (1977). *Sampling techniques* (3rd ed.). New York: Wiley.

Dodge, R. W. (1981). "The Washington D.C. recall study." Reprinted in R. G. Lehnen & W. G. Skogan (Eds.), *The National Crime Survey: Working papers, volume I: Current and historical perspectives* (NCJ-75374). Washington, DC: U.S. Department of Justice. (Original work published 1970) pp. 12–15.

Dodge, R. W., & Balog, F. D. (1987). *Series crimes: Report of a field test* (NCJ-104615). Washington, DC: U.S. Department of Justice.

Dodge, R. W., & Turner, A. (1981). "Methodological foundations for establishing a national survey of victimization." Reprinted in R. G. Lehnen & W. G. Skogan (Eds.), *The National Crime Survey: Working papers, volume I: Current and historical perspectives* (NCJ-75374). Washington, DC: U.S. Department of Justice. (Original work published 1971) pp. 2–6.

Groves, R. M., Fowler, F. J., Couper, M. P., Lepkowski, J. M., Singer, E., & Tourangeau, R. (2004). *Survey methodology.* Hoboken, NJ: Wiley.

Hart, T. C., & Rennison, C. M. (2003). *Reporting crime to police, 1992–2000* (NCJ-195710). Washington, DC: U.S. Department of Justice.

Hubble, D. L. (1995). *The National Crime Victimization Survey redesign: New questionnaire and procedures development and phase-in methodology.* Paper presented at the annual meeting of the American Statistical Association, Orlando, Florida, August 1995.

Hubble, D. L., & Wilder, B. E. (1995). *Preliminary results from the National Crime Survey CATI experiment.* New Orleans, LA: Proceedings of the American Statistical Association, Survey Methods Section, 1995.

Kindermann, C., Lynch, J. P., & Cantor, D. (1997). *The effects of the redesign on victimization estimates* (NCJ-164381). Washington, DC: U.S. Department of Justice.

Klaus, P., & Rennison, C. M. (2002). *Age patterns of violent victimization, 1976–2000* (NCJ-190104). Washington, DC: U.S. Department of Justice.

Lauritsen, J. L. (2005). "Social and scientific influences on the measurement of criminal victimization." *Journal of Quantitative Criminology* 21:245–266.

Law Enforcement Assistance Administration. (circa 1974). *National sample survey documentation, appendix D. NCP classification scheme description.* Unpublished memo.

Law Enforcement Assistance Administration. (1976a). *Criminal victimization in the United States 1973* (SD-NCP-N4). Washington, DC: U.S. Department of Justice.

Law Enforcement Assistance Administration. (1976b). *Criminal victimization in the United States 1974* (SD-NCS-N-6). Washington, DC: U.S. Department of Justice.

Law Enforcement Assistance Administration. (1976c). *Criminal victimization surveys in eight American cities: A comparison of 1971/72 and 1974/75 findings.* Washington, DC: U.S. Department of Justice.

Law Enforcement Assistance Administration. (circa 1977–1978). *Report concerning the future of the National Crime Survey (NCS).* Unpublished internal memo written in response to an October 21, 1977, directive from the deputy attorney general.

Lehnen, R. G., & Reiss, A. J. (1978). "Response effects in the National Crime Survey." *Victimology* 3:110–160.

Lehnen, R. G., & Skogan, W. G. (1981). *The National Crime Survey: Working papers, volume I: Current and historical perspectives* (NCJ-75374). Washington, DC: U.S. Department of Justice.

Lehnen, R. G., & Skogan, W. G. (1984). *The National Crime Survey: Working papers volume II: Methodological studies* (NCJ-90307). Washington, DC: U.S. Department of Justice.

Martin, E. (1982). *Procedural history of changes in NCS instruments, interviewing procedures, and definitions.* Unpublished memo, Bureau of Social Science Research, Washington, DC.

Mosher, C. J., Miethe, T. D., & Phillips, D. M. (2002). *The mismeasure of crime.* Thousand Oaks, CA: Sage.

Murphy, L. R., & Cowan, C. D. (1984). "Effects of bounding on telescoping in the National Crime Survey." Reprinted in R. G. Lehnen & W. G. Skogan (Eds.), *The National Crime Survey: Working papers volume II: Methodological studies* (NCJ-90307). Washington, DC: U.S. Department of Justice. (Original work published 1976) pp. 83–89.

Murphy, L. R., & Dodge, R. (1981). "The Baltimore recall study." Reprinted in R. G. Lehnen & W. G. Skogan (Eds.), *The National Crime Survey: Working papers, volume I: Current and historical perspectives* (NCJ-75374). Washington, DC: U.S. Department of Justice. (Original work published 1970) pp. 16–21.

Neter, J., & Waksberg, J. (1964). "Conditioning effects from repeated household interviews." *Journal of Marketing* 29:51–56.

Penick, B., & Owens, M. (1976). *Surveying crime.* Washington, DC: National Academy Press.

President's Commission on Law Enforcement and the Administration of Justice. (1967a). *The challenge of crime in a free society.* Washington, DC: U.S. Government Printing Office.

President's Commission on Law Enforcement and the Administration of Justice. (1967b). *Task force report: Crime and its impact – an assessment.*

Rand, M. R., Lynch, J. P., & Cantor, D. (1997). *Criminal victimization 1973–95* (NCJ-163069). Washington, DC: U.S. Department of Justice.

Rennison, C. M. (2001a). *Intimate partner violence and age of victim* (NCJ-187635). Washington, DC: U.S. Department of Justice.

Rennison, C. M. (2001b). *Violent victimization and race, 1993–98* (NCJ-176354). Washington, DC: U.S. Department of Justice.

Rennison, C. M. (2002a). *Rape and sexual assault: Reporting to police and medical attention, 1992–2000* (NCJ-194530). Washington, DC: U.S. Department of Justice.

Rennison, C. M. (2002b). *Hispanic victims of violent crime, 1993–2000/ Víctimas hispanas de crímenes violentos, 1993–2000* (NCJ-191208). Washington, DC: U.S. Department of Justice.

Rennison, C. M. (2003). *Intimate partner violence, 1993–2001* (NCJ-197838). Washington, DC: U.S. Department of Justice.

Rennison, C. M., & Welchans, S. (2000). *Intimate partner violence* (NCJ-178247). Washington, DC: U.S. Department of Justice.

Ringel, C. (1997). *Criminal victimization 1996, changes 1995–96 with trends 1993–96* (NCJ-165812). Washington, DC: U.S. Department of Justice.

Rosenthal, M. D., & Hubble, D. L. (1993). "Results from the National Crime Victimization Survey (NCVS) CATI experiment." In *American Statistical Association 1993 Proceedings of the Section in Survey Research Methods, Volume II* (pp. 742–747). Arlington, VA: American Statistical Association.

Sellin, T. (1931). "The basis of a crime index." *Journal of the American Institute of Criminal Law and Criminology* 22:52–64.

Skogan, W. G. (1981). *Issues in the measurement of victimization* (NCJ-74682). Washington, DC: U.S. Department of Justice.

Strack, F., & Martin, L. L. (1987). "Thinking, judging, and communicating: A process account of context effects in attitude surveys." In H. J. Hippler, N. Schwarz, & S. Sudman (Eds.), *Social information processing and survey methodology* (pp. 123–148). New York: Springer-Verlag.

Sudman, S., Bradburn, N. M., & Schwarz, N. (1996). *Thinking about answers: The application of cognitive processes to survey methodology.* San Francisco: Jossey-Bass.

Taylor, B. (1989). *Redesign of the National Crime Survey* (NCJ-111457). Washington, DC: U.S. Department of Justice.

Taylor, B., & Rand, M. R. (1995). "The National Crime Victimization Survey redesign: New understandings of victimization dynamics and measurement." Paper presented at the Joint Statistical Meetings of the American Statistical Association, Orlando, FL, August 1995.

Tourengeau, R. (1984). "Cognitive sciences and survey methods." In T. Jabine, M. Straf, J. M. Tanur, & R. Tourangeau (Eds.), *Cognitive aspects of survey methodology: Building a bridge between disciplines* (pp. 73–100). Washington, DC: National Academy Press.

Turner, A. G. (1972). *San Jose methods test of known crime victims.* Washington, DC: Law Enforcement Assistance Administration.

U.S. Census Bureau. (2004). *National Crime Victimization Survey regional office manual* (NCVS-570). Washington, DC: U.S. Government Printing Office.

U.S. Department of Commerce. (1968). *Report on national needs for criminal justice statistics.* Washington, DC: U.S. Government Printing Office.

CHAPTER THREE

Introduction to the Uniform Crime Reporting Program

Cynthia Barnett-Ryan

In 1927, the International Association of Chiefs of Police convened the Committee on Uniform Crime Records to provide much-needed information on crime trends for the nation. This small beginning was the result of years of contemplation and expressed desires by law enforcement to create a program that would afford a unified vision of the crime problem in the United States as well as provide law enforcement executives the means to compare their jurisdiction with others more easily. One of the first official mentions of the need to create a crime statistics program occurred in 1871 at a convention in St. Louis. Police executives approved a resolution "to procure and digest statistics for the use of police departments" (Official Proceedings of the National Police Convention, 1871, p. 30).

Ultimately, the creation of the Uniform Crime Reporting Program would require more than 50 years of continual effort to secure support and funding before the IACP formed the Committee on Uniform Crime Records to fulfill this need. One of the major issues that arose during the Committee's deliberations concerned the creation of a uniform data collection method that would convert the disparate state and local laws and definitions into one standardized system. In its finalized format, the IACP created a program based on seven standardized offense definitions, which became the centerpiece of the Uniform Crime Reporting (UCR) Program.

In 1930, the UCR Program's first year of data collection, 400 law enforcement agencies in 43 states reported data to the Federal Bureau of Investigation. Currently, the UCR Program has grown to encompass nearly 17,000 law enforcement agencies from all 50 states, the District of Columbia, and some U.S. territories. Although the scope of the UCR Program has both expanded and contracted since its inception in 1929, the driving force behind adjustments has always been to serve the strategic needs of law enforcement.

To meet these needs, the UCR Program required participating law enforcement agencies to report data via a series of standardized data collection forms that constitute the organizational framework for the Program. In addition to the form-driven Summary Reporting System, the current UCR Program also provides an alternate track for reporting crime data through the National Incident-Based Reporting System (NIBRS).

The stated purpose of this volume is to consider the myriad reasons underlying the convergence or divergence between official reports of crime and victim self-reports of crime. To understand how official reports of crime contribute to the process of convergence or divergence, one needs to consider both the information contained in the current UCR Program as well as a longitudinal perspective of the history of this long-lived statistical program. The goal of this chapter is to give the reader that broad understanding of what the UCR Program is, what data are collected and the manner in which they are collected, how missing data are handled by the UCR Program, and, finally, how we arrived at the system we have today.

As a starting point for any discussion of a data collection program, it is helpful to begin with the basic questionnaire, survey, or form. In the UCR Program, more particularly the Summary Reporting System, there is no questionnaire directed at a particular respondent as such, but there are a series of administrative forms on which, ultimately, the data sets are built.

SUMMARY REPORTING SYSTEM

In recent years, the term Summary Reporting System (SRS) has been adopted to distinguish the traditional data collection methods from the newer incident-based system. The data reporting forms that had their inception in the beginning of the UCR Program are as follows: Return A – Report of Offenses Known to the Police; Supplement to Return A; Age, Sex, and Race of Persons Arrested; Supplementary

Homicide Report; the Law Enforcement Officers Killed and Assaulted forms; the Hate Crime Data Collection forms; Monthly Return of Arson Offenses Known to Law Enforcement; and Law Enforcement Employees Report (see Table 3.1).

Return A – Report of Offenses Known
Many consider the Return A form to be the backbone of the UCR System. Contributing agencies use it to report offenses known to the police and the number of offenses resolved through investigation, or cleared, for a particular month. The Part I offenses reported on the Return A are murder and nonnegligent manslaughter; manslaughter by negligence; rape by force; attempts to commit forcible rape; robbery by weapon type; aggravated assault by weapon type; other assaults; burglary – forcible entry; burglary – unlawful entry (no force); attempted forcible entry; larceny-theft; and motor vehicle theft by type of vehicle. For each offense on the Return A, an agency forwards how many reports of offenses it received, as well as how many were found to be baseless or unfounded after law enforcement investigation. The number of actual offenses is calculated by removing unfounded offenses from the original total of known offenses (Federal Bureau of Investigation, 2004).

In addition to numbers of offenses, the Return A captures information on clearances by arrest or exceptional means. The UCR Program considers an offense cleared when at least one individual has been arrested in connection with it or the identity of the offender is well established and could be arrested because of sufficient evidence and his or her location is known, but circumstances beyond the control of law enforcement prevent that arrest from being made. In the latter situation, the offense would be exceptionally cleared. Some examples of situations that would result in an exceptional clearance involve the death of the offender, denied extradition, or the offender already being in custody. The clearances on the Return A are captured by two categories: total clearances and those offenses cleared involving only persons under the age of 18. It is important to understand that the clearances reported on any given month's Return A do not necessarily bear any relationship to the offenses reported for that month. Arrests or exceptional clearances denoted could be connected to an

TABLE 3.1. *Uniform Crime Reporting Program publications by information included*

Publication[a]	Forms included	Information collected
Crime in the United States	Return A – Report of Offenses Known	Offenses reported to law enforcement and any associated clearances for criminal homicide, forcible rape, robbery, assault, burglary, larceny-theft, and motor vehicle theft. Includes weapon and additional breakdown information (depending on the offense). Reported monthly.
	Supplement to Return A	Offenses by type and value of property loss and locations or circumstances (depending on the offense). Reported monthly.
	Arson	Offenses reported to law enforcement and any associated clearances for arson. Includes property type breakdowns. Reported monthly.
	Age, Sex, and Race of Persons Arrested	Arrestees by age and sex combined and race for all Part I and Part II offenses. Collected separately for adults and juveniles. Reported monthly.
	Supplementary Homicide Report	Incident-level information on criminal homicides. Includes details on victims, offenders, and circumstances of the homicide. Reported monthly.
	Police Employee Form	Annual counts of police employees (as of October 1) by civilian or sworn and gender.
Law Enforcement Officers Killed and Assaulted	Law Enforcement Officers Killed and Assaulted (Monthly Return)	Counts of any in-the-line-of-duty assaults committed against law enforcement by circumstances, type of assignment, time of day, and weapon. Totals provided for in-the-line-of-duty deaths due to felonious act or accident or negligence. Reported monthly.
	Analysis of Law Enforcement Officers Killed and Assault	Detailed information collected on all in-the-line-of-duty deaths of law enforcement and assaults with injury by firearm or knife/cutting instrument. Reported as needed.
Hate Crime Statistics	Hate Crime Incident Form	Incident-level information on hate crimes. Includes details on offenses, victims, offenders, and bias motivation. Reported monthly.

[a] All publications include data submitted by National Incident-Based Reporting System agencies that have been converted into a Summary Reporting System format.

offense reported on a previous month's Return A (Federal Bureau of Investigation, 2004).

Supplement to Return A
The Supplement to Return A is a separate form used to capture information on the value and type of the property stolen and recovered and the nature of the offenses reported on the Return A. The form begins with property type divided into broad categories such as currency and notes; jewelry and precious metals; clothing and furs; locally stolen motor vehicles; office equipment; televisions, radios, stereos, and so on; firearms; household goods; consumable goods; livestock; and miscellaneous. However, these categories are not separated by offense. Additional information captured on the Supplement to Return A is classified by offense and include breakdowns of the information on robbery locations, burglaries by time of day and location, and types of larceny-thefts. Although the Supplement does provide additional information on offenses reported through the Return A and should agree with the total on the Return A, it is not possible to cross-reference the offenses reported on the two forms (Federal Bureau of Investigation, 2004).

Arson
Although arson data collection is relatively new to the UCR Program (added in 1979), given the Program's lengthy history, the arson report retains many of the same features as the Return A form for the other Part I offenses. In addition to the same information on reported offenses, unfounded offenses, and clearances, the arson report also includes information on whether the structures were inhabited and the estimated value of the property damage. The breakdown of the arson offenses are divided broadly into structural arsons, mobile arsons, or *other*. Within those broad categories, additional information is collected on type and use of the structures and the type of mobile property. The *other* category encompasses such arsons as the burning of crops, timber, fences, or signs. Because the arson information is collected separately from other Part I information collected on the Return A, the number of agencies reporting this data has been historically lower than the Return A (Federal Bureau of Investigation, 2004).

Age, Sex, and Race of Persons Arrested

The Age, Sex, and Race of Persons Arrested (ASR) information consists of two separate forms: one for individuals 18 years of age or older and another for juveniles, defined by UCR as those under the age of 18. On either ASR form, monthly tallies of arrestees are recorded by a combination of age and sex and a separate tally of arrestees by race. They are essentially the same forms; however, the juvenile form includes the additional offense categories of curfew violations and runaways. Although there is no collection of arrestee information by race and age, the fact that the collection is broken into two forms does allow for general statements of race for juveniles and adults as separate totals. There is no ability to look at arrestees by race and sex (Federal Bureau of Investigation, 2004).

The Juvenile ASR also has additional information of the handling of juveniles by law enforcement such as handled within the department and released, referred to juvenile court, referred to welfare agency, referred to another police agency, or referred to criminal or adult court. The offense categories on the ASR include both Part I and Part II crimes. There are 26 Part II offenses and subcategories. The collection of information on Part II offenses has traditionally been limited to arrest information because, in the majority of cases, law enforcement learns of its commission at the time of arrest (e.g., drug offenses). A list of Part II offenses is provided in the Appendix to this chapter (Federal Bureau of Investigation, 2004).

Supplementary Homicide Report

The information collected on the Supplementary Homicide Report focuses on additional details of both murder/nonnegligent manslaughters and negligent manslaughters reported on the Return A form. These details include demographic information on offenders and victims, weapons used, relationship between victims and offenders, and the circumstances surrounding the incident. Although this level of detail is not received for all murders reported on the Return A, the vast majority of the agencies provide these additional details. This form provides one of two incident-level data collections in the Summary Reporting System (the other being the Hate Crime Incident Form). Again, however, as is the case with all of the Summary forms, the homicides reported in the SHR cannot be directly tied to the offenses reported on the Return A or Supplement to Return A (Federal Bureau of Investigation, 2004).

Law Enforcement Officers Killed and Assaulted

The Law Enforcement Officers Killed and Assaulted (LEOKA) Program consists of two separate data collections. On a monthly report, agencies forward tallies of law enforcement officers killed in the line of duty by either felonious act or accident/negligence. The tallies of assaults of law enforcement officers that occurred in the line of duty are described by type of assignment, type of weapon, and type of investigative or enforcement activity. Additionally, totals of assaults are collected by time of day. Once information about a death or serious assault of a law enforcement officer is received by the National Program, a second form, the Analysis of Law Enforcement Officers Killed and Assaulted, is forwarded to the appropriate agency to collect additional details on the incident (Federal Bureau of Investigation, 2004).

The Analysis of LEOKA form elicits eight pages of detailed questions concerning the circumstances surrounding the in-the-line-of-duty death by felonious act or accident or serious assault. A serious assault is defined as one in which an injury is sustained by the officer through the use of either a firearm or knife or other cutting instrument. The agency provides both standardized responses to questions and a narrative report of the incident and the circumstances surrounding it. The details ascertained through this program are published in the annual LEOKA publication and, more importantly, used to develop training materials for law enforcement officers' safety (Federal Bureau of Investigation, 2004).

Hate Crime

The Hate Crime Data Collection was added to the UCR Program by congressional mandate in 1990. The Hate Crime Data Collection focuses on the identification of incidents motivated in whole or in part by biases against race, ethnicity, religion, sexual orientation, or disability. In its Summary form, agencies forward information on the date of the incident, multiple offenses connected to the incident, and the location type by offense. Additionally, the incident report provides information on the type of bias motivating the hate incident, victim type, the number of offenders, and the race of the offenders as an individual or group. The types of victims collected on the Hate Crime form include individuals, businesses, financial institutions, government, religious organizations, society or public, other, or unknown. In the case of an individual victim type, the agency is to note the number of victims (Federal Bureau of Investigation, 1999).

Police Employees
The final Summary data collection is the Law Enforcement Employee Report and is commonly referred to as the Police Employee Form. This is an annual data collection in which agencies forward their full-time employee totals as of October 31 of a given year. These totals are broken down by gender, as well as how many are sworn or civilian employees (Federal Bureau of Investigation, 2004).

NATIONAL INCIDENT-BASED REPORTING SYSTEM

The second track in which crime data are forwarded from agencies to the National Program is the NIBRS. Although the design of the NIBRS was intended to provide an enhanced, new-generation system, it is still deeply rooted within the UCR Program. With the primary exceptions of the Analysis of LEOKA and the Police Employee forms, nearly everything that can be found in the diffused and disparate forms of the Summary Reporting System can be found in the NIBRS as well.

The major strength and enhancement of the NIBRS is the availability of all that information in a single incident; this provides the user with greater knowledge of the interconnectedness of these details, which was not possible when they were condensed into totals on separate forms (Federal Bureau of Investigation, 2000).

To reflect changes in the criminal justice community and its understanding of criminality, revisions included an expanded list of offenses for incident-level reporting to include 46 offenses, which required that new definitions be devised or other definitions be updated. Most notably, the definition of forcible rape was revised to allow an agency to apply the definition in situations with a male victim as well as a female victim. The Hierarchy Rule was also suspended altogether, and the Hotel Rule was modified to allow for its application in burglaries of self-storage warehouses (a discussion of the Hierarchy and Hotel Rules appears later in the chapter). The NIBRS also expands on certain information collected in the SRS. Whereas in the SRS, victim-to-offender relationships and circumstances are only captured on homicides through the SHR, the NIBRS allows for the reporting of relationship on all crimes against persons and circumstances on homicides and aggravated assaults (Federal Bureau of Investigation, 2000).

The NIBRS uses a new crime category called crime against society that was created to capture information on such offenses as drug violations, gambling offenses, prostitution, and other vice crimes. These crimes are scored as one offense per distinct operation. Additionally, it is possible to distinguish attempted crimes from completed ones in NIBRS with the exception of attempted murders and attempted rapes, which would be reported as a completed aggravated assault (Federal Bureau of Investigation, 2000).

For the purposes of publication in the three major volumes of *Crime in the United States*, *Hate Crime Statistics*, and *Law Enforcement Officers Killed and Assaulted*, the UCR Program converts an agency's NIBRS data into Summary data. The UCR Program has published several special studies and monographs using NIBRS data in its collected format, however.

WHAT ARE THE RULES OF DATA SUBMISSION?

Given the intended uniformity of the UCR data collection, one would expect certain rules regarding the manner and form in which criminal justice data are collected and received by the FBI. Most professionals in the criminal justice field are somewhat familiar with the definitions of offenses provided by the FBI. Beyond the uniform definitions, however, are additional factors that have an effect on published agency data. These factors are both directly and indirectly related to the procedures behind the flow of data from the actual criminal event until the data are forwarded to the National UCR Program. The process of collecting crime data can be thought of as a system of decision points, all of which can affect the level and type of crime data that ultimately make it to the FBI. These decision points can be crystallized into six major issues that are discussed in this section.

There Is a Prescribed Manner in Which the Data Are Classified and Scored

The collection of UCR data begins with the two-step process of classification of offenses (deciding on the type of offense reported) and the scoring of those offenses (the counting of offenses). The standard definitions of the UCR Part I offenses are as follows:

Murder and Nonnegligent Manslaughter – the willful (nonnegligent) killing of one human being by another

Manslaughter by Negligence – the killing of another person through gross negligence

Justifiable Homicide – the killing of a felon by a peace officer in the line of duty or the killing of a felon, during the commission of a felony, by a private citizen (not a crime)

Forcible Rape – the carnal knowledge of a female forcibly and against her will

Robbery – the taking or attempted taking of anything of value from the care, custody, or control of a person or persons by force or threat of force or violence and/or by putting the victim in fear

Aggravated Assault – an unlawful attack by one person upon another for the purpose of inflicting severe or aggravated bodily injury. This type of assault usually is accompanied by the use of a weapon or by means likely to produce death or great bodily harm

Other Assaults, Simple, Not Aggravated – an unlawful attack by one person upon another that did not involve the use of a firearm, knife, cutting instrument, or other dangerous weapon and in which the victim did not sustain serious or aggravated injuries[1]

Burglary – an unlawful entry of a structure to commit a felony or a theft

Larceny-theft – the unlawful taking, carrying, leading, or riding away of property from the possession or constructive possession of another

Motor Vehicle Theft – the theft or attempted theft of a motor vehicle

---

[1] Currently, simple assaults are used by the UCR Program to identify agencies that may be misclassifying aggravated assaults as simple assaults or vice versa. They are not published in *Crime in the United States*.

Arson – any willful or malicious burning or attempt to burn, with or without intent to defraud, a dwelling house, public building, motor vehicle or aircraft, personal property of another, etc. (Federal Bureau of Investigation, 2004)

Part I offenses can also be categorized as crimes against persons or crimes against property. The crimes against persons are criminal homicides, forcible rape, and the assaults. The crimes against property are those offenses in which the target of the crime is the property of another. The Part I crimes against property are robbery, burglary, larceny-theft, and motor vehicle theft. These concepts are crucial to the correct classification and scoring of offenses (Federal Bureau of Investigation, 2004).

The standard practice of agencies converting their own crime information into UCR data begins with the classification of the criminal event into one of eight UCR Part I offenses. Because on occasion more than one offense occurs in a criminal incident, it is necessary to understand the Hierarchy Rule and the Separation of Time and Place Rule and how those rules impact on the final numbers received from reporting agencies (Federal Bureau of Investigation, 2004).

The Hierarchy Rule was instituted to prevent counting the same criminal incident more than once due to multiple offenses as it is reported to the FBI. In essence, this rule requires the agency to determine the most serious offense in a criminal incident and report only that offense. The hierarchy of offenses is in this order: criminal homicide, forcible rape, robbery, aggravated assault, burglary, larceny-theft, and motor vehicle theft. For example, if an individual breaks into a home and proceeds to assault the owner, law enforcement would only report the aggravated assault. The burglary would not be reported and, therefore, would remain unknown to users of the data. Arson falls outside of the hierarchy and should be reported independently of the remaining seven Part I offenses. The two remaining exceptions to the Hierarchy Rule involve the reporting of motor vehicle theft and of justifiable homicides. If there is a criminal incident containing both a motor vehicle theft and, by extension, the contents of the vehicle constitutes a larceny-theft, only the motor vehicle theft should be reported. In the case of a justifiable homicide, two separate incidents/offenses would be reported: one reflecting the felonious act connected to the offender and another incident of the justifiable homicide, which is reported as a murder/nonnegligent manslaughter and unfounded (Federal Bureau of Investigation, 2004).

There is also a hierarchy associated with the reporting of arrest information as well. Beyond the already specified Part I hierarchy, however, the reporting agency is left to decide the most serious charge associated with an arrest. As mentioned earlier, the Hierarchy Rule was eliminated in the NIBRS because it allows for the reporting of multiple offenses within one incident. An agency reporting an arrest through the NIBRS would still need to determine the most serious offense to report as the arrest offense, however (Federal Bureau of Investigation, 2000, 2004).

Multiple offenses and the application of the Hierarchy Rule raise the question of what specifically constitutes an incident in the UCR Program to determine which offenses apply. The Separation of Time and Place Rule states that if there is a separation of time and place between multiple offenses, the agency should consider them separate events or incidents to be classified and reported individually. The *Uniform Crime Reporting Handbook* provides the following example of the application of the Separation of Time and Place Rule:

> A robber entered a bank, stole $5,000 from a teller at gunpoint, and then escaped in a getaway care. At a shopping center parking lot across town, the robber and an accomplice stole a car in their effort to elude police. (p. 12)

In this scenario, there are two offenses occurring both in different locations and at different times. The law enforcement agency should report both a robbery and a motor vehicle theft. Occasionally there are circumstances that separation of time and place occurs, but the actions could be considered continuing criminal activity of the same incident. For example, an offender or group of offenders steals the contents of a series of coin-operated devices or parking meters in a one-block area during one night. Such occasions are rare, however, and agencies are cautioned as such (Federal Bureau of Investigation, 2004).

After the classification of the offenses occurring in the criminal incident and the application of the Hierarchy Rule, agencies then score, or count, the number of offenses. Scoring rules in UCR dictate that for all crimes against persons, one offense is counted for every victim connected to that offense. For all crimes against property, one offense is counted for every "distinct operation" or incident. In the case of motor vehicle theft, one offense is to be counted for every vehicle stolen. The main exception to these standards involves the Hotel Rule. The Hotel Rule is only applicable in cases of burglary and states that where multiple units are burglarized in a facility under a single manager (such as a hotel or lodging house) and the burglaries are most likely to be reported by the manager rather than the tenants, the incidents should be treated and counted as one incident/offense. In the NIBRS, the Hotel Rule has been extended to also include self-storage warehouses (Federal Bureau of Investigation, 2000, 2004).

Not All Crime Is Known and Recorded by Law Enforcement

Beyond the set rules that determine how the data look when they finally arrive at the FBI National Program, there is the question of *if* they arrive. Within the criminological community, there are numerous discussions of the "dark figure" of crime unreported by victims and crime unrecorded by law enforcement and its implications on crime statistics. Law enforcement, like any bureaucratic process, is multilayered, and, as such, provides ample opportunity for information never to be found or to be lost before it arrives at the FBI.

Any serious student of the subject of crime and criminality is aware that not every victim chooses to report victimizations to the appropriate law enforcement agency, nor is every criminal event detected by law enforcement. Because UCR is a source of official statistics on crime, crimes that go unreported are not reflected in the figures available. Considering the wide-ranging experience of crime victims and the myriad situations that can exist in the areas policed by the almost 17,000 law enforcement agencies that report to the FBI, this important factor is incredibly complex and the discussion of its implications is beyond the scope of this chapter. Additionally, some of these practices can create situations in which an event comes to the attention to law enforcement but they do not take a report or it is handled by some other means. This includes scenarios in which law enforcement issues a simple citation for lesser offenses but does not take an incident report or when an officer chooses to warn an offender rather than cite him or her. Occasionally, agencies use information tracking systems for citations that is not a part of their standard record management system for incident reports. In these eventualities, the data would simply never be recorded in the local databases and could not be included as crime data are forwarded to either the State Program or the FBI.

There Is a Given Set of Information That Is Reported Through the UCR Program

Assuming that an incident was reported by a victim or came to the attention to law enforcement and that agency participates in the UCR Program, there is still a possibility that the information would not be reported to the FBI. As was delineated in earlier sections, data are collected only on designated offenses. If a criminal activity is not one of those offenses, it would not be reported to the FBI or reflected in its crime counts.

There Are Rules About Who Can Participate (i.e., Not Every Agency That Learns About Criminal Activity Can Report It to the FBI)

Once a victim has decided to report a criminal incident to the appropriate authority, there is still not a guarantee that the information will ultimately be reported to the FBI. The UCR Program will only accept data from agencies that are considered to be *law enforcement*. The UCR Program defines a law enforcement agency as one in which the sworn officers have full arrest powers. This would eliminate a number of administrative agencies that have jurisdiction over certain offenses (such as the Security and Exchange Commission's jurisdiction over certain white-collar offenses) or facilities that use private security firms or officers who have limited arrest powers.

There Are No Laws on the Federal Level That Require Participation in the UCR Program (i.e., Not Every Law Enforcement Agency Participates)

In any given year, there are law enforcement agencies that choose not to participate in the UCR Program. Since 1994, participation has ranged from 16,522 to 17,381 law enforcement agencies. From its inception, the UCR Program has been a voluntary program. Law enforcement agencies choose to participate at their own discretion with no extra funding provided to them by the FBI for that purpose. Many agencies have begun to participate, however, because of requirements associated with non-FBI funding or because reporting facilitates the awarding of that funding. There are also many states that have enacted laws requiring their agencies participate in the UCR Program.

There Are No Rules That Specify a Mandatory Amount of Data to Submit

In addition to the voluntary nature of the UCR Program, agencies also are not required to submit a full year's worth of data. There are many occasions that agencies will give the Program only a few months of data or be just shy by 1 month of the full 12. Alternatively, there are some agencies that will only submit Return A (offense) data but not participate in the remaining data collections associated with the UCR Program. Given these two scenarios, it becomes necessary for the FBI to estimate[2] the missing pieces (nonparticipation, incomplete participation, and limited participation) to provide the nation with a complete picture of crime in the United States (Federal Bureau of Investigation, 2004).

In the situation where a nonparticipating agency chooses not to submit any crime data to the UCR Program, the crime experience for the population served should still be accounted for in national and regional estimates on the status of crime. For agencies that participate in the UCR Program but fall short of 12 complete months (or incomplete participation), the UCR Program uses a method to "fill in" those missing months. Finally, there are agencies that provide complete data but on a limited number of reports. In all but a few exceptions, these agencies and their populations are not accounted for in particular tables in UCR publications or are treated as a nonparticipant within the estimation process.

---

[2] Although the terms *estimate* and *estimation* have very specific definitions within the methods of sample-based statistics, the UCR Program uses *estimation* to describe the process of imputing values for missing data. This chapter uses the terminology employed by the UCR Program and its documentation.

ESTIMATING CRIME

Although it is always possible for an interested party to receive copies of the actual submitted data from the FBI or other data clearinghouses, most users of UCR data learn crime information from the FBI's publications such as *Crime in the United States*. For its publications, the FBI provides estimated crime information to compensate for incomplete reporting. Depending on the type of data and the amount of missing data, the techniques for that estimation vary.

Offense Data

Most of the estimated data published by the FBI are offense data. Historically, there are two primary estimation techniques used by the FBI depending on the amount of data received from the agency. For agencies that have submitted at least 3 months of offense data, the FBI applies a simple weighting technique that inflates the submitted data to what would be expected for 12 months at the same rate. This technique would not be possible if the agency failed to submit any data at all or submitted too little data, however. In those circumstances, the UCR Program uses an estimation procedure based on population rather than time. Population is used because it is readily available and is highly correlated with crime.

If an agency submitted less than three months or is completely absent, the missing data are estimated based on the experience of other similar agencies based upon population. For core, or principal, cities in a Metropolitan Statistical Area (MSA),[3] the current year rate for the agency's population group for the nation is applied to the agency's population to calculate an estimated volume. It should be noted, however, that the UCR Program pursues the acquisition of actual data from principal cities in an effort to avoid estimating their crime experience. The remaining agencies that have submitted less than three months are estimated by using the state rate for the agency's population group from the current year. In the absence of a state rate, the UCR Program will apply the division or regional rate.

---

[3] A Metropolitan Statistical Area is a designated area consisting of a principal city of at least 50,000 inhabitants and the surrounding counties that have strong economic ties.

These agency-level estimates are always aggregated into larger geographic areas. The smallest unit published is that of the MSA. Other aggregate levels of estimates include state, geographic division, region, and the nation.

In addition to these two primary means of estimation, there are occasions when a differing technique is introduced for the estimation of agencies from a particular state. The UCR Program documents those procedures as far back as 1985 and is specified annually in the *Crime in the United States.*

There is also one table in *Crime in the United States* that represents categories collected on the Supplement to Return A and contains estimated figures for crime. The UCR Program first ascertains the current proportions of the subcategories of location and circumstances of offenses that are captured on the Supplement to Return A by using the data from agencies that supplied at least six months of Supplement to Return A data. The estimates for the "Offense Analysis" table (currently table 7 in *Crime in the United States*) are then calculated by applying these proportions to the estimated offense totals. The remaining published offense tables in *Crime in the United States* have differing established criteria for completeness to be included. The most common is to limit the table to only include agencies that submitted complete data for 12 months.

Critical to the understanding of the estimation process in the UCR publications is the concept of population groups. The UCR Program assigns an agency to one of nine groups based on the population of the jurisdiction it serves. The largest population group comprises agencies that serve cities with 250,000 or more in population. That single group can also be divided into three subgroups of 1,000,000 or more, 500,000 to 999,999, and 250,000 to 499,999 in population. The agencies that serve cities are then divided into six remaining groups of 100,000 to 249,999, 50,000 to 99,999, 25,000 to 49,999, 10,000 to 24,999, 2,500 to 9,999, and under 2,500 in population. In practice, the two smallest population groups are often combined into an "under 10,000 in population" group. Agencies that serve university and college populations or other similar type agencies are usually assigned to the smallest city population group category. County and state police agencies are divided into two remaining population groups for counties that are divided by whether the agency serves a metropolitan or nonmetropolitan population on the basis of membership in an MSA (Federal Bureau of Investigation, 1960–2004).

In many cases, there are agencies that serve a constituency in which the population is already accounted for by another agency. These "zero-population" agencies are still assigned a population group. If the agency serves a county area, the UCR Program categorizes the agency into the appropriate county group. Those agencies that serve in incorporated places are placed in the smallest city population group category. The fact that these agencies have no population attributed to them places them in a unique situation for the estimation of nonparticipating agencies. Although it is not possible to estimate for a nonparticipating zero-population agency, the crime rate that is employed during the estimation procedure incorporates any reported data from other zero-population agencies. Thus, each agency-level estimate for the smallest city and county population groups would be slightly inflated by the crime reports of other zero-population agencies. This is one of many reasons that the stated UCR estimation procedures would be inappropriate for agency-level estimates. The bias that this inflation creates disappears once the data are aggregated, however.

Arrest Data

Arrest data have little estimation applied to them. There is one table in *Crime in the United States* that provides estimated arrest data. Estimated arrests are based on a rate from agencies reporting a full 12 months of arrest data. The rate for each population group and each arrest offense is multiplied by the total population base for each population group in the UCR database. This population base would include both participating and nonparticipating agencies. The volume calculated for each population group is then aggregated by arrest offense to reflect a national estimate (Federal Bureau of Investigation, 1960–2004).

Many of the arrest tables in *Crime in the United States* illustrate the trends observed at 2-, 5-, and 10-year intervals. To be included in these tables, an agency must have submitted at least six of the same months for both of the years in question (Federal Bureau of Investigation, 1960–2004).

In addition to the annual published arrest data in *Crime in the United States,* the FBI published *Age-Specific Arrest Rates and Race-Specific Arrest Rates for Specific Offenses* on an ad hoc basis in early editions and currently provides updates annually. The basic methodology used by the FBI is to use only agencies that submit 12 months of complete arrest data within either age and sex categories or race categories as the set of admissible agencies. Because there are agencies that provide age and sex arrest data but not race data, the universe of admissible agencies for each set of calculations is different. In the case of age-specific arrests, the age and gender distribution provided by the Census Bureau for a given year is applied to the UCR population from the set of admissible agencies. This estimated population is then used to calculate a rate using the reported number of arrests within a specific age or gender category and within arrest offense. The same procedure is followed to calculate race-specific arrest rates beginning with a different universe of admissible agencies and using the race distribution as reported by the Census Bureau for a given year. Because the estimation procedure used in *Age-Specific Arrest Rates and Race-Specific Arrest Rates* is based on an age and gender stratification or race stratification, one should not expect that total estimates derived from these rates would match the estimates and rates published in *Crime in the United States* (Federal Bureau of Investigation, 1993, 2003)

Other Data

Other data collected by the UCR Program can also be in various states of completion. The UCR Program does not have any estimation procedure in place for Supplementary Homicide or Arson data. Most commonly, the FBI will restrict the tabulation to only agencies that have submitted 12 months of data (Federal Bureau of Investigation, 1960–2004).

In addition to crime data, the UCR Program must estimate population data for its publications because the Census Bureau does not release its estimates in time for the UCR publications. These populations are used in the calculation of any rates that are published by the UCR Program. The UCR Program derives population estimates by applying the growth rate of each state using population data from the Census Bureau for the current and prior year to each agency's

population from the prior year. To reconcile UCR population estimates with the published Census totals for the states and the nation,
adjustments are made to the population of the largest city agency
within the state. This ensures that the sum of the agency populations is equivalent to the published Census figures (Federal Bureau
of Investigation, 1960–2004).

HOW DID WE ARRIVE AT THE SYSTEM WE HAVE TODAY?

It may be the general understanding of the users of crime data that
the UCR Program has been relatively unaltered from its inception
in 1929. This has often been touted as the justification behind the
creation of the NIBRS. However, there have been many occasions for
the expansion and contraction of the data collections associated with
the UCR Program in its history (see Table 3.2).

Original Components of the Data Collection

At the advent of the UCR Program, the collection of crime data consisted of a set of monthly returns and a set of annual returns. Participating agencies provided counts of Part I offenses on the Return A on a
monthly basis. Originally, information associated with these counts was
limited because the breakdowns of offense data, such as weapons or
manner of criminal activity, was not included on the Return A. There
were versions of the Supplement to Return A and the Supplementary
Homicide Report, but the collection of this information was limited
to only agencies with 25,000 or more in population.

Prior to 1952, the UCR Program used fingerprint submissions to
the Bureau for the identification of arrest information. The collection
included such information as type of crime committed, place and date
of arrest, place of birth, age, sex, race, nationality, and the criminal
history of the arrestee. The original racial categories included White,
Negro, Indian, Chinese, Japanese, Mexican, and All Other. While the
category of Mexican was dropped in 1942, the other race categories
remained unchanged until 1980. In 1952, the annual returns of the
UCR Program incorporated a version of the Age, Sex and Race of
Persons Arrested. It included many of the Part I offenses that are seen
on the current version of the ASR.

TABLE 3.2. *Highlights of Uniform Crime Reporting (UCR) Program history*

1950s and 1960s	• The Consultant Committee on the Uniform Crime Reports formed to review the Program and formulate any changes needed to improve and modernize the UCR Program. • *Crime in the United States* became an annual publication rather than quarterly releases. • *Crime in the United States* included estimated figures to account for missing or incomplete data submissions. • UCR Program was expanded to include data from unincorporated areas (i.e., sheriffs' offices). • The Crime Index was created based on the submission of Part I offense data. • Collections of both offense and arrest data were adjusted. • The FBI began to shift much of its responsibilities of day-to-day data collection from law enforcement agencies to state-level organizations called State Programs.
1970s	• State Programs grew, with the addition of 44 new states added by the end of the decade. • Both the traffic collection data and the charge and disposition data comprising the Return C eliminated from the Program. • The Crime Index was simplified to include all larceny-thefts as opposed to those with a value of $50 or more. • Two new aggregate counts debuted: violent crime and property crime. • The collection of offense information was revised focusing on extending the breakdown information collected on the Return A and the Supplement to Return A. • Age, sex, and race of the offender and the relationship of the victim to the offender began to be collected on the Supplementary Homicide Report. • Age, Sex and Race of Persons Arrested (ASR) went from an annual collection to a monthly collection. • The juvenile ASR form added two new age categories for the youngest arrestees – under 10 and 10–12. • Drug violations were expanded on the ASR to include categories to reflect either the sales or possession of one of the collected drug types. • The estimation procedures stated in *Crime in the United States* were revised to include application of information from similar areas in addition to the original weighting procedure.

(continued)

TABLE 3.2 *(continued)*

1980s	• The Federal Crime Reporting Act was passed to capture crime data from federal law enforcement agencies that had not traditionally participated in the UCR Program. • The Hate Crime Statistics Act authorized the collection of bias-motivated offenses for a five-year period. • The newly authorized collection of arson data was made a permanent part of the list of Index and Part I crimes in the UCR Program. • The NIBRS Program was created. • The UCR Program changed its race and ethnicity designations to conform to the Office of Management and Budget racial categories for the federal statistical systems. • The quarterly preliminary releases were scaled back to semiannual releases.
1990s	• Piloting and initial implementation of the NIBRS Program occurred. • The Hate Crime Data Collection Program was made a permanent fixture in the UCR Program. • LEOKA analysis collection was expanded to include serious assaults with injury as a result of the use of a firearm or knife. • Violent Crime Control and Law Enforcement Act enabled data collections in topic areas including stalking, domestic violence, and gang violence. • The first pilot of a Quality Assurance Review was conducted in efforts to understand the amount of classification and scoring error at local agencies and to provide the agencies with guidance in improving these same processes.
2000s	• The Crime Index was suspended until a more refined methodology is developed. • Twenty-six states are certified to submit NIBRS data to the UCR Program. • In association with changes to the structures of Metropolitan Statistical Areas, the new terminology of *metropolitan* and *nonmetropolitan* is to replace the use of *suburban* and *rural*.

Note: LEOKA = Law Enforcement Officers Killed and Assaulted; NIBRS = National Incident-Based Reporting System.

Additional annual returns included the Return B and the Return C. The Return B was an annual version of the Return A for the agency to report its yearly totals. The Return C was used to collect information on the charges and dispositions of individuals arrested for Part I and Part II offenses.

The IACP, being the original steward of the UCR Program, was responsible for the first reports issued from the UCR Program. Those duties were shifted to the Bureau of Investigation, which later became the FBI, by 1930. The first publication of UCR data from the Bureau of Investigation consisted of only five tables and could be purchased for 10 cents. Originally these reports were issued on a monthly basis, but the UCR Program converted to quarterly issues in 1932.

Changes in the 1950s and 1960s – Results of the 1958 Consultant Committee

In 1957, a Consultant Committee on the UCR was formed to review the Program and formulate any changes needed to improve and modernize the UCR Program. With the exception of the creation of the NIBRS, this effort resulted in the most comprehensive revision to the UCR Program in its history. The changes recommended by the Consultant Committee were phased in over a number of years and constituted the majority of modifications seen through the late-1950s and the 1960s (Federal Bureau of Investigation, 1958).

In terms of the overall release of crime data from the FBI, the Consultant Committee recommended that there be an annual publication rather than quarterly releases. Additionally, the publication would begin to include estimated figures to account for missing or incomplete data submissions. The first published estimates were confined to the "Index of Crime" section, which displayed data from Standard Metropolitan Statistical Areas (later called Metropolitan Statistical Areas). Estimation procedures consisted of weighting data from agencies that had contributed at least nine months of data and were associated with at least 25 percent of the area being tabulated. In the case of fewer months of data being submitted, the crime figures were estimated on the basis of reports of other agencies within the same area (Federal Bureau of Investigation, 1958).

The UCR Program was expanded to include data from unincorporated areas (i.e., sheriffs' offices) in addition to the already collected information from the police departments of cities and towns. To better delineate the differences between rural and urban crime, the Consultant Committee recommended that the FBI use the newly created category of a Standard Metropolitan Statistical Area to define the urban areas. In addition, the 1958 publication reported for the first time monetary values for losses associated with offenses (Federal Bureau of Investigation, 1958).

The Consultant Committee also recommended the creation of a Crime Index[4] based on the submission of Part I offense data. Because this Index was to be a simple additive one, it was recommended offenses similar in terms of severity be included. For this reason, the Part I offenses of negligent manslaughter and larcenies under $50 in value were not counted in the Index. Assaults were also limited to aggravated assaults in the Index (Federal Bureau of Investigation, 1958).

There were additional adjustments to the data collections of both offenses and arrests during these decades. One major revision included the elimination of statutory rape from the rape collection. This provided that motivation to use the term *forcible* in connection to rape for the first time. There was also the first inclusion of offense breakdowns on the Return A during the 1960s. The first breakdown of offense information included rape by force or attempted rape, robbery with a weapon (armed) or no weapon (strong-arm), aggravated assaults by weapon type (gun, knife, other, or hands, fists, feet, etc.), the inclusion of simple assault, and burglary by force, unlawful entry, or attempted (Federal Bureau of Investigation, 1960–2004).

The supplemental offense reports – Supplement to Return A and the Supplementary Homicide Report – were also amended during this time period. The Supplement to Return A eliminated joyriding from the automobile theft categories, and additional categories of larceny-theft were added to include those from buildings and from coin-operated devices or machines. The Supplementary Homicide Report began collecting age, sex, and race information on victims, as

---

4 Currently, the UCR Program has opted to suspend the Crime Index and the Modified Crime Index to develop and implement a more valid measure of criminality of place.

well as weapon information (Federal Bureau of Investigation, 1960–2004).

Arrest data underwent major modifications to include the creation of two forms, one for juveniles and one for adults. On the juvenile form, the offense categories of curfew/loitering law, runaway, vandalism, and arson were added to the original list of Part II offenses. Although both vandalism and arson were also included on the adult form, a different set of offense categories to include drug offense breakdowns by type, and gambling offense breakdowns were added at this time (Federal Bureau of Investigation, 1960–2004).

Toward the end of the 1960s, the FBI began to shift much of its responsibilities of day-to-day data collection from law enforcement agencies to state-level organizations called State Programs. In 1968, the FBI established 10 requirements that must be met for the recognition of a UCR State Program. In that same year, New Jersey and California became the first states to establish State Programs, followed quickly by Michigan, which established its State Program in 1969 (Federal Bureau of Investigation, 1960–2004).

Changes in the 1970s

The UCR Program continued to see growth in State Programs with the addition of 44 new states added by the end of the decade. The 1970s also saw examples of simplifications to the data collection process. Two major aspects of the UCR Program, the traffic collection data and the charge and disposition data comprising the Return C, were eliminated from the Program during this time because of difficulties in ascertaining the data. The same difficulties were also cited as the reason for simplifying the Index to include all larceny-thefts as opposed to those with a value of $50 or more (Federal Bureau of Investigation, 1960–2004).

Two new aggregate counts also debuted in this decade: violent crime and property crime. Although similar in terminology, these categories should not be confused with the crimes against persons and crimes against property, which are crucial to proper scoring of offenses. The new aggregate categories were created solely for the tabulation and publication of crime data. The violent crimes are murder and nonnegligent manslaughter, forcible rape, robbery, and aggravated assaults.

The property crimes are burglary, larceny-theft, and motor vehicle theft. This results in the classification of robbery as a violent crime for tabulation and publication purposes and as a crime against property for scoring the offense (Federal Bureau of Investigation, 1960–2004).

Revisions to the collection of offense information focused on extending the breakdown information collected on the Return A and the Supplement to Return A. The classification of robbery weapons was expanded to include firearm, knife or cutting instrument, or other serious weapon. The category of strong-arm robbery remained. Automobile theft was renamed motor vehicle theft, and the breakdowns of automobiles, trucks and buses, or other were added to the Return A. The Supplement revised the larceny-theft values to account for inflation, changing them from "Less than $5," "$5 to $50," and "Over $50" to "Less than $50," "$50 to $200," and "Over $200." The collection of the value of stolen property on the Supplement was expanded to include murder and rape along with the other Part I crimes (Federal Bureau of Investigation, 1960–2004).

The detailed homicide data also saw some additions to its data collection. The FBI began collecting information on the age, sex, and race of the offender and the relationship of the victim to the offender on the Supplementary Homicide Report (Federal Bureau of Investigation, 1960–2004).

The arrest information also went through some revisions in the 1970s. Starting in 1974, the age, sex, and race of persons arrested went from an annual collection to a monthly collection. The juvenile arrest form also saw the addition of two new age categories for the youngest arrestees: under 10 and 10–12. Drug violations were also expanded to include categories to reflect either the sales or possession of one of the collected drug types (Federal Bureau of Investigation, 1960–2004).

The publications released by the FBI continued to evolve during the 1970s. The estimated procedures stated in *Crime in the United States* were based on applying information from similar areas in addition to the original weighting procedure (see *Estimating Crime*). The UCR Program also began to produce its own population estimates rather than trying to collect them from the Census and other sources. This decade also saw dramatic changes to the Crime Index. In addition to the inclusion of all larceny-thefts to the Index, Congress ordered that offense data on arson be added to the list of Index crimes. The FBI published for the first time aggregate measures on violent crime and property crime. It was also during this period that the Law Enforcement Officers Killed and Assaulted Program was created (Federal Bureau of Investigation, 1960–2004).

Changes in the 1980s

In the 1980s, the Congress and its legislative agenda had a significant impact on the role of crime statistics and reporting. Two legislative acts were passed authorizing the creation of new data collection systems. The Federal Crime Reporting Act was passed in 1988 to begin capturing crime data from federal law enforcement agencies that had not traditionally participated in the UCR Program. The Hate Crime Statistics Act authorized the collection of bias-motivated offenses for a five-year period. There were also several pending legislative initiatives impacting the UCR Program. The subject areas included arson, law enforcement officers killed, bombings, assaults on federal officers, and parental kidnappings (Federal Bureau of Investigation, 1960–2004).

The newly authorized collection of arson data was also made a permanent part of the list of Index and Part I crimes in the UCR Program. As these statistics began to show improvement, more of the data were published in this decade. Because reporting of arson was still spotty, however, the UCR Program published arson along with the other seven Index crimes as a Modified Crime Index rather than incorporate it in its traditional Crime Index. There were also plans to incorporate the arson data collection with the data collected by Federal Emergency Management Administration's National Fire Data Center. As priorities within the Bureau shifted toward the development of a new generation of data collection for the UCR Program, the project was eventually abandoned (Federal Bureau of Investigation, 1960–2004).

It was during the 1980s that the UCR Program began to consider seriously the future of the Program and where it needed to go for the benefit of law enforcement and its other users. The FBI, through the Bureau of Justice Statistics (BJS), contracted for a phased study of the UCR Program that would ultimately make recommendations for the next generation of the UCR Program. From this study, summarized in the *Blueprint for the Future of the Uniform Crime Reporting Program: Final*

Report of the UCR Study, the NIBRS came into being. The study and
the ratification of its recommendations was a process that took the
majority of this decade to conclude. By the end of the process, the law
enforcement community reaffirmed its desire to have the FBI manage
the program. Additionally, even though the recommendation was to
have only a sample of agencies implement the full version of the NIBRS
with a "lighter version" for the remainder of the nation's agencies, the
law enforcement community endorsed the ambitious goal of having
all law enforcement agencies implement the full version of the NIBRS
(Federal Bureau of Investigation, 1960–2004).

There were other ongoing adjustments to the UCR Program during
this time period. The UCR Program changed its race and ethnicity
designations in 1980 to conform to the Office of Management and
Budget racial categories for the federal statistical systems. The new race
designations were White, Black, American Indian or Alaskan Native,
and Asian or Pacific Islander. The ethnic categories implemented on
the ASR (arrest) and SHR (homicide) collections were Hispanic or
not Hispanic. These ethnic designations were only in effect until 1987
(Federal Bureau of Investigation, 1960–2004).

The publications issued by the UCR Program were adjusted for
changing circumstances during the 1980s. The quarterly preliminary
releases were scaled back to semiannual releases. The Program also
began estimating rape figures for the state of Illinois because of
changes in their data collection, including the rape of males under
their forcible rape category. It was also during this time that State Programs went through a period of retraction with many states choosing
to close their State Programs due to lack of support (Federal Bureau
of Investigation, 1960–2004).

Changes in the 1990s
Whereas there were signs of contraction during the 1980s, the UCR
Program went through a general period of expansion during the
1990s. Many of the states that had dissolved State Programs began
the process of reinstating them. Three major data collection initiatives
began during this decade as well. During the years following 1990, the
FBI UCR Program began to pilot and implement the NIBRS. South
Carolina was the pilot state and the first to participate officially. By the

TABLE 3.3. *National Incident-Based Reporting System (NIBRS) certification by year*

Year certified	NIBRS-certified state
1991	North Dakota
	South Carolina
1992	Iowa
	Idaho
1994	Utah
	Virginia
	Vermont
1995	Massachusetts
1996	Michigan
1997	Colorado
	Kentucky[a]
	Nebraska
	Wisconsin
1998	Tennessee
	Texas
	West Virginia
1999	Connecticut
	Ohio
2000	Arkansas
2001	District of Columbia[a]
	Delaware
	Kansas
	South Dakota
2003	Louisiana
	New Hampshire
2004	Arizona
	Maine
2005	Missouri
	Oregon
2006	Montana

[a] Kentucky and the District of Columbia are not NIBRS-certified states; however, there are agencies within the states certified to submit NIBRS data directly to the FBI.

end of the 1990s, the FBI was accepting NIBRS data from 18 states (see Table 3.3; Federal Bureau of Investigation, 1960–2004).

Other major expansions to the UCR Program include the implementation of the Hate Crime Data Collection Program and the expansion of the LEOKA analysis collection to include serious assaults with injury as a result of the use of a firearm or knife. The Hate Crime

Data Collection, which began as a five-year initiative, published data for the first times in 1991 and included 3,000 participating agencies from 32 states. In 1994, disability bias was added to its data collection through the Violent Crime Control and Law Enforcement Act, and with the passage of the Church Arson Prevention Act in 1996, the Hate Crime Data Collection Program was made a permanent part of the UCR Program (Federal Bureau of Investigation, 1960–2004).

The legislative agenda begun in the 1980s came to fruition in the 1990s. In addition to the changes in the Hate Crime Data Collection, the Violent Crime Control and Law Enforcement Act enabled data collections in topic areas including stalking, domestic violence, and gang violence. Most of these newer data collections were either already available in the NIBRS or, as in the case of gang violence, the NIBRS was adjusted to include new data values to capture the involvement of juvenile gangs and adult gangs. Legislation also required colleges and universities to maintain reports of crime in accordance with UCR definitions (Federal Bureau of Investigation, 1960–2004).

The UCR Program also began to initiate changes from within. In 1996, the first pilot of a Quality Assurance Review (QAR) was conducted. The QAR sends representatives into law enforcement agencies, on a voluntary basis and at the request of the State Program, to review the agencies' information contained in their record management system and compare it with their original UCR reports. These efforts by the UCR Program sought to understand the amount of classification and scoring error at local agencies, as well as to provide the agencies with guidance in improving these same processes (Federal Bureau of Investigation, 1960–2004).

Changes in 2000 and Beyond

The most significant change to the UCR Program since 2000 has been the suspension of the Crime Index. Through discussions with contributing agencies, State Program managers, and other learned professionals, the UCR Program decided that the Crime Index in its current form did not provide the precision of measurement that had come to be expected in indices. Because the Crime Index and the Modified Crime Index are only simple additive indices, they did not provide any way to ascertain the severity of the type of crime experienced by a location. For example, two agencies could have the same Crime Index with one having problems focusing on petty theft and the other having a more pervasive problem with violent crime. That information could not be ascertained through the Crime Index number. The UCR Program is in the process of studying alternative means of calculating a Crime Index with the idea of reintroducing the concept at a later date with more refined methodology. Unlike other indices that are more closely tied to market processes and the value of goods and services, developing a crime index has inherent difficulties associated with defining a metric that can quantify the severity or impact of a crime (Federal Bureau of Investigation, 1960–2004).

Additional changes to the UCR publications include the revising of the terminology in association with changes to the structures of MSAs. Because OMB changed the criteria of MSAs to factor in only commuting information, they advised agencies to discontinue any reference to urban or rural in association with MSAs. The 2003 *Crime in the United States* marked the debut of the new terminology of *metropolitan* and *nonmetropolitan* to be used instead of *suburban* and *rural* (Federal Bureau of Investigation, 1960–2004).

Finally, the UCR Program has seen slow but steady growth in participation in the continued growth of the NIBRS. As of 2004, 5,616 agencies from 28 states are currently submitting NIBRS data to the UCR Program through this collection system. The FBI has also made the Quality Assurance Review process a permanent part of the UCR Program (Federal Bureau of Investigation, 1960–2004).

THE LEGACY OF UCR

The legacy of the UCR Program is difficult to quantify. In addition to its direct impact on the day-to-day operations of law enforcement, the UCR Program indirectly contributes to the acquisition of law enforcement resources and staff through the Local Law Enforcement Block Grants (LLEBG), Community Oriented Policing Services (COPS) Grants, and Byrne Grants. The COPS office estimates that 114,648 law enforcement officers have been put on the street since 1992 (Office of Community Oriented Policing Services, October 19, 2004). Individuals and investors in local communities also use UCR crime data heavily. The level of crime in a particular area is a factor in decisions such as where to buy a house, build schools, and locate businesses and other developments. Finally, the amount of research generated by both criminal justice practitioners and academic researchers with the aid of UCR data is invaluable both in its contribution to the general understanding of criminality and crime and in its contribution to the formulation of criminal justice policy.

The future of the UCR Program is in the NIBRS and its continued growth. As more data become available, there is a growing interest in the generation of research and analysis with the NIBRS. With its incident-based format, this data collection system will allow for the exponential expansion in the amount of knowledge on criminal activity in the United States.

APPENDIX – PART II OFFENSES

Other assaults (simple) – assaults and attempted assaults which are not of an aggravated nature and do not result in serious injury to the victim.

Forgery and counterfeiting – the altering, copying, or imitating of something without authority or right, with the intent to deceive or defraud by passing the copy or thing altered or imitated as that which is original or genuine; or the selling, buying, or possession of an altered, copied, or imitated thing with the intent to deceive or defraud. Attempts are included.

Fraud – the intentional perversion of the truth for the purpose of inducing another person or other entity in reliance upon it to part with something of value or to surrender a legal right. Fraudulent conversion and obtaining of money or property by false pretenses. Confidence games and bad checks, except forgeries and counterfeiting, are included.

Embezzlement – the unlawful misappropriation or misapplication by an offender to his/her own use or purpose of money, property, or some other thing of value entrusted to his/her care, custody, or control.

Stolen property; buying, receiving, possessing – buying, receiving, possessing, selling, concealing, or transporting any property with the knowledge that it has been unlawfully taken, as by burglary, embezzlement, fraud, larceny, robbery, etc. Attempts are included.

Vandalism – to willfully or maliciously destroy, injure, disfigure, or deface any public or private property, real or personal, without the consent of the owner or person having custody or control by cutting, tearing, breaking, marking, painting, drawing, covering with filth, or any other such means as may be specified by local law. Attempts are included.

Weapons; carrying, possessing, etc. – the violation of laws or ordinances prohibiting the manufacture, sale, purchase, transportation, possession, concealment, or use of firearms, cutting instruments, explosives, incendiary devices, or other deadly weapons. Attempts are included.

Prostitution and commercialized vice – the unlawful promotion of or participation in sexual activities for profit, including attempts. Sex offenses (except forcible rape, prostitution, and commercialized vice), statutory rape, offenses against chastity, common decency, morals, and the like. Attempts are included.

Drug abuse violations – the violation of laws prohibiting the production, distribution, and/or use of certain controlled substances and the equipment or devices utilized in their preparation and/or use. The unlawful cultivation, manufacture, distribution, sale, purchase, use, possession, transportation, or importation of any controlled drug or narcotic substance. Arrests for violations of state and local laws, specifically those relating to the unlawful possession, sale, use, growing, manufacturing, and making of narcotic drugs. The following drug categories are specified: opium or cocaine and their derivatives (morphine, heroin, codeine); marijuana; synthetic narcotics – manufactured narcotics that can cause true addiction (Demerol, methadone); and dangerous nonnarcotic drugs (barbiturates, Benzedrine).

Gambling – to unlawfully bet or wager money or something else of value; assist, promote, or operate a game of chance for money or some other stake; possess or transmit wagering information; manufacture, sell, purchase, possess, or transport gambling equipment, devices or goods; or tamper with the outcome of a sporting event or contest to gain a gambling advantage.

Offenses against the family and children – unlawful nonviolent acts by a family member (or legal guardian) that threaten the physical, mental, or economic well-being or morals of another family member and which are not classifiable as other offenses, such as Assault or Sex Offenses. Attempts are included.

Driving under the influence – driving or operating a motor vehicle or common carrier while mentally or physically impaired as the result of consuming an alcoholic beverage or using a drug or narcotic.

Liquor laws – the violation of state or local laws or ordinances prohibiting the manufacture, sale, purchase, transportation, possession, or use of alcoholic beverages, not including driving under the influence and drunkenness. Federal violations are excluded.

Drunkenness – to drink alcoholic beverages to the extent that one's mental faculties and physical coordination are substantially impaired. Exclude driving under the influence.

Disorderly conduct – any behavior that tends to disturb the public peace or decorum, scandalize the community, or shock the public sense of morality.

Vagrancy – the violation of a court order, regulation, ordinance, or law requiring the withdrawal of persons from the streets or other specified areas; prohibiting persons from remaining in an area or place in an idle or aimless manner; or prohibiting persons from going from place to place without visible means of support.

All other offenses – all violations of state or local laws not specifically identified as Part I or Part II offenses, except traffic violations.

Suspicion – arrested for no specific offense and released without formal charges being placed.

Curfew and loitering laws (persons under age 18) – violations by juveniles of local curfew or loitering ordinances.

Runaways (persons under age 18) – limited to juveniles taken into protective custody under the provisions of local statutes.

References

Bureau of Justice Statistics and Federal Bureau of Investigation. (1985, May). *Blueprint for the future of the Uniform Crime Reporting Program: Final report of the UCR Study.* Washington, DC: U.S. Department of Justice.

Federal Bureau of Investigation. (1958). *Uniform Crime Reports for the United States: Special issue.* Washington, DC: U.S. Department of Justice.

Federal Bureau of Investigation. (1960–2004). *Crime in the United States 1959–2003.* Washington, DC: U.S. Department of Justice.

Federal Bureau of Investigation. (1993). *Age-specific arrest rates and race-specific arrest rates for selected offenses, 1965–1992.* Washington, DC: U.S. Department of Justice.

Federal Bureau of Investigation. (1999). *Hate crime data collection guidelines.* Washington, DC: U.S. Department of Justice.

Federal Bureau of Investigation. (2000). *National Incident-Based Reporting System, Volume 1: Data collection guidelines.* Washington, DC: U.S. Department of Justice.

Federal Bureau of Investigation. (2003). *Age-specific arrest rates and race-specific arrest rates for selected offenses, 1993–2001.* Washington, DC: U.S. Department of Justice.

Federal Bureau of Investigation. (2004). *Uniform Crime Reporting handbook.* Washington, DC: U.S. Department of Justice.

Office of Community Oriented Policing Services. (2004, October 19). Quick state facts. Retrieved January 19, 2005, from http://www.cops.usdoj.gov/print.asp?Item=108.

Official Proceedings of the National Police Convention, St. Louis, 1871. Reprinted in *Uniform Crime Reporting: A complete manual for police,* Committee on Uniform Crime Records, International Association of Chiefs of Police, New York, 1929.

DEFINING DIVERGENCE AND CONVERGENCE

CHAPTER FOUR

What Is Convergence, and What Do We Know About It?

David McDowall and Colin Loftin

Whether crime rates from the Uniform Crime Reporting System (UCR) and National Crime Victimization Survey (NCVS) converge with each other has been a matter of substantial research interest since before the NCVS formally began. Lack of convergence would not necessarily raise questions about the validity of either data system because each might measure a different set of phenomena. The UCR and NCVS nevertheless share almost identical definitions of criminal offenses, and agreement between them would support the idea that neither is hopelessly in error. Strong evidence that they diverge would correspondingly complicate policy and academic uses of the data because one's findings might vary with the system.

A selective list of studies that consider convergence appears in Table 4.1. Perhaps the most notable feature of the list is the steady pace of research, beginning with early developmental work on the NCVS and continuing to the present. One might take this as showing that the convergence–divergence issue is important to criminologists and that it remains largely unresolved.

This chapter considers how one might define and measure convergence. Others have already evaluated the most straightforward definitions, and much of the chapter therefore reviews the existing literature.[1] Throughout, the presentation uses the terms *convergence* and

---

[1] Because of the volume of work on the issue, this is necessarily a selective review, using only a few representative studies to illustrate general points. Omitting a study does not imply criticism of its quality or significance.

TABLE 4.1. *Studies that compare estimates from the Uniform Crime Reporting System and National Crime Victimization Survey, by year of publication*

1967	1983	1992
Biderman, Johnson, and Weir	O'Brien	Blumstein, Cohen, and
Ennis	Zedlewski	Rosenfeld
Reiss	**1984**	McDowall and Loftin
1974	Cohen and Land	Menard
Hindelang	Messner	**1993**
Skogan	**1985**	Jensen and Karpos
1975	Gove, Hughes, and	Steffensmeier and Harer
Maltz	Geerken	**1996**
Skogan	Green	O'Brien
1976	O'Brien	**1997**
Decker	**1987**	Boggess and Bound
1977	Menard	**1998**
Booth, Johnson, and Choldin	Steffensmeier and	Levett
S. H. Decker	Harer	**1999**
Skogan	**1988**	Steffensmeier and Harer
1978	Messner and South	Bernard
Hindelang	Menard and Covey	**2000**
1979	**1990**	Wiersema, McDowall,
Eck and Riccio	O'Brien	and Loftin
Hindelang	**1991**	**2002**
Nelson	Biderman and Lynch	Rand and Rennison
Shichor, Decker, and O'Brien	Blumstein, Cohen, and	**2003**
1980	Rosenfeld	O'Brien
Nelson	Jencks	
O'Brien, Shichor, and	Menard	
Decker	O'Brien	
Shichor, Decker, and O'Brien		
1982		
Cohen and Lichbach		
D. L. Decker, Shichor, and		
O'Brien		

divergence as antonyms, employing whichever term is more convenient in context.

The next sections present a series of four definitions that follow a rough progression from more demanding to less demanding in their requirements for how closely the systems must agree. As the definitions become less demanding, support for convergence becomes stronger. At the same time, however, the less demanding definitions become less valuable for research and policy purposes. After discussing the definitions and their empirical support, the chapter examines an important complicating factor: the possibility that convergence levels have systematically changed over time. The final section offers some conclusions.

DEFINITION 1: CONVERGENCE AS IDENTICAL RATES

The most obvious definition of convergence, and the most demanding one, is that the UCR and NCVS should produce identical results. In a cross-sectional comparison of individual jurisdictions, the NCVS rates for each crime should equal those from the UCR.[2] In a longitudinal comparison of estimates for the entire United States, trend plots of UCR crimes should lie exactly on top of their counterparts from the NCVS. One would, of course, wish to allow for limited divergences due to sampling and recording errors. These minor sources of variation aside, the NCVS and UCR would mirror each other.

From the earliest pilot surveys onward (Biderman et al., 1967; Ennis, 1967; Reiss, 1967; U.S. Department of Justice, 1974), the UCR and NCVS have never converged under this definition. Both cross-sectional studies of city-level data and time series studies of the nation as a whole have consistently found much higher rates from the NCVS than from the UCR.

A small but troublesome limitation on the cross-sectional findings is that most comparisons did not analyze the NCVS as the Census Bureau actually fields it. This research instead relied on NCVS-*like* estimates, usually from surveys conducted in 26 cities during the early 1970s (U.S. Department of Justice, 1975a, 1975b, 1976). The 26-city surveys lacked bounding interviews and other basic features of the regular NCVS, and they used one-year reference periods for crime reports instead of the NCVS's six-month reference periods.

---

[2] Conventional terminology distinguishes the "NCS" (the survey before its 1992 redesign) from the "NCVS" (the survey after its redesign). Although the chapter considers both NCS and NCVS data, it will use "NCVS" throughout to avoid distractingly cumbersome prose.

The cross-sectional comparisons are also hampered by an incomplete overlap in the geographic coverage of the UCR and NCVS data. The NCVS counts crimes against persons who *reside* in a given area, and it includes offenses against sample members if they occurred elsewhere. In contrast, the UCR counts crimes that *occur* within a given area, and it necessarily includes victims who do not live there.

The gap between the NCVS and UCR estimates is very large, and these differences seem unlikely to account for more than a modest fraction of it. Even so, it deserves emphasis that few data points are available and that such features would limit the amount of convergence one would expect to find.

The cross-sectional lack of convergence between the UCR and NCVS is also apparent in national-level data over time. These trend studies use the field NCVS, eliminating any influence that unique features of the city surveys might have had on the results. Because they cover the entire United States, the trend studies additionally avoid most geographic mismatches between the two systems. Figure 4.1 shows UCR and NCVS rates for six crimes between 1973 and 2003. The gap has narrowed considerably, but even in 2003 the NCVS rates were 60% higher (assaults) to 500% higher (larceny-thefts) than were rates from the UCR.

The absence of support for the identical rates definition is well known to anyone who is even modestly familiar with the data. If the two systems did meet this definition, convergence would never have become a matter of concern in the first place. Yet a perfect match is the tightest and least problematic standard, and any alternative will be a significant retreat from it. In the strictest sense, the UCR and NCVS do not converge.

DEFINITION 2: CONVERGENCE AS CORRELATED RATES

If the UCR and NCVS do not converge in their absolute levels, a less demanding definition requires them to agree only up to a scale factor. Here the *relative* distribution of crimes across geographic areas or time will be the same, making rates from the systems highly correlated.

Differences in procedures and definitions could produce this type of agreement. The NCVS includes offenses that victims did not report to

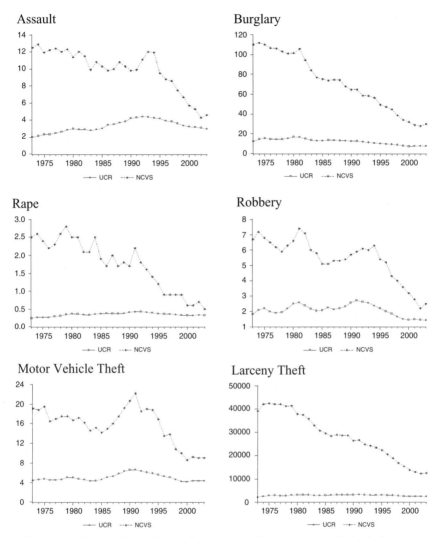

Figure 4.1. Rates of assault, burglary, rape, robbery, motor vehicle theft, and larceny-theft, Uniform Crime Reporting System (UCR) and National Crime Victimization Survey (NCVS) 1973–2003 (same scales).

the police, and its estimates should thus be higher than those from the UCR. If the proportion of unreported offenses is temporally and spatially constant, however, the UCR rates should have large correlations with their NCVS counterparts. This definition is not as stringent as the previous one because it allows an imperfect relationship between the systems. Still, if UCR and NCVS had sufficiently large correlations with each other, they would be interchangeable for most research and policy applications.

A problem with the correlational definition – and with any definition that permits less than perfect agreement – is how large the correlation must be to support convergence. Viewing essentially the same results, some researchers (e.g., S. H. Decker, 1977) have seen substantial correspondence between the systems, whereas others (e.g., Menard and Covey, 1988) have seen little or none.

One possibility is to use standards from reliability theory, where authorities often suggest that a correlation of .80 or higher indicates acceptable agreement (e.g., Nunnally and Bernstein, 1994, pp. 264–265). This solution is not entirely satisfactory because convergence is a matter more of validity than of reliability, and anything less than a perfect relationship is cause for concern. Still, the .80 criterion gives rough guidance about what convergence might involve, and some UCR–NCVS comparisons have used it in the past (e.g., Menard, 1992).[3]

Convergence as correlated rates has received far more research attention than have any of the other definitions. For purposes of presentation, it is therefore useful to examine city level cross-sectional analyses separately from time series analyses of the nation as a whole.

Cross-Sectional Comparisons

Under the .80 standard, the NCVS and UCR converge cross-sectionally for a few crimes. In an early analysis of the 26-city surveys, S. H. Decker (1977) found correlations this large for motor vehicle theft and for burglary. Nelson (1979), with different transformations of the same

[3] Demanding analysts might regard a correlation of $r = .80$ as too small to show convergence. As a case in point, the Current Population Survey (CPS) and the Current Employment Statistics survey (CES) provide separate measures of employment levels in the United States. Since the mid-1990s, estimates from the surveys have become increasingly divergent, and this difference has been a matter of concern to labor economists (e.g., Juhn and Potter, 1999). Yet the correlation between the monthly CPS and CES series was $r = .99$ over the period 1973–1996, and it dropped only to $r = .88$ between 1997 and 2003. The .80 benchmark seems a low hurdle in comparison, but data collection procedures vary much more between the UCR and NCVS than between the CPS and CES.

data, found such values for motor vehicle theft and for robbery with a weapon. Menard and Covey (1988), again working with basically the same data, obtained such a correlation only for motor vehicle theft. Although most correlations were .50 or more in all of the studies, a few were zero and a few were negative. Overall, the cross-sectional data offer some support for convergence under the correlational definition, but this evidence is uncomfortably weak.

A variation on the definition of convergence as correlation is to compare the relationships of the UCR and NCVS across major crime covariates. Similar correlations between a given covariate – median income, for example – and crime rates from the UCR and NCVS would support the idea that the systems converge. Many studies have applied this definition to the 26-city surveys, and they have obtained results even less encouraging than those from correlating the rates themselves. Variables such as crowding, demographic composition, unemployment, poverty, police expenditures, and residential mobility have markedly different relationships with the UCR and the NCVS (Booth et al., 1977; Nelson, 1980; O'Brien et al., 1980; Zedlewski, 1983). These differences are often large enough that they could affect inferences about the causes of crime, particularly in more complex models.

To consider only one example, Booth et al. (1977) found similar correlations between population density and robbery rates from the UCR ($r = .66$) and the NCVS ($r = .68$). In contrast, the correlations between population density and motor vehicle thefts heavily depended on the data system ($r = .34$ for the UCR and $r = .06$ for the NCVS). In models that controlled for seven other variables, density had a statistically significant influence on the UCR robbery rate but not on the NCVS robbery rate. Although density significantly affected both the UCR and NCVS vehicle theft rates, the signs of the coefficients were opposite of each other. For these crimes, and especially for vehicle thefts, one would reach different conclusions about the impact of density depending on the system.

Almost all cross-sectional convergence studies used the 26-city surveys in place of the field version of the NCVS, and any idiosyncrasies of these data will influence the results. Yet two additional comparisons provide some evidence that problems with the 26-city surveys cannot explain the pattern of small and conflicting correlations.

The first comparison used 12-city-level surveys conducted by the Bureau of Justice Statistics in 1998 (Smith et al., 1999). Like the 26-city data, the 12-city surveys lacked many features of the field NCVS. Among other differences, the surveys were conducted entirely by telephone, specified a one-year reference period, and did not use bounding interviews. The data collection instruments were nevertheless largely identical to the regular NCVS questionnaires. An analysis of the 12-city surveys produced correlations with the UCR that were broadly comparable to those from the 26 cities, although slightly smaller.[4]

The other comparison took advantage of the NCVS sample design to compute separate rates for each of its 40 self-representing units (Wiersema et al., 2000). The boundaries of the self-representing units coincide with the nation's 40 largest metropolitan areas, and the respondents within them are probability samples of each area's residents. Unlike the other cross-sectional convergence studies, the data for this comparison came from the full field version of the NCVS. This is an important advantage for comparability purposes, but the small sample sizes in each area limited the accuracy of the estimates. Wiersema and colleagues again obtained correlations similar to those from the other comparisons, although this time slightly larger.[5]

It is worth repeating again that, in all cross-sectional comparisons, the UCR and NCVS differed in the types of incidents they included. The UCR measures crimes that occur in a given geographic area, regardless of whether the victims live there. The NCVS measures crimes against residents of a given geographic area, regardless of whether the offenses occur there. These differences in coverage will restrict the size of the maximum possible correlations between the two systems.

Time Series Comparisons

Time series comparisons consider the United States as a whole, and they are not as vulnerable to the geographic differences that affect

---

[4] The correlations were $r = .50$ for robbery, $r = .41$ for motor vehicle theft, $r = .42$ for burglary, and $r = -.08$ for assault.
[5] The correlations were $r = .48$ for robbery, $r = .88$ for motor vehicle theft, $r = .64$ for burglary, and $r = .25$ for assault.

the cross-sectional correlations. The time series studies also use the field NCVS, avoiding the uncertainties introduced by data collected with different procedures. On the other hand, many of these studies are hampered by the few annual observations from which to generate estimates. Despite their differences from the cross-sectional comparisons, the time series studies produce similarly modest evidence of convergence.

Analyzing UCR and NCVS rates for the period between 1973 and 1982, Menard and Covey (1988) found no correlation of .80 or more for any pair of crimes. The largest correlation, for robbery, was .59, and three offenses (assault, burglary, and motor vehicle theft) were correlated negatively. Extending the time series to 1986, O'Brien (1990) found no positive correlations larger than .65 (for burglary with forcible entry), and some associations were again substantially negative.

Several studies examined convergence after allowing for linear trends. Menard (1987) used counter variables to estimate separate trends for UCR and NCVS crimes between 1973 and 1982. He found that whereas the NCVS series tended to fluctuate around constant means, most of the UCR series trended strongly upward. These patterns are obviously inconsistent with convergent relationships. Estimating the associations more directly, O'Brien (1990) analyzed a slightly longer series (1973–1986) after removing trends with counter variables and first-differences. He found correlations of more than .80 for total burglaries and forcible entry burglaries and correlations of .5 or more for some of the other crimes.

The existing time series studies used a shorter string of data than is currently available, but an analysis over a longer period yields essentially the same results. For the years 1973–2003, the correlations between the UCR and NCVS series were $r = -.21$ for assault; $r = -.16$ for rape; $r = .76$ for robbery; $r = .93$ for burglary; $r = .67$ for motor vehicle theft; and $r = .20$ for larceny-theft. Of these, only the burglary and (for practical purposes) robbery correlations meet the .80 standard.

Their correlations notwithstanding, the two data systems visually appear to agree reasonably closely over the full time period available for study. Figure 4.2 contains the same information as in Figure 4.1

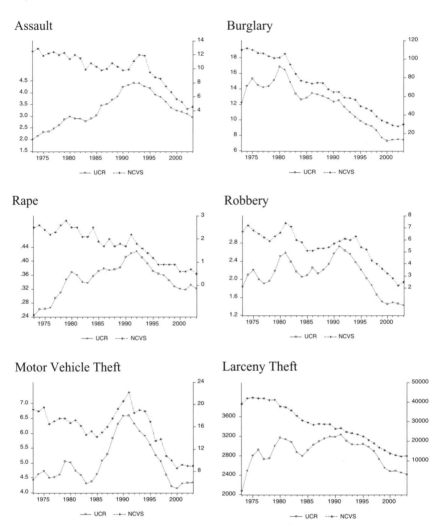

Figure 4.2. Rates of rape, robbery, assault, burglary, motor vehicle theft, and larceny-theft, Uniform Crime Reporting System (UCR) and National Crime Victimization Survey (NCVS) 1973–2003 (separate scales).

but with the series rescaled to allow finer comparisons. The burglary, robbery, and vehicle theft series show a good deal of correspondence between the UCR and NCVS, and even assaults, larcenies, and rapes follow similar paths after about 1990. This suggests that the systems may have common features that the simple correlations do not capture, and a later definition of convergence will consider this possibility in more detail.

In general, the UCR and NCVS display more signs of convergence under the correlational definition than under a definition that requires perfect agreement. Yet few correlations are as large as .80, and most are far short of it. Although the .80 cutoff is arbitrary, one could perhaps more easily argue for a higher standard than for a lower one. Even allowing considerable room for judgment, support for convergence under this definition is not as persuasive as one would wish.

DEFINITION 3: CONVERGENCE AS IDENTICAL RATES AFTER ADJUSTMENT

If the UCR and NCVS do not converge absolutely or up to a scale factor, a third definition requires that they agree only after removing major differences. Like the previous two, this definition can set a high standard for the degree of correspondence necessary to support a claim of convergence. It is less demanding (and perhaps more realistic), however, in acknowledging that the UCR and NCVS both have large components of variation specific to themselves. The raw rates are therefore not directly comparable with each other, and one cannot translate from one system to the other without allowing for the unique features.

The most thorough examination of this definition was by Biderman and Lynch (1991), who studied how differences in coverage and measurement procedures might operate to make the systems diverge. Biderman and Lynch noted that the UCR and NCVS differ in their population bases, in the nature of the offenses that they include, and in their methods for defining criminal events. The NCVS samples only persons aged 12 and over, and it estimates property crimes against households rather than against individuals. The UCR includes crimes against business establishments, and it necessarily omits offenses that victims do not report to the police. The systems are also not uniform in their measurement quality. Police agencies vary in how well they record UCR crimes, and NCVS victimization reports depend partly on how much time the respondents have spent in the sample.

Using national time series data between 1973 and 1986, Biderman and Lynch adjusted UCR and NCVS estimates for several of these differences in population bases and universes of events. They found a much higher degree of convergence after the adjustments, and major changes in the NCVS rates tended to coincide with those in the UCR. Their procedures did not completely reconcile the series, but they could not allow for all of the differences that they had identified. In Chapter 8 of this volume, Addington shows that the some of the adjustments that Biderman and Lynch used were unavoidably crude. More generally, their study called attention to the many incompatible features of the data systems, and it raised questions about how much convergence one might reasonably expect from them.

Other researchers have also studied convergence between adjusted series. Blumstein et al. (1991) adjusted UCR rates between 1973 and 1985 for changes in reporting behavior, and they allowed for differences in UCR and NCVS population bases. After these modifications, and controlling for linear trends, they found a considerable degree of similarity in the fluctuations of UCR and NCVS robberies and burglaries.

Rand and Rennison (2002) applied a broadly similar set of adjustments to UCR and NCVS total violent crime rates. They removed offenses that victims did not report to the police from the NCVS estimates, and they dropped commercial robberies and victims under age 12 from the UCR counts. With these revisions, the series followed each other much more closely than did their raw counterparts.

Overall, the UCR and NCVS are more consistent with the definition of convergence as agreement after adjustment than they are with the previous two definitions. Exactly how much correspondence may exist is more difficult to gauge with this definition than with the others, because no comparison could simultaneously hold constant all known sources of divergence. This limitation aside, the evidence suggests that even a handful of well-chosen modifications can bring the systems into close agreement. Biderman and Lynch's adjustments, for example, reduced by 80% the root mean square error in predicting annual changes in one system from those in the other.[6] If the divergence

---

[6] Computed from tables 2.2 and 2.4 in Biderman and Lynch (1991).

becomes this much less marked after a few revisions, one might reasonably conclude that the remaining difference would disappear with a more thorough set of controls. This definition therefore appears largely to support the idea that the systems converge.

DEFINITION 4: CONVERGENCE AS A LONG-TERM EQUILIBRIUM

A final definition of convergence is that the data systems converge if they trace out the same long-run time path. Both systems may contain large amounts of unique variation, and this will allow them temporarily to drift away from each other. Over a sufficiently long period, however, they will tend to move in concert, varying together in an equilibrium relationship.[7]

If the UCR and NCVS have the same set of criminal acts at their core, their rates should follow a common trend. Still, the measurement methodologies and coverage of the systems only partially overlap, and this makes it possible for them to diverge from each other for periods of several years or more. The plots of the series in Figure 4.2 seem generally consistent with this possibility.

This definition is the least demanding of the four. It is inherently a time series definition, and it does not require strong cross-sectional associations. Rates from the UCR and NCVS can frequently depart from the equilibrium, and the series need only mirror each other in their long-run patterns. The other definitions assume a much higher level of agreement than this.

An advantage of the definition of convergence as a long-term equilibrium is that it fits easily into the framework of cointegration analysis (see, e.g., Enders, 2004, pp. 319–386). A pair of time series is

---

[7] Another possibility would be to determine whether the ratio of each pair of series follows a trend. A positive trend in the ratio would imply that the series diverge (that is, that their relative differences are increasing), and a negative trend would imply convergence. O'Brien (1999) used this strategy to test for convergence between male and female arrest rates for serious offenses. Unless a pair of series possesses a long-run relationship, however, their ratio will vary over time. Any statements about convergence will then hold only for the observed sample period, and the analysis will be entirely descriptive. The goal of this chapter is to make inferences about long-run patterns in the UCR and NCVS, and O'Brien's approach is unsuitable for this purpose.

cointegrated if each is nonstationary (lacks a constant mean), and if this nonstationarity has a common source. Because of these features, cointegrated series will share a trend, toward which each series will return when external shocks push it away. A well-developed methodology exists to test for the presence of cointegration and to estimate cointegrating relationships (see, e.g., Enders, 2004, pp. 319–386).

Convergence as cointegration leads in a somewhat different direction than do the other definitions. A cointegration analysis tests the null hypothesis that a pair of series is not cointegrated. Rejecting this hypothesis supports only the existence of a long-run relationship between the series, and it implies very little about their association at any specific moment. In contrast, the other definitions implicitly test the null hypothesis that the correspondence between a pair of series is perfect at all time points. Less-than-perfect correlations are inconsistent with convergence under these definitions, and they result in the problem of how to define perfection in practice.

Although cointegration is less demanding than the standards set by the other definitions, it is not an easy criterion to satisfy. One will reject the null hypothesis only with strong evidence of a common trend, and findings of cointegration are rare in criminology (e.g., Greenberg, 2001; Witt and Witte, 2000).

Table 4.2 presents the results of cointegration tests for each pair of UCR and NCVS crimes. Time series must be nonstationary for cointegration to be possible, and the first panel of the table presents augmented Dickey-Fuller tests of the null hypothesis of nonstationarity. In all cases, the tests fail to reject the null. The second panel of the table shows the results of Johansen tests of zero versus one cointegrating relationship for each series pair. The analysis considered three possible models: no trend in the data and an intercept in the cointegrating equation; a linear trend in the data and an intercept in the cointegrating equation; and a linear trend in both the data and the cointegrating equation. The table reports the results for the models that best fit each crime.

The tests reject the null hypothesis of no cointegration for all offenses except robberies. The series are short for this type of analysis, and the results are suspiciously variable across the tests. Motor

TABLE 4.2. *Unit root and cointegration tests, Uniform Crime Reporting System (UCR) and National Crime Victimization Survey (NCVS), 1973–2003*

Series	p Value
NCVS rapes	.8868
NCVS robberies	.9680
NCVS assaults	.9694
NCVS burglaries	.9378
NCVS larceny-thefts	.9916
NCVS motor vehicle thefts	.8741
UCR rapes	.5518
UCR robberies	.4285
UCR assaults	.3949
UCR burglaries	.9761
UCR larceny-thefts	.4332
UCR motor vehicle thefts	.2368

Cointegration null hypothesis: Each series pair does not have a cointegrating relationship

Series	Trace statistic	Model
Rapes	22.6645*	No trend in data, intercept in cointegrating equation
Robberies	10.3950	No trend in data, intercept in cointegrating equation
Assaults	16.6422*	No trend in data, no intercept in cointegrating equation
Burglaries	27.7424*	No trend in data, intercept in cointegrating equation
Larceny-thefts	24.1800*	No trend in data, intercept in cointegrating equation
Motor vehicle thefts	27.1182*	Linear trend in data, intercept and trend in cointegrating equation

Note: Unit root null hypothesis: Each series is nonstationary.
* Reject null hypothesis, $p < .05$.

vehicle thefts require a linear trend in the data and cointegrating equation, but these trends are not obvious in Figure 4.1 or Figure 4.2. The test indicates no cointegration between the robbery series, but visually robberies appear as closely related as any pair of crimes. These and other anomalies suggest that one should interpret the results with more than the usual amount of caution. Still, taken on their face, the tests show that five of the six sets of series do possess an equilibrium relationship.

Despite their long-run correspondence, cointegrated series can move away from each other for extended periods. Table 4.3 presents estimates of the vector error correction models that describe the short-term dynamics between the UCR and NCVS rates.[8] The results of most interest are the coefficients for the error correction terms, which measure how rapidly a series moves back to equilibrium after an exogenous shock pushes it away. These coefficients are small in all cases, indicating that the return to equilibrium will be extremely slow. NCVS assaults, for example, will make up only about 9% of a one unit (1 crime per 1,000) movement away from equilibrium in the previous year. UCR assaults will adjust to shocks away from equilibrium even more gradually, enough so that the error correction coefficient is statistically insignificant. This general pattern also characterizes the other offenses. In broadest terms, pairs of series will move together, eventually converging to a common path. At any point short of the long run, the rates can considerably diverge.

Fully convincing support for a cointegrating relationship will require more observations than the NCVS now provides. The logic that underlies cointegration analysis nevertheless seems well suited to the relationship between the UCR and NCVS, and the statistical evidence is generally consistent with it. Remaining mindful of the uncertainties, one might tentatively conclude that the data systems show convergence under this definition.

ARE THE UCR AND NCVS BECOMING MORE CONVERGENT?

The comparisons and analysis in this chapter have assumed that any relationship between the UCR and NCVS will be constant over the entire period available for study. Questioning this idea, Figure 4.1

---

[8] The estimates are maximum likelihood, using Johansen's method. Table 4.3 presents regression models, with dependent variables, rather than measurement models. Cointegration analysis can accommodate measurement models (e.g., Durbin and Koopman, 2001; Harvey, 1989), but regression specifications should be satisfactory with two variables. The NCVS series is dependent in each model, but the inferences would be identical if the UCR series were dependent.

TABLE 4.3. *Error correction models, Uniform Crime Reporting System (UCR) and National Crime Victimization Survey (NCVS), 1973–2003*

Rape

Variable	Coefficient	Standard Error	t
Dependent variable: ΔUCR_t			
Error correction term	0.0047	0.0025	1.88
$\Delta NCVS_{t-1}$	0.0158	0.0106	1.49
ΔUCR_{t-1}	0.5180	0.2146	2.41
$\Delta NCVS_{t-2}$	0.0012	0.0112	0.10
ΔUCR_{t-2}	−0.3204	0.2014	−1.59
Dependent variable: $\Delta NCVS_t$			
Error correction term	−0.1051	0.0446	−2.35
$\Delta NCVS_{t-1}$	−0.4172	.1906	−2.19
ΔUCR_{t-1} 11.2997	3.8563	2.93	
$\Delta NCVS_{t-2}$ −.4117	0.2018	−2.04	
ΔUCR_{t-2} −2.6490	3.6202	−0.73	
Assault			
Dependent variable: ΔUCR_t			
Error correction term	−0.0001	0.0052	−0.02
$\Delta NCVS_{t-1}$	0.0193	0.0349	0.55
ΔUCR_{t-1}	0.3529	0.2038	1.73
$\Delta NCVS_{t-2}$	−0.0008	0.0352	−0.02
ΔUCR_{t-2}	0.3455	0.2064	1.67
Dependent variable: $\Delta NCVS_t$			
Error correction term	−0.0870	0.0219	−3.97
$\Delta NCVS_{t-1}$	−0.0977	0.1469	−0.66
ΔUCR_{t-1}	0.4152	0.8455	0.49
$\Delta NCVS_{t-2}$	−0.2566	0.1482	−1.73
ΔUCR_{t-2}	3.5958	0.8698	4.13
Burglary			
Dependent variable: UCR_t			
Error correction term	−0.0028	0.0030	−0.93
$NCVS_{t-1}$	−0.0068	0.0416	−0.16
UCR_{t-1}	−0.6388	0.2036	3.14
$NCVS_{t-2}$	−0.0128	0.0397	−0.32
UCR_{t-2}	−0.4016	0.2134	−1.88
Dependent variable: $NCVS_t$			
Error correction term	−0.0652	−0.0152	−4.30
$NCVS_{t-1}$	−0.3178	−0.2072	−1.53
UCR_{t-1}	3.8056	1.0141	3.75
$NCVS_{t-2}$	−0.3858	−0.1976	−1.95
UCR_{t-2}	−0.9520	1.0631	0.89

(*continued*)

TABLE 4.3 *(continued)*

Rape

Variable	Coefficient	Standard Error	t
Larceny-Theft			
Dependent variable: UCR_t			
Error correction term	0.0031	0.0015	2.07
$NCVS_{t-1}$	0.0209	0.0157	1.33
UCR_{t-1}	0.4889	0.1741	2.81
$NCVS_{t-2}$	0.0244	0.0148	1.65
UCR_{t-2}	−0.5690	0.1618	−3.52
Dependent variable: $NCVS_t$			
Error correction term	−0.0457	0.0173	−2.65
$NCVS_{t-1}$	0.0422	0.1848	0.23
UCR_{t-1}	0.0719	2.0515	0.03
$NCVS_{t-2}$	0.3217	0.1746	1.84
UCR_{t-2}	1.4950	1.9062	0.78
Motor Vehicle Theft			
Dependent variable: UCR_t			
Error correction term	−.1165	.1006	−1.16
$NCVS_{t-1}$	.0414	.0730	.57
UCR_{t-1}	.5164	.3809	1.36
$NCVS_{t-2}$	.0229	.0505	.45
UCR_{t-2}	−.3617	.3386	−1.06
Constant	.0120	.0556	.22
Dependent variable: $NCVS_t$			
Error correction term	−1.8876	0.4348	−4.34
$NCVS_{t-1}$	0.4439	0.3156	1.40
UCR_{t-1}	−1.3793	1.6458	−0.84
$NCVS_{t-2}$	−0.1419	0.2180	0.65
UCR_{t-2}	−1.6448	1.4628	−1.12

and (especially) Figure 4.2 appear to show greater convergence in more recent years. UCR and NCVS burglaries display little correlation before about 1980, but they have tracked each other closely since then. A similarly strong association for most of the other crimes begins to become apparent during the 1990s. This suggests that a structural break might have altered the relationship between the systems and that they now and will in the future more closely agree.

The source of a structural break could lie in the UCR, in the NCVS, or in both. Of these possibilities, researchers have given most attention to the UCR. The case for a break in the UCR begins from the claim that it is less complete in its coverage than is the NCVS. UCR measurement methods have nevertheless improved over time, whereas NCVS methods have remained essentially constant. The UCR therefore appears to show rising crime rates through the 1980s only because it was including larger and larger fractions of eligible offenses. The stability or declines in the NCVS are the patterns that the UCR would have followed if it had been equally accurate. By the 1990s, the UCR improvements were mostly in place, and estimates from the two systems were in general agreement.

Proponents of this view (e.g., Jencks, 1991; O'Brien, 2003) point out that police departments have invested heavily in record-keeping systems and that technological developments and new personnel have enhanced crime reporting efficiency. With these changes, the gap between the number of crimes NCVS respondents say that they reported to the police and the number of police-recorded crimes in the UCR has considerably narrowed (Rand and Rennison, 2002).

Although a break in the NCVS is a less widely considered possibility, the closer correspondence between the systems loosely coincides with the redesign of the NCVS in 1992. The redesign involved major alterations to the NCVS questionnaire, and these changes significantly increased estimates in several crime categories (Kindermann et al., 1997). The comparisons in this chapter, and in most other post-redesign studies, use recalibrated series that attempt to allow for the new features (Rand et al., 1997). Yet data limitations constrained the scope of the calibration adjustments, and it is conceivable that differences due to the redesign remain. Even without a strong theory, the change in NCVS methodology would be a logical suspect if a break occurred.

Almost no research has examined breaks in the NCVS, the Catalano and Rosenfeld contributions to this volume being notable exceptions. Several careful studies have focused on breaks in the UCR, however, and they provide suggestive support for the hypothesis that improved UCR accuracy has made the systems more convergent. In particular, Jensen and Karpos (1993) found that increased UCR rape rates between 1973 and 1990 paralleled three developments that might have encouraged higher levels of reporting: greater availability of rape crisis centers, new policies for handing sexual assaults, and more female police personnel. The generally decreasing NCVS rape rates over the period were consistent with several other social indicators, such as reductions in fear of crime and higher rape clearance rates. Falling NCVS rape rates may then have reflected changes in the incidence of the crime, while rising UCR rates may have been due to improvements in measurement.

O'Brien (1996, 2003) similarly showed that year-to-year fluctuations in UCR homicide rates have always closely paralleled year-to-year fluctuations in the rates of other UCR violent crimes. In contrast, multi-year trends in the series began to depart from each other during the 1970s, with the other violent crime rates moving steadily upward while homicide rates remained constant. O'Brien noted that the UCR has always recorded homicide accurately and that its lack of increase may have reflected a pattern common to all types of criminal violence. The apparently rising rates of the other offenses would then have been a consequence of better measurement.

In agreement with the other studies, Rosenfeld (this volume) found evidence that recording practices help explain the differences between UCR and NCVS aggravated assault rates. Rosenfeld pointed out that although gun assaults are uniformly serious crimes, other types of assault often cause relatively little harm. He suggested that, for a variety of reasons, police departments have progressively reduced the threshold of harm that they require before they classify an assault into the aggravated (seriously harmful) category. If this were true, UCR aggravated assault rates should rise over time, and most of the increase should involve assaults without guns. The NCVS should not show a similarly divergent pattern between gun and other weapon assaults because NCVS definitions and recording procedures have remained constant. Consistent with these hypotheses, Rosenfeld found that UCR and NCVS gun assault rates exhibited similar trends, whereas trends in UCR and NCVS nongun assaults diverged.

The idea that the divergence between the UCR and NCVS was due to low UCR accuracy is an intriguing possibility, but several problems complicate efforts to test it convincingly. First and most obviously, only 31 annual NCVS observations are available through 2003. The limited amount of data makes trend estimates tenuous even for the full period, and tests for a break require dividing each series into two pieces. The existing research partially avoided this problem by concentrating on changing temporal patterns in the longer UCR series. Yet satisfactory tests of the measurement change hypothesis will ultimately require direct comparisons between the UCR and NCVS, and this will be possible only with more data.

Second, and relatedly, the break explanation is necessarily vague about the timing of the changes in the UCR, dating them as occurring between the "mid-1970s" and the "early 1990s." This lack of precision makes it easier to obtain suggestive support for the hypothesis and more difficult to subject it to a conclusive test. Although any effects of changes in UCR measurement accuracy should become apparent over a long enough period, the hypothesis's limited specificity could extend this period well into the future.

Finally, and again similar to the other problems, the idea that the series are becoming more convergent is in part the fruit of "data snooping." Simply, the series *look* like they are now coming together, and increased UCR measurement accuracy is a convenient mechanism to account for the apparent change. The lack of exogenously given dates for the beginning and end of the UCR improvements can make the measurement hypothesis difficult to falsify. Methods for blindly finding a break in a cointegrating relationship potentially offer a way to resolve this problem (Gregory and Hansen, 1996; Hansen, 1992), but they did not prove useful with the UCR and NCVS series through 2003.[9]

Overall, the UCR and NCVS may be moving toward a higher degree of convergence than they have displayed in the past. The structural break that this implies is nevertheless far from certain, and the greater

---

[9] Separate tests of each series for a structural break at an unknown date (Andrews, 1993; Andrews and Ploberger, 1994) yielded no evidence (at $p < .05$) of level changes in any UCR or NCVS crime. More powerful tests for NCVS breaks coinciding with the 1992 redesign found a significant downward shift in motor vehicle thefts. This suggests that the Rand et al. (1997) adjustments to the vehicle theft series may have overcorrected for the redesign's impact.

agreement between the series is only about a decade old. Although some evidence supports the idea that changes to the UCR have made the series move toward convergence, any strong conclusion is probably premature.

CONCLUSIONS

This chapter has considered four ways in which the UCR and NCVS might converge. The strictest and most straightforward definition specifies identical rates, and the relationship between the two data systems clearly does not satisfy its requirements. The slightly less demanding definition of convergence as correlated rates is complicated by the need for a standard of how large the correlation must be. The chapter has used a correlation of .80 or more, but one could easily impose a higher or lower cutoff value. High standards seem most consistent with a commonsense understanding of convergence, and even with the somewhat lenient .80, support for convergence is uncomfortably weak. Some studies find convergence for some crimes, but these are exceptions to a general pattern of small or even negative relationships.

The other two definitions allow the data systems more noticeably to depart from each other. The definition of convergence as agreement after adjustment emphasizes that the UCR and NCVS have fundamental differences in their definitions and measurement methods. One must therefore hold these differences constant before one can reasonably expect that estimates from the systems will agree. The definition of convergence as long-term equilibrium looks for a single time path toward which the UCR and NCVS rates will both move. It attributes all remaining variation to unique characteristics of the data systems, which it leaves unexamined.

Perhaps because they allow weaker relationships, these two definitions are more consistent with the data than are the first two. The adequacy of the evidence for convergence as agreement after adjustment is in part a matter of opinion, because the definition stresses features of the systems that are often unmeasurable. Still, after making adjustments where they are possible, the UCR and NCVS show a very high degree of correspondence. The case for convergence as a long-term equilibrium rests on a shaky foundation of limited data, but the available observations also generally support the idea of the cointe-grating relationship that it requires.

Yet if one uses the two less demanding definitions, the concept of convergence begins to become fuzzy enough that it can lose practical significance. If the UCR and NCVS converge under the stricter defi-nitions, one will be able accurately to predict one system's rates from those of the other. When the UCR increases or decreases, the NCVS will increase or decrease with it. This would be a desirable outcome for criminologists because it would suggest that measurements from both systems were generally valid. It would also be a desirable situation for policy makers and the press because either system would provide the same answers to questions about variations in crime.

Defining convergence as agreement after adjustment or as a long-run equilibrium does not offer this level of comfort. For criminolo-gists, convergence under either definition would still suggest that the UCR and NCVS were valid measures of crime. Yet as the annual NCVS observations begin to accumulate, researchers will increasingly have a choice between using UCR or NCVS data for their macrolevel anal-yses. If the two series are cointegrated, over a very long period they should both provide the same conclusions. Over less than a very long period, the results of an analysis could depend on the system that one chooses to examine. Knowing that the UCR and NCVS diverge because of definitions and procedures will also be unhelpful to crimi-nologists if they cannot measure and control these differences in their studies.

For policy makers and the press, the less demanding definitions of convergence are even more problematic. The definitions allow the possibility that rates from one data system will rise in a given period, while those from the other system fall. The divergences will some-times be minor, but practical experience and the error correction models show that they can also be very large. Even simple descriptions of short-term changes in crime rates might then vary with the data source.

Convergence may ultimately hold only under conditions that most users will find unsuitable for their purposes. Knowing that the UCR and NCVS converge could be a matter of theoretical interest to scholars but of little practical importance to them or to anyone else.

As the chapter has suggested, the relationships between the data systems may not be immutable, and their closer agreement since the mid-1990s might continue into the future. Here the convergence between the UCR and NCVS could be tight enough to satisfy the more demanding definitions, especially the definition of convergence as correlation. This would again be an ideal situation for all interested parties. Although the data are currently insufficient to evaluate the break hypothesis with much confidence, eventually a definitive test should be possible.

The limited uses of the less demanding definitions also raise questions about how much importance one should attach to convergence in the first place. An alternative to focusing on convergence would be to accept that both systems contain multiple unique components, and to emphasize their complementarities instead of their correspondence (Biderman and Lynch, 1991).

The UCR and NCVS could both accurately measure crime and still diverge from each other. Although the systems employ similar definitions of criminal offenses, they have many differences in their scope and measurement methodologies. The logic of convergence is to minimize these differences or to work around them. Researchers could instead take advantage of the variations and use the UCR and NCVS to answer the types of questions for which each is best suited. In the end, understanding the differences between the systems might be more helpful in deciding which to use in a particular situation than in proving that they converge under some esoteric definition.

References

Andrews, D. W. K. (1993). "Tests for parameter instability and structural change with unknown change point." *Econometrica* 61:821–826.

Andrews, D. W. K., & Ploberger, W. (1994). "Optimal tests when a nuisance parameter is present only under the alternative." *Econometrica* 62:1383–1414.

Bernard, T. J. (1999). "Juvenile crime and the transformation of juvenile justice: Is there a juvenile crime wave?" *Justice Quarterly* 16:337–356.

Biderman, A. D., Johnson, L. A., McIntyre, J., & Weir, A. W. (1967). *Report on a pilot study in the District of Columbia on victimization and attitudes toward law enforcement; Field Surveys I, a report of a research study submitted to the President's Commission on Law Enforcement and Administration of Justice.* Washington, DC: U.S. Government Printing Office.

Biderman, A. D., & Lynch, J. P. (1991). *Understanding crime incidence statistics: Why the UCR diverges from the NCS.* New York: Springer-Verlag.

Blumstein, A., Cohen, J., & Rosenfeld, R. (1991). "Trend and deviation in crime rates: A comparison of UCR and NCS data for burglary and robbery." *Criminology* 29:237–263.

Blumstein, A., Cohen, J., & Rosenfeld, R. (1992). "The UCR-NCS relationship revisited: A reply to Menard." *Criminology* 30:115–124.

Boggess, S., & Bound, J. (1997). "Did criminal activity increase during the 1980s? Comparisons across data sources." *Social Science Quarterly* 78:725–739.

Booth, A., Johnson, D. R., & Choldin, H. M. (1977). "Correlates of city crime rates: Victimization surveys versus official statistics." *Social Problems* 25:187–197.

Cohen, L. E., & Land, K. C. (1984). "Discrepancies between crime reports and crime surveys: Urban and structural determinants." *Criminology* 22:499–530.

Cohen, L. J., & Lichbach, M. I. (1982). "Alternative measures of crime: A statistical evaluation." *Sociological Quarterly* 23:253–266.

Decker, D. L., Shichor, D., & O'Brien, R. M. (1982). *Urban structure and victimization.* Lexington, MA: Lexington Books.

Decker, S. H. (1976). *Criminalization, Victimization and Structural Correlates of Twenty-Six American Cities.* Dissertation, School of Criminal Justice, Florida State University.

Decker, S. H. (1977). "Official crime rates and victim surveys: An empirical comparison." *Journal of Criminal Justice* 5:47–54.

Durbin, J., & Koopman, S. J. (2001). *Time series analysis by state space methods.* New York: Oxford University Press.

Eck, J. E., & Riccio, L. J. (1979). "Relationship between reported crime rates and victimization survey results: An empirical and analytical study." *Journal of Criminal Justice* 7:293–308.

Enders, W. (2004). *Applied econometric time series* (2nd ed.). New York: Wiley.

Ennis, P. H. (1967). *Criminal victimization in the United States: A report of a national survey; Field Surveys II, a report of a research study submitted to the President's Commission on Law Enforcement and Administration of Justice.* Washington, DC: U.S. Government Printing Office.

Gove, W. R., Hughes, M., & Geerken, M. (1985). "Are Uniform Crime Reports a valid indicator of the Index Crimes? An affirmative answer with minor qualifications." *Criminology* 23:451–500.

Green, G. S. (1985). "The representativeness of the Uniform Crime Reports: Ages of persons arrested." *Journal of Police Science and Administration* 13:46–52.

Greenberg, D. F. (2001). "Time series analysis of crime rates." *Journal of Quantitative Criminology* 17:291–327.

Gregory, A. W., & Hansen, B. E. (1996). "Residual-based tests for cointegration in models with regime shifts." *Journal of Econometrics* 70:99–126.

Hansen, B. E. (1992). "Tests for parameter instability in regressions with I(1) processes." *Journal of Business and Economic Statistics* 10:321–335.

Harvey, A. C. (1989). *Forecasting, structural time series models and the Kalman filter.* New York: Cambridge University Press.

Hindelang, M. J. (1974). "The Uniform Crime Reports revisited." *Journal of Criminal Justice* 2:1–17.

Hindelang, M. J. (1978). "Race and involvement in crimes." *American Sociological Review* 43:93–109.

Hindelang, M. J. (1979). "Sex differences in criminal activity." *Social Problems* 27:143–156.

Jencks, C. (1991, winter). "Behind the numbers: Is violent crime increasing?" *American Prospect* 4:98–109.

Jensen, G. F., & Karpos, M. (1993). "Managing rape: Exploratory research on the behavior of rape statistics." *Criminology* 31:368–385.

Juhn, C., & Potter, S. (1999). "Explaining the recent divergence in payroll and household employment growth." *Current Issues in Economics and Finance* 16(5):1–6.

Kindermann, C., Lynch, J., & Cantor, D. (1997). *Effects of the redesign on victimization estimates.* Washington, DC: U.S. Government Printing Office.

Levitt, Steven S. D. (1998). "The relationship between crime reporting and police: Implications for the use of Uniform Crime Reports." *Journal of Quantitative Criminology* 14:61–81.

Maltz, M. D. (1975). "Crime statistics: A mathematical perspective." *Journal of Criminal Justice* 3:177–194.

McDowall, D., & Loftin, C. (1992). "Comparing the UCR and NCS over time." *Criminology* 30:125–132.

Menard, S. (1987). "Short-term trends in crime and delinquency: A comparison of UCR, NCS, and Self-Report Data." *Justice Quarterly* 4:455–474.

Menard, S. (1991). "Encouraging news for criminologists (in the year 2050)? A comment on O'Brien (1990)." *Journal of Criminal Justice* 19:563–567.

Menard, S. (1992). "Residual gains, reliability, and the UCR-NCS relationship: A comment on Blumstein, Cohen, and Rosenfeld." *Criminology* 30:105–113.

Menard, S., & Covey, H. (1988). "UCR and NCS: Comparisons over space and time." *Journal of Criminal Justice* 16:371–384.

Messner, S. F. (1984). "The 'dark figure' and composite indexes of crime: Some empirical explorations of alternative data sources." *Journal of Criminal Justice* 12:435–444.

Messner, S. F., & South, S. J. (1988). "Estimating race-specific offending rates: An intercity comparisons of arrest data and victim reports." *Journal of Crime and Justice* 11:25–45.

Nelson, J. F. (1979). "Implications for the ecological study of crime: A research note." In Willard Parsonage (Ed.), *Perspectives on victimology* (pp. 21–28). Newbury Park, CA: Sage.

Nelson, J. F. (1980). "Alternative measures of crime: A comparison of the Uniform Crime Reports and the National Crime Survey in twenty-six American cities." In D. E. Georges-Abeyie & K. D. Harries (Eds.), *Crime, a spatial perspective* (pp. 77–92). New York: Columbia University Press.

Nunnally, J. C., & Bernstein, I. H. (1994). *Psychometric theory* (3rd ed.). New York: McGraw-Hill.

O'Brien, R. M. (1983). "Metropolitan structure and violent crime: Which measure of crime? (comment on Blau and Blau, ASR, February 1982)." *American Sociological Review* 48:434–437.

O'Brien, R. M. (1985). *Crime and victimization data.* Beverly Hills, CA: Sage.

O'Brien, R. M. (1990). "Comparing detrended UCR and NCS crime rates over time: 1973–1986." *Journal of Criminal Justice* 18:229–238.

O'Brien, R. M. (1991). "Detrended UCR and NCS crime rates: Their utility and meaning." *Journal of Criminal Justice* 19:569–574.

O'Brien, R. M. (1996). "Police productivity and crime rates: 1983–1992." *Criminology* 34:183–207.

O'Brien, R. M. (1999). "Measuring the convergence/divergence of 'serious crime' arrest rates for males and females: 1960–1995." *Journal of Quantitative Criminology* 15:97–114.

O'Brien, R. M. (2003). "UCR violent crime rates, 1958–2000: Recorded and offender-generated trends." *Social Science Research* 32:499–518.

O'Brien, R. M., Shichor, D., & Decker, D. L. (1980). "An empirical comparison of the validity of UCR and NCS crime rates." *Sociological Quarterly* 21:391–401.

Rand, M., Lynch, J. P., & Cantor, D. (1997). *Criminal victimization, 1973–95.* Washington, DC: U.S. Government Printing Office.

Rand, M. R., & Rennison, C. M. (2002). "True crime stories? Accounting for differences in our national crime indicators." *Chance* 15:47–51.

Reiss, Albert J., Jr. (1967). *Studies in crime and law enforcement in major metropolitan areas, field survey III, volume I; a report of a research study submitted to the U.S. President's Commission on Law Enforcement and Administration of Justice.* Washington, DC: U.S. Government Printing Office.

Shichor, D., Decker, D. L., & O'Brien, R. M. (1979). "Population density and criminal victimization: Some unexpected findings in central cities." *Criminology* 17:184–193.

Shichor, D., Decker, D. L., & O'Brien, R. M. (1980). "The relationship of criminal victimization, police per capita and population density in twenty-six cities." *Journal of Criminal Justice* 8:309–316.

Skogan, W. G. (1974). "The validity of official crime statistics: An empirical investigation." *Social Science Quarterly* 55:25–38.

Skogan, W. G. (1975). "Measurement problems in official and survey crime rates." *Journal of Criminal Justice* 3:17–31.

Skogan, W. G. (1977). "Dimensions of the dark figure of unreported crime." *Crime and Delinquency* 23:41–50.

Smith, S. K., Steadman, G. W., Minton, T. D., & Townsend, M. (1999). *Criminal victimization and perceptions of community safety in 12 cities, 1998.* Washington, DC: U.S. Government Printing Office.

Steffensmeier, D., & Harer, M. D. (1987). "Is the crime rate really falling? An aging U.S. population and its impact on the nation's crime rate, 1980–1984." *Journal of Research in Crime and Delinquency* 24:23–48.

Steffensmeier, D., & Harer, M. D. (1993). "Bulging prisons, an aging U.S. population, and the nation's violent crime rate." *Federal Probation* 57:3–10.

Steffensmeier, D., & Harer, M. D. (1999). "Making sense of recent U.S. crime trends, 1980 to 1996/1998." *Journal of Research in Crime and Delinquency* 36:235–274.

U.S. Department of Justice. (1974). *Crimes and victims: A report on the Dayton–San Jose Pilot Survey of Victimization.* Washington, DC: U.S. Government Printing Office.

U.S. Department of Justice. (1975a). *Criminal victimization surveys in the nation's five largest cities.* Washington, DC: U.S. Government Printing Office.

U.S. Department of Justice. (1975b). *Criminal victimization in 13 American cities.* Washington, DC: U.S. Government Printing Office.

U.S. Department of Justice. (1976). *Criminal victimization surveys in eight American cities.* Washington, DC: U.S. Government Printing Office.

Wiersema, B., McDowall, D., & Loftin, C. (2000). "Comparing metropolitan area estimates of crime from the National Crime Victimization Survey and the Uniform Crime Reports." Paper presented at the Joint Statistical Meetings, American Statistical Association, Indianapolis, Indiana, August 13–17.

Witt, R., & Witte, A. (2000). "Crime, prison, and female labor supply." *Journal of Quantitative Criminology* 16:69–85.

Zedlewski, E. (1983). "Deterrence findings and data sources: A comparison of the Uniform Crime Reports and the National Crime Survey." *Journal of Research in Crime and Delinquency* 20:262–276.

SOURCES OF DIVERGENCE
IN THE NCVS

CHAPTER FIVE

Methodological Change in the NCVS and the Effect on Convergence

Shannan M. Catalano

Historically the National Crime Victimization Survey (NCVS) and the Uniform Crime Reports (UCR) have provided different estimates of crime at the national level. Of the two, the NCVS traditionally reported more crime than recorded by police. In 2001, however, the number of serious violent crimes recorded by the police *exceeded* the number of crimes that victims said they reported to the police in the NCVS. This recent correspondence is the culmination of more than a decade of gradual convergence and raises important issues regarding the measurement of serious violent crime, particularly over time.[1]

One of these issues is whether changes in the methodology employed in the NCVS could be contributing to the convergence with UCR estimates. Research shows that methodological change in the NCVS creates within series variation over time (Biderman and Lynch, 1991), yet the effect of such change remains largely ignored since the NCVS redesign in the early 1990s. This chapter examines whether the recent convergence between reported crimes in the NCVS and recorded crimes in the UCR is influenced by long-term methodological change in the victimization survey.

---

[1] *UCR* and *police recorded* are used interchangeably to denote officially generated police data. *NCVS, victim survey,* and *victim reported* are used interchangeably to denote victimizations in the NCVS survey that respondents indicate were reported to the police. Similarly, *correspondence* and *convergence* are used interchangeably for purposes of this chapter. Use of the term convergence does not imply a statistical relationship but rather a convergence in absolute number of crimes measured by each data program.

The chapter opens with an outline of the methodological changes to the survey and their potential effect on correspondence;[2] a discussion of data sources and the construction of the variables used in the subsequent analysis follows.[3] The results indicate that, except for changes in response rates and to a lesser extent computer-assisted telephone interviewing (CATI), changes in the NCVS design had minimal effect on the observed correspondence of the two series. A brief discussion and concluding remarks follow.

BACKGROUND AND SIGNIFICANCE

Until 30 years ago, the UCR was the only indicator of crime in the United States. In 1973, the NCVS, partly in response to limitations of the UCR, was implemented in an effort to augment and expand available knowledge on the nature and extent of crime. As the nation's two indicators of crime, the UCR and NCVS were expected to provide identical estimates of crime, but absolute correspondence between the two series was impossible without taking into consideration important differences between the two data collection programs (see Chapters 2 and 3, this volume). Most important among these is the fact that the NCVS measures crimes both reported and not reported to the police. In contrast, the UCR represents only those crimes coming to the attention of law enforcement. Once these differences are controlled for, correspondence between the two series improved markedly, although the volume of crime measured by each program still differed substantially (Biderman and Lynch, 1991). The remaining gap continued as the subject of much debate (Biderman and Lynch, 1991; Blumstein et al., 1991; Langan and Farrington, 1998; McDowall and Loftin, 1992; O'Brien et al., 1980; see also Chapter 4, this volume). The result of subsequent research on the issue was an unsteady truce between the NCVS and UCR based on the understanding that each provided valuable, albeit not directly comparable, data on the crime.

---

[2] See Lauritsen and Catalano (2005) for an overview of methodological characteristics of the NCVS.

[3] Not every methodological change in the survey is included in this analysis. Specifically, changes in undercoverage in the household sampling frame are not explicitly addressed in this chapter. This issue is addressed in Chapter 7 of this volume.

Since 2000, the Bureau of Justice Statistics (BJS) has made publicly available a Fact Sheet illustrating the gap between UCR and NCVS estimates (U.S. Department of Justice [USDOJ], 2004). As presented in Figure 5.1, estimates of victimizations reported to the police in the survey are nearly double those recorded by police in official statistics during the early years of the survey. Notable, however, are changes in the pattern of the two trends over time, particularly during the last decade. From 1973 until 1993, a stable upward trend in police recording is observed, in contrast to a fairly stable trend in reported victimizations. In 1993, the volume of serious violent crime measured by each series began to decline, with a more pronounced decrease in victimization counts.

The steeper decline in survey estimates opens the possibility that factors other than an actual decline in crime are driving victimization counts down, and one of those factors could be methodological changes in the survey. This chapter evaluates the hypothesis that changes in NCVS methodology have resulted in an underestimate of crime over time, thereby bringing the NCVS into closer correspondence with the UCR, even to the point of having the UCR counts exceed the relevant counts from the NCVS.[4] The conjecture that changes in survey methodology are contributing to the steeper decline in victimization counts gains credibility in light of the fact that the survey has undergone substantial changes in the past decade.

Methodological Changes in the NCVS

Since its inception in 1973, the NCVS has gone through a number of changes, some large and many small, some by design and others due to changes in the world in which the survey exists (see Chapter 2, this volume). Throughout the period 1973 to 1992, there were gradual changes in the mode of interviewing and very modest changes in instrumentation and procedures, largely introduced in 1986. In 1992, there was a major change in both mode of interviewing (with the

---

4 In 2001, the UCR recorded 1.3 million serious violent Crime Index offenses (homicide, rape, robbery, and aggravated assault). If the crime of homicide is added into total NCVS crime counts for 2001, the survey recorded 1.2 million crimes. There are a number of explanations of this "overlap," some of which are discussed in Chapters 6, 7, 9, and 10, this volume.

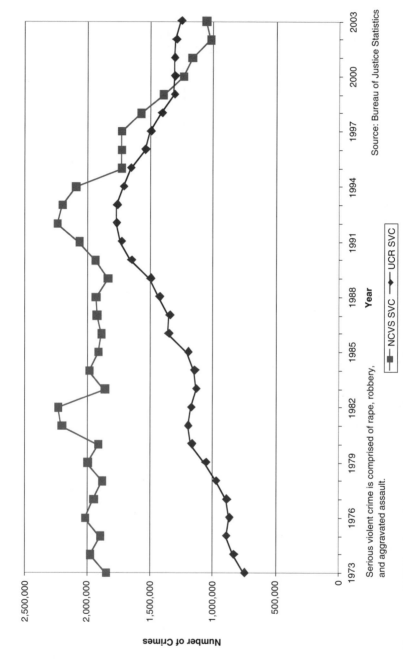

Serious violent crime is comprised of rape, robbery, and aggravated assault.

Source: Bureau of Justice Statistics

Figure 5.1. NCVS serious violence reported to the police and UCR serious violent crime, 1973–2003.

introduction of CATI) and major changes in instrumentation. Throughout the life of the survey, there have been changes in the response rate due to variations in the ability to locate respondents and gain their cooperation. Similarly, there have been changes in the mobility of the U.S. population that have affected the number of unbounded interview contributing to NCVS annual estimates. All of these changes have the potential to influence the count of victimization produced by the survey and, as a result, the convergence of the NCVS and UCR estimates.

Telephone and Computer-Assisted Telephone Interviewing

Up to the early 1980s, nearly all NCVS respondents were interviewed in person. In response to increasing budgetary constraints, over time a greater proportion of interviews were conducted by telephone. CATI began as a test in the late 1980s and was introduced on a broad scale with the redesign in 1992 (Groves and Nicholls, 1986; House, 1985; Hubble and Wilder, 1995). The percentage of telephone interviewing varies between 20 and 80 percent over the past 30 years. Currently, 75 percent of all NCVS interviews are administered via telephone. The percentage of CATI shows similar increases varying between 0 prior to the late 1980s and increasing to between 20 and 40 percentage points after the redesign.

Research on the effect of telephone interviewing is mixed, with some research indicating little impact on survey estimates (Roman and Sliwa, 1982) and contradictory research suggesting variable influence by crime type and population subgroup. CATI is associated with the increased reporting of events due to the reduction of interviewer error when following skip patterns within the instrument (Groves and Couper, 1998; Hubble and Wilder, 1995). Yet with the advent of telephone options such as call blocking and caller identification, reaching often reluctant participants has become increasingly difficult (Groves and Couper, 1998; Oldendick, 1993), possibly negating any benefit derived from the format. Thus, the effect of increased CATI and telephone usage at the national level remains uncertain, and to date no research directly examines the influence of increased telephone and CATI usage in the production of national-level crime estimates

(M. Monahan, Bureau of the Census, Washington, DC, personal communication, 2005).[5]

Response Rates

In the early years of the crime survey, response rates for both persons and households hovered near 100 percent, but within the last 10 years, person response rates for the survey declined from approximately 99 percent to 86 percent. Although not as drastic, household response rates have likewise declined steadily from approximately 96 percent in 1973 to 92 percent in 2003. The NCVS instrument is administered by the Census Bureau, which is known for producing extremely high survey participation rates among households and individuals.[6] The Census Bureau adjusts for nonresponse through the use of weighting procedures. Weighting is a common survey practice in which individual responses are multiplied by a factor to provide an estimate equivalent to the general population. As nonresponse increases, weights are applied to compensate for the decreased number of respondents. The effect of long-term declining response rates on estimated victimization remains unknown, however. The level at which weighting of data ceases to provide a representative reflection of the larger population is unclear and the subject of much debate (see Groves and Couper, 1998). Unfortunately for the victimization survey, declining response rates are associated with groups at the highest risk of violent victimization: the young, poor, and transient. Regardless of weights applied, as fewer individuals participate in the survey, the burden of representation falls on a decreasing number of responders.

Further, lower survey response rates for high-risk groups produce unknown effects for estimates as crime incidence in general declines, especially for relatively rare offenses such as rape or robbery (Atrostic et al., 2001; Groves, 1989; Groves and Couper, 1998; but see also

---

[5] Census conducted tests of the effects telephone interviewing in the late 1970s and early 1980s, but no tests have been conducted since the redesign in 1992.

[6] Individual response rates are calculated from households that agree to participate in the survey. Therefore, personal response rates may be higher during a given year depending on the number of individuals residing within the average household on an annual basis.

DeHeer, 1999; Smith, 1995).[7] The empirical literature supports the proposition that survey nonresponse is an undesirable but tolerable aspect of survey research (Groves and Couper, 1998; Steeh et al., 2001). The level of acceptable response generally varies depending on the methodological preference of the researcher and the purpose of the survey (Steeh et al., 2001).

Unbounded Interviews

An important characteristic of the NCVS is that bounding is used to limit the "telescoping" of crime events into the reference period (see Chapter 2 of this volume for a more complete description of bounding). Seven interviews are conducted for each household sampled in the survey. After the first interview in a household, prior interviews are used to "bound" subsequent interviews. Early research on the effect of unbounded interviews suggests that interviews not temporally bounded are characterized by inflated estimates (Biderman and Cantor, 1984; Biderman et al., 1986; Penick and Owens, 1976). This occurs for two reasons, the first of which is "telescoping." The second reason stems from the fact that bounding status is correlated with residential mobility, which is, in turn, correlated with criminal victimization. Individuals at the highest risk of victimization are very transient, and bounding in the NVCS is tied to a household rather than to residents residing *within* a household (Dugan, 1999; Hindelang et al., 1978; Penick and Owens, 1976). Thus, first-time interviews with members of replacement households, that is, households moving into units vacated by NCVS respondents, are not bounded by a previous interview, but they are included in victimization estimates. The inclusion of these participants has the potential to generate inflated estimates that vary depending on whether mobility among the population is increasing or decreasing (Addington, 2005; Biderman and Lynch, 1991; Dugan, 1999). This type of bounding procedure has the potential to affect the NCVS trend because the presence of unbounded interviews in the

---

[7] Calculations done by Cohen and Lynch in Chapter 7 (this volume) suggest that the effects of nonresponse on counts of serious violence could be substantial for specific subgroups of the population, but the effect on crime rates for the general population should not be great because the subgroups are such a small part of the overall population.

NCVS has fluctuated between 10.7 and 14.7 percentage points during the course of the survey.

Proxy Interviews

Proxy interviews refer to the practice of interviewing eligible respondents through a proxy, an available adult within the sampled household (see Chapter 2 for a more complete discussion of proxy interviewing). Between 1973 and 1986, the bulk of proxy interviews were conducted of 12 and 13 year olds because Census had a policy of not directly interviewing household members of this age. Beginning in 1986, however, children of these ages were interviewed directly in the NCVS. Proxy interviews were implemented within the survey for two reasons. During the developmental stage of the NCVS research, it was believed that children were cognitively unable to comprehend and respond to questions regarding victimization and, additionally, that parents would object to the questioning of children regarding the sensitive topic of victimization (M. Rand, BJS, personal communication, 2005).

In 1974, a test of proxy interviewing was conducted in San Francisco to evaluate the feasibility of interviewing children under age 13 directly rather than through the proxy format. The results indicated that slightly higher victimization rates were reported in the self-response format, with children reporting higher rates of minor events such as simple assault and petty theft (Gray, 1974; Rand, 1974). Anecdotal accounts suggested that children were unlikely to report these minor events to adults because the event was viewed as insignificant and the child simply forgot until prompted directly (Gray, 1974). The validity of these results was initially called into question because of the small sample tested (Turner, 1974). Subsequent research supported the proposition that incidents of victimization were substantially underreported using a proxy-interviewing format (Reiss, 1982). Lastly, adults within tested households did not object to the type of survey questions asked of youngsters during the San Francisco test. Ultimately, the decision to use a direct interviewing format for 12 and 13 year olds was based on this second finding (Gray, 1974; P. Klaus, BJS, personal communication, 2005; Rand, 1974; M. Rand, BJS, personal communication, 2005), and in 1986 the change in direct interviewing of children was implemented. Since 1986, the proportion of proxy interviews in the NCVS is low.

Questionnaire
In a 1976 review of the NCVS's predecessor, the National Academy of Science recommended that several aspects of the survey should be improved. Specifically, the academy suggested that an improved screening section would better stimulate victim recall of crime and help reduce the subjectivity often associated with certain survey questions. For example, victims often downplayed a victimization if the offender was an intimate or acquaintance. Once implemented, the enhanced screening questions improved the measurement of traditionally underreported crimes such as rape and those committed by acquaintances, family members, and intimates (Biderman et al., 1986; Kinderman et al., 1997; Penick and Owen, 1976). Higher counts of rape and aggravated assaults were reported, although robbery showed no appreciable change. In general, the available evidence suggests the questionnaire redesign produced the desired effect (Kindermann et al., 1997). Not only were victims of crime able to recall victimizations that were reported to the police, but the recalled events also included the offenses of rape and aggravated assault that were less likely to be captured in the previous surveys.

Other Factors
The influence of additional factors on NCVS estimates of crime should also be noted. The design and implementation of the NCVS does not address changes in society although they are likely to affect survey estimates by interacting with survey procedures. Potential factors include changes in public attitudes, demographic composition of the population, characteristics related to households, and changes related to high-risk populations not traditionally captured in the NCVS sample. Each of these factors may influence victimization rates at the national level by influencing survey estimates (Biderman and Lynch, 1991; Groves and Couper, 1998). For example, a variable that affects the likelihood of victimization and the subsequent decision to report the event to the police may affect survey estimates of crime. Change in the demographic composition of the U.S. population can produce

these effects, especially for generational influences such as the postwar baby boom experienced in this country (Biderman and Lynch, 1991). Although much research has focused on individual characteristics of age, gender, and racial composition, undeniably more knowledge is gained when these factors are examined in tandem rather than alone (Biderman and Lynch, 1991; Hindelang et al., 1978). Although not discussed in further detail here, research suggests that at the national level, such change contributes negligibly to the observed convergence between police-recorded and victim-reported crime (Catalano, 2004a).[8]

THE PRESENT STUDY

The principle question guiding this study is, *what effect does broad methodological change in the NCVS have on recent correspondence between the nation's two measures of crime?* Whether changes in the survey ultimately exert a negative or positive effect is unknown. Although we may have some information on the effects of these changes individually (e.g., CATI; Hubble and Wilder, 1995), the net effect of the factors cited here on correspondence is unclear. For some, the effect is clearly positive (e.g., proxy interviews, questionnaire redesign), and for others the effect may be negative (e.g., nonresponse) or even unclear (e.g., CATI, telephone). When the effects of changes in these procedures are combined in the actual survey, they may cancel each other out. Further, survey estimates may be affected by variables not examined here (e.g., demographic characteristics of the population, social attitudes). Based on the evidence considered here, the following hypothesis is evaluated:

> H_1: *Greater correspondence between the UCR and NCVS rape, robbery, and aggravated assault counts is an artifact of methodological change in the NCVS.*

---

[8] Catalano (2004a) finds that additional factors such as mobility (the percentage of renters, households moving in the last year), nonsampled populations (prison and jail populations, victims aged under 12 years), and demographic characteristics (age, race, ethnicity, gender, English proficiency, educational attainment, homeowners, single-person households) do not contribute to greater NCVS and UCR correspondence at the national level.

The summary measure "serious violent crime" is disaggregated into its three component crimes for two reasons. First, aggregate measures of violent crime are driven by the crime of aggravated assault, particularly at the national level (Blumstein, 2000). Second, methodological change may affect subclasses of serious violent crime in different ways. Figure 5.2 presents the trend for serious violent crime disaggregated into the offenses of rape, robbery, and aggravated assault. Once disaggregated, greater correspondence clearly differs based on crime type, with correspondence at the national level motivated primarily by rape and aggravated assault. Indeed, convergence between the trends is evident in rape and aggravated assault, and although increasing correspondence is present for robbery, the effect is notably less pronounced. Design change in the victimization survey may differentially affect correspondence for the three crime types.

This study examines the recent convergence between the UCR and NCVS. Little is known regarding the recent fluctuations of UCR and NCVS trends. Therefore, this study begins the discussion by approaching the question broadly. Crime counts rather than rates are used so that the known correspondence as disseminated by the Bureau of Justice Statistics may be examined (USDOJ, 2004). In keeping with this approach, this study uses the few consistently measured methodological variables that are available since the survey's inception. First, multivariate models are estimated to examine the effect of methodological change on NCVS rape, robbery, and aggravated assault. Second, predicted estimates from the models are retained and graphed with observed NCVS and UCR estimates. These graphs are examined to see whether the predicted estimates that take account of methodological changes in the survey bring the two series into closer correspondence.

Data and Methods
Data. Data used in this study were derived from published sources. Table 5.1 presents a list of the variables used, the method in which they are constructed, and the original source of the variable. With the exception of the indicator for unbounded interviews, all data were collected from the annual publication of Criminal Victimization in the United States between the years of 1973 and 2003. The

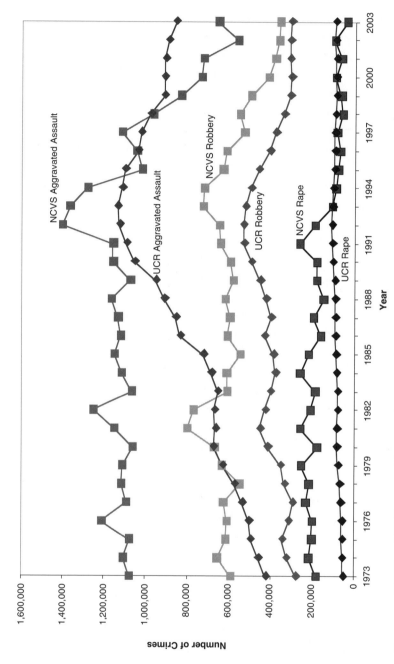

Figure 5.2. NCVS and UCR rape, robbery, and aggravated assault, 1973–2003.

TABLE 5.1. *Variables, measurement, and data sources used in the analysis of NCVS and UCR correspondence, 1973–2003*

Variable	Measurement	Description
Dependent Variables		
Rape	NCVS rape	Annual count of rapes reported to police
Robbery	NCVS reported robbery	Annual count of robberies reported to police
Aggravated assault	NCVS reported aggravated assaults	Annual count of aggravated assaults reported to police
Explanatory Variables		
Survey response	Percent households and individuals response rates	Factor score for annual household and individuals responding to the survey
Technology	Percent telephone and CATI interviews	Factor score for percent telephone and CATI at national level
CATI	Percent CATI interviews	Percent of interviews conducted by CATI
Telephone	Percent interviewed by phone	Percent interviewed by telephone
Unbounded interviews	Percent of households not interviewed in previous period	Annual percentage of households without a bounding interview
Change in proxy interview	Dummy variable (0 = no; 1 = yes)	Pre-1986 coded 0; Post-1986 coded 1
Questionnaire design	Dummy variable (0 = no; 1 = yes)	Pre-redesign coded 0; Post-redesign coded 1

variable for unbounded interviews was generated from the annual NCVS data files obtained from the public use files archived by the Inter-University Consortium for Political and Social Research.

Measures Used
Dependent Variable. Three dependent variables were used: rape, robbery, and aggravated assault. Homicide is not measured in the NCVS and was therefore dropped from further consideration. Each dependent variable reflected the raw count of victimizations that NCVS survey respondents reported to police during a given data year.[9] Victims

9 The distinction between NCVS data year and collection year is discussed in Chapter 2 in this volume and not addressed further here.

of crime need not report directly to police. Witnesses and others knowledgeable of the offense also report crimes to law enforcement officials.
Because the survey is probability based, the extent of sampling errors
is a function of the sample size and the relative rarity of the event.
This becomes increasingly problematic when rates of victimization are
already low and is exacerbated for rare crimes such as rape. Taking this
into consideration, the results for rape must be viewed with caution.

Explanatory Variables

Telephone and CATI Interviews. These variables were measured individually as the percentage of telephone and CATI interviews administered
annually.

Response Rates. Household and individual response rates were measured as the percentage of households and individual respondents
that complete the survey during the course of a year.

Unbounded Interviews. This variable was the annual percentage of
household occupants who were not present in a sampled household
during the previous interview cycle. The percentage is calculated using
the Household Status variable present in the annual NCVS public use
files between 1973 and 2003.

Proxy Interviews. The change in proxy interviewing was coded as a
dichotomous variable. Years prior to 1986 were coded 0, and years
following the implementation of direct interviewing were coded 1.

Questionnaire Design. This variable was indicated as pre- and post-
redesign periods and measured as a dichotomous variable.

Factor Analysis

The number of variables under examination, limited number of data
points, and presence of multicollinearity among the variables made
standard statistical models unwieldy. Factor analysis is a method of data
reduction that distills the essence of interrelated variables into summary indices that retain a linear relationship to the original variables

TABLE 5.2. *Descriptive statistics of variables used in the analysis of NCVS and UCR correspondence, 1973–2003*

	N	Min.	Max.	Mean	Std. dev.
NCVS rape	31	38,223	261,899	159,349	69,174
Predicted rape	30	35,468	227,752	158,642	64,789
NCVS robbery	31	360,659	796,539	590,607	104,897
Predicted robbery	30	336,453	753,103	590,681	93,423
NCVS aggravated assault	31	560,402	1,400,594	1,065,816	189,719
Predicted aggravated assault	30	520,447	1,358,121	1,065,500	179,920
Person response rate	31	86.30	98.70	94.42	3.77
Household response rate	31	91.60	97.00	95.30	1.40
Telephone interviews	31	20.00	75.00	57.45	22.66
CATI interviews	31	.00	40.00	12.26	14.48
Unbounded interviews	31	10.70	14.70	12.73	1.32
Proxy interview	31	0	1	.58	.50
Redesign	31	0	1	.40	.50

(Gugarati, 1995). Additionally, this technique increases the degrees of freedom within a multivariate model with limited data points.

Four variables were identified as candidates for data reduction during preliminary analyses: telephone and CATI interviewing and household and individual response rates. The extraction method used was principal components analysis with Varimax rotation using SPSS software. Two factor analyses were conducted and two factor scores retained for further analysis in the regression format. The variables for telephone and CATI interviewing loaded highly on one factor and were operationalized as NCVS technology ($\alpha = .80$). An additional factor was extracted from the NCVS person and household response rate variables. This factor was operationalized as NCVS survey response ($\alpha = .94$). The results of the factor analyses are presented in Appendix 1.

Descriptive Statistics

Table 5.2 presents descriptive statistics for the variables included in the analysis. For the dependent variables, mean levels of crime are inversely related to the relative rarity of the event, with aggravated assault clearly the most prevalent offense. More informative are the estimates between the observed and predicted values for each crime type. With the exception of maximum values for rape, predicted values for each crime are within 5 percentage points of observed values.

Two variables capture technological change in the survey since 1973. Initial use of CATI was implemented in 1988, at which time 5 percent of all NCVS interviews were conducted in this manner. By 2003, the percentage of CATI usage had increased to 40 percent. Parallel increases are observed in the proportion of telephone interviews. In 1973, roughly 20 percent of all interviews were conducted over the telephone. The percentage of telephone interviewing is now 75 percent, an increase of nearly fourfold.

Individual response rates for the NCVS were at the highest level in 1973, when 98.7 percent of all contacted individuals responded to the survey. Since that time, a slow and steady decline is observed until reaching a low of 86 percent in 2003. Household response rates decline similarly, although less drastically, over time. In 1973, a full 96 percent of sampled households responded to the survey yet by 2003, this number had declined to 92 percent.

The percentage of unbounded interviews varies between 11 and 15 percent, with steady increases evident from during the initial years of the survey. In 1977, the proportion of such interviews reached a high of 15 percent. Currently the percentage is at the lowest level since the late 1980s. Dichotomous variables are used to indicate pre- and post changes in proxy interviews as well as questionnaire design. Mean values for each variable represent the percentage of years for which the variable is scored 1. Bivariate correlations for the variables examined are presented in Appendix 2.

Analytic Procedures
The analysis consists of two components. AR(1) models are estimated to examine the effect of broad scale methodological change on estimates of rape, robbery, and aggravated assault.[10] Second, predicated estimates of NCVS crime counts are retained from the models. These are subsequently graphed against observed NCVS and UCR annual

---

[10] The modeling procedure was iterative and multiple specifications were examined. In addition to AR(1) models, other specifications included ordinary least squares, differenced models, and combinations of the two. Regression coefficients across the various models were compared to check for changes in magnitude, direction, and

crime counts. These graphs allow for inspection of the trends over time with explanatory variables held constant at 1973 levels.

Preliminary models are first estimated using the ordinary least squares (OLS) version of a linear estimator. In general, using factor scores assists considerably with degrees of freedom. However, the Durbin–Watson statistics indicate that the models are autocorrelated. The time series data were characterized with few degrees of freedom, so little modeling maneuverability was available. Rather than lose additional observations through differencing, the lagged dependent variable is introduced on the right side of the equation. Subsequent examination of the residuals indicated that the autocorrelation function (ACF) and partial autocorrelation function (PACF) were within tolerable parameters. The general form of the AR(1) model is as follows:

$$y = \alpha + \beta(y_{t-1}) + \beta x_1 \cdots + \beta x_k + e.$$

Further diagnostics in preliminary models indicated the present of high levels of collinearity among the explanatory variables. Multicollinearity will produce erroneous conclusions regarding the significance of explanatory variables. Examination of the F-change statistic is one method of ascertaining the relative influence of explanatory variables that is not affected by collinearity. Investigators are subsequently able to evaluate change in a model's R^2, F statistic, and, most important, whether change in the F score significantly improves the explanatory power of the model (Granato and Suzuki, 1996; Pindyck and Rubinfeld, 1998).

RESULTS

Multivariate Models

Table 5.3 presents findings for the rape and aggravated assault multivariate models. The results for the robbery models are not presented here because, with the exception of survey response and lagged crime counts, coefficients in the robbery models do not attain conventional levels of significance. The coefficient for the lagged crime counts was

significance levels. Although levels in magnitude changed across different specifications, significant effects observed in the final models were consistently robust. In no instance were changes in sign observed.

TABLE 5.3. *Rape and aggravated assault models including technology, CATI, and telephone methodological changes, NCVS 1973–2003*

	Unstandardized	Standard error	Standardized
Rape With Technology Variable			
1. Constant	92,356.26	153,831.94	–
Lagged NCVS variable	.06***	.19	.06
2. NCVS response	23,797.39***	20,896.66	.34
3. NCVS technology	−9,195.97**	21,051.58	−.13
4. Unbounded interviews	7,589.33	12,569.53	.15
5. Change in proxy interview	−27,819.19	35,233.17	−.20
6. Redesign	−56,143.03	39,854.33	−.40
adj.R^2 .81			
Rape With CATI Variable			
1. Constant	42,758.28	150,196.46	–
Lagged NCVS variable	.00***	.18	.00
2. NCVS response	9,069.10***	22,142.84	.13
3. NCVS CATI	−2,669.49**	1,679.81	−.55
4. Unbounded interviews	4,743.29	12,704.47	.28
5. Change in proxy interview	−40,823.88	24,610.17	−.29
6. Redesign	−34,702.18	39,466.54	−.25
adj. R^2 .83			
Rape With Telephone Variable			
1. Constant	79,016.57	164,069.60	–
Lagged NCVS variable	.06***	.19	.06
2. NCVS response	24,781.87***	20,730.02	.35
3. NCVS telephone	185.49	620.37	.06
4. Unbounded interviews	8,949.16	13,030.49	.17
5. Change in proxy interview	−47,370.60	39,796.91	−.34
6. Redesign	−64,753.47	37,978.19	−.50
adj. R^2 .81			
Aggravated Assault With Technology Variable			
1. Constant	647,030.31	320,897.15	
Lagged NCVS variable	.28***	.15	.25
2. NCVS response	240,146.10**	50,756.68	1.26
3. NCVS technology	32,226.23	55,579.67	.16
4. Unbounded interviews	2,704.60	30,550.58	.02
5. Change in proxy interview	−677.47	92,414.65	−.00
6. Redesign	229,338.61*	96,556.04	.59
adj. R^2 .84			

	Unstandardized	Standard error	Standardized
Aggravated Assault With CATI Variable			
1. Constant	634,041.33	351,664.38	
Lagged NCVS variable	.30***	.15	.27
2. NCVS response	232,963.74**	62,046.74	1.23
3. NCVS CATI	354.69*	4,510.95	.03
4. Unbounded interviews	−391.87	33,258.02	.00
5. Change in proxy interview	37,400.19	66,432.04	.10
6. Redesign	244,532.76*	96,556.04	.59
adj. R^2 .83			
Aggravated Assault With Telephone Variable			
1. Constant	520,931.92	353,095.33	
Lagged NCVS variable	.28***	.15	.25
2. NCVS response	229,389.09**	47,464.15	1.19
3. NCVS telephone	1,064.88	1,618.17	.12
4. Unbounded interviews	8,316.16	32,448.62	.06
5. Change in proxy interview	−16,604.46	104,568.7	−.04
6. Redesign	235,999.47*	92,842.82	.61
adj. R^2 84			

Note: CATI = computer-assisted telephone interviewing.

significant in each model in Table 5.3.[11] The first three models in Table 5.3 present results for the crime of rape. Standard statistical tests do not reveal significant effects of the explanatory variables on reported rape counts. F-change statistics indicate, however, that the addition of survey response and technology does add significant explanatory power to the model. The summary measures of NCVS technology and NCVS response exert significant influence on NCVS crime counts, albeit in opposing directions.

Survey response is positively associated with estimates of rape ($\beta = 23,797$; $p > .001$), whereas technology is inversely related to the presence of reported rapes in the victim survey. The effect of survey response is intuitively appealing. Net of other factors, increases in response rates should be associated with the survey's capacity to detect crime *whether* NCVS nonrespondents are indeed at higher risk of victimization.

[11] Results of the autocorrelation function and partial autocorrelation function residuals were within tolerable parameters. These results suggest that time dependency is adequately controlled for by the current specification.

Less intuitive is the result for the impact of NCVS technology on the dependent variable. The coefficient indicates a negative relationship between the summary measure of technology and survey counts of reported rape ($\beta = -9,196$; $p > .01$). To understand this counterintuitive result better, we distinguished changes in telephone interviewing from changes in CATI usage. When CATI usage was entered into the model without the proportion of interviews conducted by telephone, there was a negative effect of CATI on the reporting of rape. When the proportion of telephone interviews was entered without CATI, it had no significant affect on reporting, although the sign of the coefficient was negative. Traditionally CATI usage is associated with increases in control over interviewers and the reduction of interviewer error, which should increase accuracy or, at minimum, produce a null effect on the crime counts. Although decreases in interviewer error need not translate into higher estimates, the *negative* relationship between CATI usage and the reporting of rape is puzzling. The observed relationship may be spurious; increases in CATI may be occurring when there are genuine decreases in rapes. Or it is plausible that qualitative differences exist for the crime of rape. Although CATI interviewing is associated with higher NCVS estimates generally, a difference may exist for the crime of rape. Because CATI is administered from a central facility and non-CATI telephone interviewing is not, CATI interviews are more likely to be conducted by different interviewers over time. In-person interviews and non-CATI telephone interviews are more likely to be conducted by the same interviewer over time. The familiarity between interviewers and respondents that results from repeated interviewing may encourage more complete reporting of this sensitive crime. A question for future research is whether victimized individuals are more likely to report rape when interviews are conducted with the same interviewer over time. These issues are not explored here and the data do not permit further examination of the proposition. Most important, the annual estimates for rape examined here are volatile, as noted previously, and must be viewed with caution.

The last three models in Table 5.3 concern aggravated assault. As observed for the crime of rape, increased survey response is positively related to survey counts of aggravated assault. As with rape, survey response is positively associated with counts of aggravated assault and

CATI usage has a significant positive effect on counts of aggregated assault. The coefficient for the redesign variable is significant only for the crime of aggravated assault. This is consistent with earlier work that found no significant effect of the redesign for robbery and significant positive effects for aggravated assault (Kinderman et al., 1997; Persley, 1995) but inconsistent with the same earlier work that found a substantial increase in reporting of rape due to the redesign. The fact that these earlier studies did not separate out the effects of new instrumentation and increased use of CATI may account for these differences in results. When they did separate the effects of CATI from the effects of the new instrumentation, Cantor and Lynch (2005) found no effects of new instrumentation for robbery but an effect of CATI for that crime. Reporting of aggravated assault was increased both by the new instrumentation and increased use of CATI. All of this is consistent with the observed positive relationship between post-redesign years and survey counts of aggravated assault.

When the technology measure is disaggregated into CATI and the proportion of telephone interviews in the aggravated assault models, we see that CATI has a positive effect on reporting and telephone interviewing has no significant effect on reporting.

Among the five variables, only survey response is consistently related to reporting in all three crime types. Some evidence exists for effects of CATI usage and questionnaire redesign for rape and aggravated assault. In general, the results of the multivariate models suggest the variables exert minimal effect on NCVS estimates at the national level. If we compare the sum of squared differences (SSD) in crime counts between the UCR and the NCVS unadjusted with those for the UCR and the counts adjusted for differences in NCVS methodology, the SSD decreases between 2.9 percent and 4.9 percent.[12] These

---

[12] Sum of squared differences were computed as follows:

UCR = UCR counts
NCVS = NCVS counts without adjustments for methodological changes
NCVSA = NCVS counts adjusted for methodological changes
$SSD = (NCVS - UCR)^2$
$SSDA = (NCVSA - UCR)^2$

The percent difference in these estimates of sum of squares were computed as follows:

$PC\ dft = (SSD - SSDA)/SSD$

improvements in correspondence between the two series are larger for rape and aggravated assault and smallest for robbery. In all instances, the effects of survey methodology on the NCVS counts are relatively small.

Graphs

Three trend lines appear in Figures 5.3–5.5. As in Figure 5.2, annual UCR and NCVS estimates are graphed but with an additional trend line included for predicted NCVS estimates. As expected, there is no discernible difference between observed and predicted NCVS estimates. Across the three crime types, the predicted estimates do little more than provide a smoothed version of the NCVS trend for the observed estimates. One notable pattern does exist, however. The smoothing effect is more prominent for the crimes of rape and aggravated assault. Most important for the purpose of this study is that the trend for NCVS predicted estimates *does not* produce a trend in closer correspondence to UCR recorded crimes.

DISCUSSION

This study examined the hypothesis that greater correspondence between the UCR and NCVS results from methodological changes in the victimization survey. At the national level, this hypothesis was not supported. Multivariate modeling suggested some effect, but, once these data were graphed, predicted NCVS estimates did little beyond smoothing the observed NCVS estimates. Indeed, the predicted values were within 10 percentage points of the observed values at every time point.

The results must be considered with caveats. First, the limited number of time points, or years available for analysis, places restrictions on the type of time series models that may be used. More fine-grained analysis that standardized annual estimates for methodological differences using household or person-level data could yield effects that are not visible with the highly aggregated data used here. The research is preliminary in nature and focuses on a limited number of available

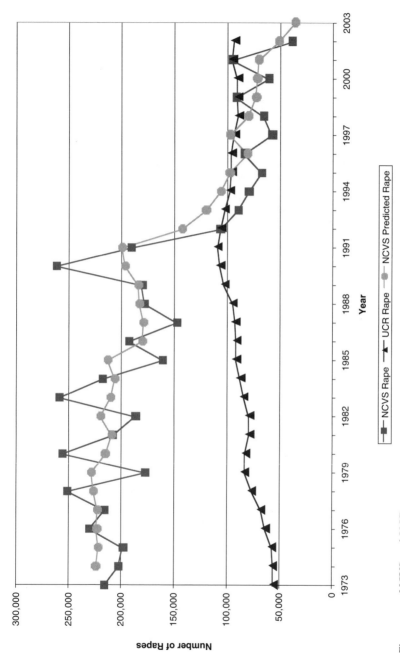

Figure 5.3. NCVS and UCR rape, 1973–2003.

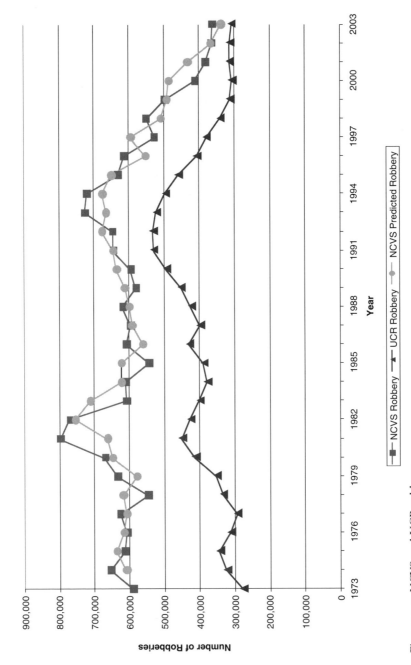

Figure 5.4. NCVS and UCR robbery.

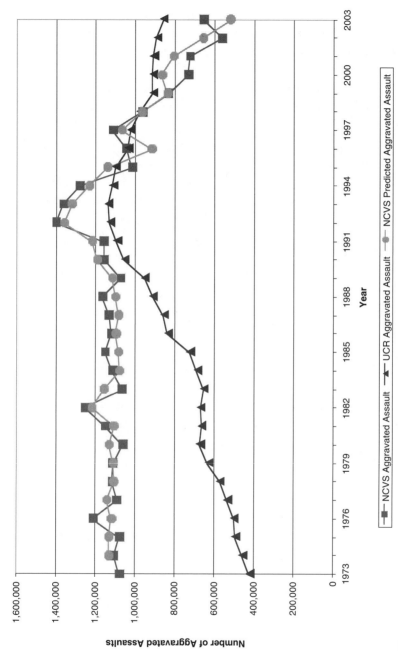

Figure 5.5. NCVS and UCR aggravated assault.

149

variables and possibly excludes relevant variables not considered here. Last, the study examines the correspondence at the national level with highly aggregated data. Such data are likely to mask variation at the regional or state level. Indeed, recent research suggests that the effect of change across counties and metropolitan statistical area units differs from that observed at the national level (Lauritsen and Schaum, 2005).

Traditionally, the nation's two indicators of crime have provided differing estimates of crime, with counts from the survey substantially exceeding those from the administrative series. Yet in 2001, an unprecedented change occurred: serious violent crime in the UCR exceeded counts of serious crimes reported to the police as measured in the NCVS. In some ways, this "overlap" has replaced divergence as an event that draws attention to the quality of crime statistics. This development is not necessarily surprising given what we know about methodological differences between the two data programs. A brief example is beneficial. Often overlooked in discussion of the two programs is the fact that the UCR and NCVS are generated from *different populations*. By design the NCVS excludes specific segments of the population, most notably children under the age of 12. In contrast, victimization of children is under the purview of law enforcement. With respect to this example alone, the police should record *more* victimizations than the survey. Addington provides some estimates of the effect of these differences in Chapter 8 of this volume. Other potential sources of this "overlap" are discussed in Chapters 6 and 9. The "overlap" will be beneficial if it results in efforts to better understand these series.

This chapter suggests that in our search for explanations of the "overlap" and for greater understanding of crime statistics more generally, methodological changes in the NCVS are not going to play a large role. The possible exception to this general conclusion is response rate. There are signs that declining response rates in the survey may be contributing to lower estimates of the count of violent victimization. This effect would be greatest for the broad and ambiguous category of aggravated assault.

APPENDIX 1. *Results of factor analyses and variables used in the analysis of NCVS and UCR correspondence,*
1973–2003

Factor Name
NCVS response

Cronbach's Alpha = .94

Component	Mean	Std. Dev.	Description	Factor Loading	Factor Score
Person response	98.70	3.77	% individuals responding to survey	.95	.97
household response	97.00	1.40	% households responding to survey	.95	.97

Pearson Correlation Matrix

	(1)	(2)
(1) Person	1.00	
(2) Household	.89**	1.00

Factor Name
NCVS technology

Cronbach's Alpha = .80

Component	Mean	Std. Dev.	Description	Factor Loading	Factor Score
CATI	12.26	14.48	% computer assisted telephone interviews	.84	.92
Telephone	57.45	22.66	% telephone interviews	.84	.92

Pearson Correlation Matrix

	(1)	(2)
(1) CATI	1.00	
(2) Telephone	.68**	1.00

APPENDIX 2. *Bivariate correlations for dependent variables used in the analysis of NCVS and UCR correspondence,*
1973–2003

	(1)	(2)	(3)	(4)	(5)	(6)	(7)	(8)
(1) NCVS rape								
(2) NCVS robbery	.536**							
(3) NCVS assault	.530**	.849**						
(4) Survey response	.881**	.771**	.760**					
(5) Technology	-.837**	-.413**	-.395**	-.815**				
(6) Unbounded interview	-.610**	-.150	-.005**	-.477**	.761**			
(7) Proxy interview	-.695**	-.366*	.248	-.620*	.891**	.818**		
(8) Redesign	-.864**	-.428*	-.394*	-.856**	.857**	.730**	.675**	

References

Addington, L. A. (2005). "Disentangling the effects of mobility and bounding on reports of criminal victimization." *Journal of Quantitative Criminology* 21:321–343.

Atrostic, B. K., Bates, N., Burt, G., & Silberstein, A. (2001). "Nonresponse in U.S. government household surveys: Consistent measures, recent trends, and new insights." *Journal of Official Statistics* 17:209–226.

Biderman, A. D., & Cantor, D. (1984, August). *A longitudinal analysis of bounding, respondent conditioning and mobility as a source of panel bias in the National Crime Survey.* Proceedings of the American Statistical Association, Philadelphia, PA.

Biderman, A., Cantor, D., Lynch, J. P., & Martin, E. (1986). *Final report of research and development for the redesign of the National Crime Survey.* Washington, DC: Bureau of Social Science Research.

Biderman, A., & Lynch, J. (1991). *Understanding crime incidence statistics: Why the UCR diverges from the NCS.* New York: Springer-Verlag.

Blumstein, A. (2000). "Disaggregating the violence trends." In A. Blumstein & J. Wallman (Eds.), *The crime drop in America* (pp. 13–44). New York: Cambridge University Press.

Blumstein, A., Cohen, J., & Rosenfeld, R. (1991). "Trend and deviation in crime rates: A comparison of UCR and NCS data for burglary and robbery." *Criminology* 29:237–263.

Cantor, D., & Lynch, J. P. (2005). "Exploring the effects of changes in design on the analytical uses of the NCVS data." *Journal of Quantitative Criminology* 30:293–319.

Catalano, S. (2004). *The convergence between police recorded and victim reported serious violent crime, 1973–2003.* Unpublished dissertation, University of Missouri – St. Louis.

DeHeer, W. (1999). "International response trends: results of an international survey." *Journal of Official Statistics* 15:129–142.

Dugan, L. (1999). "The effect of criminal victimization on a household's moving decision." *Criminology* 37:903–930.

Granato, J., & Suzuki, M. (1996). "The use of the encompassing principle to resolve empirical controversies in voting behavior: An application to voter sophistication in congressional elections." *Electoral Studies* 15:383–398.

Gray, G. (1974). National Crime Survey – cities sample – request for special tabulations for San Francisco [memorandum]. Washington, DC: United States Department of Commerce, Bureau of the Census.

Groves, R. (1989). *Survey errors and survey costs.* New York: Wiley.

Groves, R., & Couper, M. (1998). *Nonresponse in household interview surveys.* New York: Wiley.

Groves, R., & Nicholls, W. L. (1986). "The status of computer assisted telephone interviewing: Part II – data quality issues." *Journal of Official Statistics* 2:117–134.

Gugarati, D. (1995). *Basic econometrics.* New York: McGraw-Hill.

Hindelang, M., Gottfredson, M., & Garofalo, J. (1978). *Victims of personal crime: An empirical foundation for a theory of personal victimization.* Cambridge, MA: Ballinger.

House, C. (1985). "Questionnaire design with computer assisted telephone interviewing." *Journal of Official Statistics* 1:209–219.

Hubble, D., & Wilder, B. E. (1995). "Preliminary results from the National Crime Survey CATI experiment." *Proceedings of the American Statistical Association,* Survey Methods Section, New Orleans, LA, August.

Kindermann, C., Lynch, J., & Cantor, D. (1997). *Effects of the redesign on victimization estimates.* Washington, DC: U.S. Bureau of Justice Statistics.

Langan, P. A., & Farrington, D. (1998). *Crime and justice in the United States and in England and Wales, 1981–(1996)* (BJS Report NCJ 169284). Washington, DC: U.S. Department of Justice.

Lauritsen, J. L., & Catalano, S. M. (2005). "The National Crime Victimization Surveys." In *Encyclopedia of social measurement* (Vol. 2, pp. 803–808). New York: Elsevier.

Lauritsen, J., & Schaum, R. (2005). *Crime and victimization in the three largest metropolitan areas, 1980–98.* Washington, DC: U.S. Bureau of Justice Statistics.

McDowall, D., & Loftin, C. (1992). "Comparing the UCR and NCS over time." *Criminology* 30:125–132.

O'Brien, R., Shichor, D., & Decker, D. L. (1980). "An empirical comparison of the validity of UCR and NCS crime rates." *Sociological Quarterly* 21:391–401.

Oldendick, R. (1993). "The effect of answering machines on the representativeness of samples in telephone surveys." *Journal of Official Statistics* 9:663–672.

Penick, B., & Owens, M. (Eds.). (1976). *Surveying crime. A report of the Panel for the Evaluation of Crime Surveys.* Washington, DC: Washington National Academy of Science.

Persley, C. (1995, August). *The National Crime Victimization Survey redesign: Measuring the impact of new methods.* Presented at the annual meeting of the American Statistical Association, Orlando, FL.

Pindyck, R., & Rubinfeld, D. (1998). *Econometric models and economic forecasts.* Boston: McGraw-Hill.

Rand, M. (1974). *Evaluation of interview procedure test conducted in San Francisco* [memorandum]. Washington, DC: U.S. Department of Commerce, Bureau of the Census.

Reiss, A. (1982). *Victimization productivity in proxy interviews.* New Haven, CT: Institute for Social and Policy Studies, Yale University.

Roman, A., & Sliwa, G. (1982). *Study of the impact of the increased use of the telephone in the NCS: Reply to the comments of Robert Groves* [memorandum]. Washington, DC: U.S. Department of Commerce, Bureau of the Census.

Smith, T. W. (1995). "Trends in nonresponse rate." *International Journal of Public Opinion Research* 7:157–171.

Steeh, C., Kirgis, N., Cannon, B., & DeWitt, J. (2001). "Are they really as bad as they seem? Nonresponse rates at the end of the twentieth century." *Journal of Official Statistics* 17:227–247.

Turner, A. (1984). "Report on 12- and 13-year-old interviewing experiment." In R. Lehnen & W. Skogan (Eds.), *The National Crime Survey, volume II: Methodological studies* (pp. 67–68). Washington, DC: U.S. Bureau of Justice Statistics.

U.S. Department of Justice. (n.d.). *Criminal victimization in the United States, statistical tables, 1995–2003.* Washington, DC: U.S. Bureau of Justice Statistics. Retrieved January 25, 2006 from http://www.ojp.usdoj.gov/ bjs/abstract/cvusst.htm.

U.S. Department of Justice. (2004). *Four measures of serious violent crime* (BJS Fact Sheet). Washington, DC: U.S. Bureau of Justice Statistics. Retrieved January 25, 2006 from http://www.ojp.usdoj.gov/ bjs/glance/cv2.htm.

U.S. Department of Justice, Bureau of Justice Statistics. (1997). *National Crime Surveys, 1973–1991.* Conducted by U.S. Dept. of Commerce, Bureau of the Census. Ann Arbor, MI: Inter-university Consortium for Political and Social Research [producer and distributor].

U.S. Department of Justice, Bureau of Justice Statistics. (2006). *National Crime Victimization Survey, 1992–2004.* Conducted by U.S. Department of Commerce, Bureau of the Census. ICPSR ed. Ann Arbor, MI: Inter-university Consortium for Political and Social Research [producer and distributor].

CHAPTER SIX

Series Victimizations and Divergence

Mike Planty

Divergence between annual estimates of crime produced by the Uniform Crime Reports (UCR) and National Crime Victimization Survey (NCVS) may be explained, in part, by the way criminal events are classified and counted. One important type of criminal phenomenon, the repeat victim, poses a particularly challenging problem for victimization surveys. Although the definition has been operationalized in a variety of ways, the common denominator in these various definitions is one common factor: a person experiences more than one victimization in a given time period (Farrell, 1995; Pease, 1998). This is important because, unlike official police records that are often produced immediately after or within a few days of a criminal offense, the NCVS "survey method is heavily dependent upon the ability and motivation of the respondent to remember events and report them in the interview situation" (Biderman et al., 1967). Although recall accuracy is a cognitive task for all victims to some degree, it is especially difficult for the repeat victim. They must not only remember and report details of numerous crime events, but they also must not confuse aspects of different events and even treat continuous events as if they were discrete. This is a considerable burden.

To accommodate the high-volume or chronic victim who could report dozens if not hundreds of victimizations, the NCVS developed a process that classifies six or more "similar" victimizations as a series incident (see Chapter 2, this volume). When this designation is used, the number of offenses that occurred is recorded, and only the details of the most recent event are reported. The manner in which these repeat events are counted is important because this small group of repeat victims can account for a large portion of the total crime that occurs each year (Chenery et al., 1996; Ellingworth et al., 1995; Farrell and Pease, 1993; Planty, 2004; Trickett et al., 1992). Current U.S. government practices exclude series incidents in the annual cross-sectional estimates of violent victimizations. This chapter examines the implications of this counting rule for trends in aggravated assault from the NCVS and for the divergence between aggravated assault rates in the UCR and NCVS. Aggravated assault is focused on, in part, because it is the crime class defined most similarly in the survey and the UCR. In addition, aggravated assaults include a larger number of series incidents than other Crime Index categories, and it is the type of crime for which crimes recorded by the police in the UCR exceeded crimes that victims claim to have reported to the police in the NCVS. It would be useful to see whether the series incident procedure in the NCVS accounts for this oddity in crime counts.

The next section briefly reviews what we know about how police records capture repeat victimizations, identifying potential sources of error, to provide a context for understanding the consequences for the NCVS counting procedures. While recognizing that there are important questions related to the counting of offenses with police data that impact the cross-sectional UCR rates, the remainder of the chapter focuses on how the NCVS collects and counts victimizations reported from the high-volume, chronic victims – the series incidents. Because the counting of series events is clearly documented in the NCVS, it is possible, through straightforward adjustments to the data, to understand how repeat victimization counting rules affect annual victimization rates and the divergence between the two data sources. The objective of this chapter is to examine empirically how counting schema for series incidents in the NCVS serve as an explanation for the divergence from the UCR. The discrepancies between the two measures may be explained, at least in part, if reasonable procedures for including series incidents are employed.

POLICE RECORDS AND REPEAT VICTIMS

Differences in victimization risk across the population are not news to law enforcement officials and researchers who have studied police behavior. Certain locations or addresses, referred to as "hot spots," have a concentration of criminal activity and require a significant amount of police resources (Farrell and Sousa, 2001; Pease and Laycock, 1996; Sherman et al., 1989; Sherman and Rogan, 1995; Sherman and Weisburd, 1995). Sherman and his colleagues (1989) reported that about half of all calls for service in Minneapolis could be attributed to about 3 percent of the city's addresses. Like victimization surveys, how repeat offenses are counted in official statistics may have a considerable impact on the cross-sectional crime rate.

Police counts of crime are primarily driven by the reporting and recording of the criminal event. It is well recognized that not every offense comes to the attention of law enforcement officials, and when they do each responding officer has discretion as to how, if at all, the event is recorded (e.g., Biderman and Reiss, 1967; Hart and Rennison, 2003; Reiss, 1986; Skogan, 1976). In a given period of time, if repeated offenses involving the same victim or address are systematically under- or overreported to the police by the victim (or other third party), this will have a substantial impact on the quantity and quality of the crime rate. For example, if there is reason to suspect that victims of multiple assaults (e.g., domestic violence) report to the police only a fraction of the offenses they suffer, this would lead to a serious underestimation of violence in police annual estimates. Similarly, if law enforcement officials are less likely to record (or found) offenses reported by the same person, this would also lead to an underestimation of the true crime rate (Buzawa and Austin, 1993; Gondolf and McFerron, 1989). On the other hand, if the police were to record every offense brought to their attention, regardless of evidentiary merit, this would lead to an overestimation of the true crime rate. Whatever the impact, it is difficult to know directly from police data how these social filters impact the UCR.

In addition to these reporting filters, police record systems prove to have difficulty identifying repeat victims. Most police record systems are explicitly designed to identify the repeat *offender* and not the repeat *victim*. Rap sheets, fingerprints, and DNA databases are three examples. These tools are built on the assumption that offenders will commit multiple offenses but offers little or no direct information on these victims of such crimes.

Furthermore, police offense or event records are gathered based on territorial space (Reiss, 1986). That is, to administer the deployment for police resources efficiently, information about criminal events is recorded primarily by the location of the event, address of the victim, and sometimes the offender's home address. The structure and organization of this information is often fraught with recording errors or intrinsic ambiguity that prevents the expeditious identification of repeat victims, if at all (Anderson et al., 1995; Bridgeman and Hobbs, 1997; Farrell and Pease, 1993, 2003). For example, calls for service are usually attached to a household address that may be recorded differently, preventing a linkage between events (e.g., 123 N. Main St. vs. 123 Main Street). Even when the same address is entered correctly for two criminal events, victim information may be incomplete, the events could involve different parties, or the address may involve a completely different household, which is often the case in neighborhoods with high residential turnover. A strong assumption about the victim's identity is often necessary. Other factors relate to police working practices. The organizational structure of police shifts and jurisdictions increases the likelihood that different officers will deal with the same victim. This reduces the probability that an appropriate link will be made between incidents (Bridgeman and Hobbs, 1997).

There are some aspects of police data on crime that could lead to overestimates of repeat victimization in the population. Specifically, early field tests of the victim survey method found that victims identified from police records had much higher incidence rates than victims identified from the general population through the screening interviews (Biderman et al., 1967). Assuming this is true and all other things are equal, for any given unit of time, those victims identified in police records are more likely to have multiple or repeat victimizations than victims not found in police records. It is unclear whether the tendency for police records to underrepresent repeat victimization is strong enough to offset the specific limitations of police recording practices that contribute to underreporting of repeat victimization.

The general evidence from victimization surveys suggests that the reporting and founding filters related to police involvement, along with organizational procedures for recording crime, can be substantial impediments to the recording and identification of repeat victimization in police records. Subsequently, police records are likely to reflect an underestimation of the true amount of repeat victimization within a community. Even when these events are captured, the organizational hurdles prevent an efficient recognition of the repeat victim.

THE NCVS AND THE CHRONIC VICTIM

The NCVS was designed primarily to capture and count discrete criminal events from the victim's perspective in a given time period. The objective is to produce a nationally representative description of the amount and type of criminal victimization in the United States each year. Despite the seemingly straightforward process of counting, each criminal event, measurement error associated with the recall, identification, and classification of victimization is a significant challenge to surveys like the NCVS. Although these challenges are applicable to all victims, they are particularly problematic for the high-volume repeat victims – those who report a large number of similar crimes. Because the NCVS procedures require detailed information on each victimization reported by a respondent, this process quickly becomes a burden for both respondents and interviewers when it entails the documentation of a large number of events. This is not the case with repeat victims who report two or three cases of violence. With well-trained interviewer persistence, respondents are usually able to handle this amount of cognitive and survey burden (Dodge, 1984).[1] High-volume repeat victims, on the other hand, often suffer abuse and violence in a routinized manner that tends to be more of a condition or continuing event rather than a discrete occurrence (Biderman, 1980; Shenk and McInerney, 1981). Biderman and his colleagues (1967:70–71) recognized and documented this problem during formative years of the NCVS (previously known as the NCS):

> A difficulty involving counting units that could not be solved satisfactorily was encountered in the present study. This occurred where a

---

[1] It is important to note that the concern with respondent recall is not specific to victimization surveys. In fact, most retrospective surveys involve very similar challenges (for reviews, see, for example, Czaja et al., 1994; Chu et al., 1992; Mathiowetz, 2000). In general, respondents have a difficult time not only recalling events but also placing them in the correct temporal location.

respondent described what actually was a series of related acts over a period of time, where each could be classed as an offense, but where the individual either could not specify precisely how many time the offense had taken place or where so many separate instances were involved that such acts, if counted individually, would contribute highly disproportionately to the total picture of victimization at which the study aimed. . . . Usually, the victim assumed or knew the series of offenses was being committed by the same offender or group of offenders. In each instance where the respondent spoke of the matter in terms of a unitary series of identical offenses of one of the types listed above, it has been considered a single incident. . . . In this respect, consequently, the survey may lead to an undercount relative to police statistics.

Since the NCVS adopted an approach to count victimizations as a discrete, point-in-time event, the instrument is less than practical for these high-volume victims. Therefore, to accommodate the high-volume victim, the NCVS was designed to balance the need for complete data against respondent burden. A procedure was developed to allow interviewers to treat a large number of similar victimizations as a "series incident." If respondents report six or more crime events, the interviewer answers or verifies the following set of questions to determine whether the events qualify as a series incident:

1. the incident occurred six or more times in the past six months,
2. the incidents are similar to each other in detail, and
3. the respondent is unable to recall enough detail of each incident to distinguish them from each other.

When all three conditions are satisfied, the interviewer records the number of victimizations and collects detailed information on only the last occurrence in the series.[2]

The NCVS is not alone in dealing with the problem of high-volume victims. Certainly every victimization study must decide on a procedure for treating these events. The British Crime Survey (BCS) offers another perspective on the issue. The BCS is quite similar to the NCVS

---

[2] This procedure is in striking contrast to the NCVS insomuch that it affords the interviewer an exceptional level of discretion in terms of the decisions to classify a set of victimizations as a series incident. It is likely that there is extensive interviewer variance associated with what is considered "similar" in terms of event detail.

in its general purpose, which is to provide a source independent from official police records on annual crime rates. Members of the public aged 16 and over living in households are queried about their experiences with crime and violence in the past 12 months. As with the NCVS, special procedures are used to handle respondents who report being victimized multiple times under the same circumstances and probably by the same people. If a respondent does identify a set of incidents as a series crime, the interviewer collects information on the most recent incident and counts the number up to a maximum limit of five. Although any victimization over five is not counted toward the annual crime rate, unlike the NCVS, these series crimes are not excluded and do contribute to the annual crime rates. BCS does not set a minimum number of incidents (six for the NCVS) that is needed before qualifying as a series incident, however. Clearly, the BCS is not as concerned with the error of introducing similar events as characterized by the last incident as they are with excluding these events. For both surveys, the primary concern is associated with the burden that these events introduce into the data collection process.

Table 6.1 provides a description of the 1993–2002 series incidents for the NCVS (Planty, 2004). On average, there were about 174 series incidents per year, ranging from 70 in 2002 to more than 300 in 1993. The minimum threshold for being a series incident was 6 victimizations, with respondents reporting an average of 22 victimizations, or about 1 victimization a week, over the six-month reference period. The median for most years was 10, and the mode for all years was 6 victimizations.

From 1993 to 2002, the average maximum number of victimizations reported per series incident annually was 324 victimizations, with a range from 100 in 2001 to 750 victimizations in 1996. To place this range into context, a series incident at the average of 324 translates into about 2 victimizations per day over a six-month period for a victim. Some evidence exists that victims are prone to rounding their victimization estimates. For example, reported victimizations peak at 12 (twice a month), 24 (once a week), 180 (once a day), and at other common intervals (10 or 100). Such rounding is inevitable for a group of victims who experience such a large number of offenses. Even with such estimations, large estimates of greater than 100 are rare and

TABLE 6.1. *Descriptive statistics for the number of victimizations reported in a series incident (SI), by year, 1993–2002*

Year	Percentage of all violent victimizations[a]	Mean no. victimizations per SI	Mode no. victimizations per SI	Median no. victimizations per SI	Maximum reported incidents[b]	No. unweighted SIs
1993	6.4	21	6	10	480	309
1994	6.0	21	6	10	260	297
1995	5.9	27	6	10	300	247
1996	5.6	29	6	10	750	208
1997	5.2	24	6	10	500	170
1998	5.2	25	6	10	300	159
1999	4.9	22	6	12	200	126
2000	3.2	17	6	7	192	71
2001	4.1	15	6	10	100	78
2002	4.3	17	6	10	160	70
Annual average	5.1	22	6	10	324	174

[a] Series incidents counted as one victimization.
[b] Minimum number reported in a series incident is six victimizations, which is also the mode for each year.

unique. About 20 individuals out of 1.4 million interviews reported a series incident with more than 200 victimizations.

Employing the series classification procedure to reduce burden is not without its consequences for computing annual estimates of victimizations. Three primary reasons have been identified as to why series incidents cause some concern if they are included in the annual estimates of victimization (Biderman and Lynch, 1991; Penick and Owens, 1976). First, and most important, is the inability to date each event. Because only information on the last incident is recorded, there is no way of knowing whether they all occurred in the last month or in some other manner over the course of the entire six months. If one is to rely on the date associated with only the last occurrence to classify these events, this introduces error in the annual estimates by possibly including events that are outside of the time period. For annual victimization estimates, this would result in overcounting at the beginning of the year and undercounting at the end of the year.

Second, because detailed information is collected only from the last event, there is a possibility of overgeneralizing the particular characteristics of the last victimization to all victimizations reported in a series. The assumption of homogenous incident characteristics is especially problematic when the occurrence reported in a series is part of an escalation in violence. For example, if a victim reports calling the police or that a gun was used, it is assumed that this was the case for each prior occurrence in a series.

Third, an individual respondent could have a significant impact on the annual estimates. One individual could report hundreds of incidents over the past six months, having a substantial impact on overall estimates, especially when the offense is a rarely reported event in the survey, as in the case of rape. Together, these factors contribute to a significant level of imprecision and, subsequently, suspicion about taking series incidents at face value, that is, including all incidents reported in the series. At the very least, given estimate imprecision and instability, annual patterns of change are difficult to identify.

Because of these difficulties, the Bureau of Justice Statistics excludes series incidents in published annual victimization rates for the United States (Rennison, 2002). Since the inception of the NCVS, a number of researchers have challenged this "all or nothing" approach to counting high-volume repeat victims (Farrell et al., 2005; Fienberg and Reiss, 1980; Penick and Owens, 1976; Skogan, 1981). Excluding series incidents is not ideal and results in other errors. Echoing many of the earlier findings of Biderman and Lynch (1991), Planty (2004) used the redesigned NCVS 1993–2000 data and found that the series incident counting scheme had a significant impact on the quantitative and qualitative nature of annual victimization estimates for violence. Counting series incidents as one victimization had a relatively small impact on victimization counts (annual increases ranged from 7 percent in 1993 to 3 percent in 2000; Table 6.2). The dramatic change occurs when series incidents are counted by the estimated number of victimizations as reported by the victim. Here the increase in annual counts ranged from 62 percent (2000) to 174 percent (1996). In 1993, for example, the annual victimization count would rise from about 11,365,000 when series are excluded to about 27,375,000 when all victimizations reported are counted (a 141 percent increase). If the number of victimizations reported by the respondents is accurate, the current government counting rules do not include about 58 percent of all violent victimizations in 1993.

Similar findings have been reported elsewhere. Farrell and Pease (1993) demonstrated that 4 percent of the population experienced 44 percent of all victimizations using the British Crime Survey. Others have shown that 1 percent of respondents accounted for about 59 percent of all personal victimizations (Pease, 1998). In addition to simply underestimating the crime rate, exclusion of series incidents underestimates the true role and subsequent importance that repeat victims have in generating the crime rate.

The second problem when series are excluded from the cross-sectional crime rate is with the potential distortion as to how crime is characterized. If certain incidents are more likely to be counted as series than others, these characteristics will be underrepresented in the annual crime rates (Dodge, 1987; Planty, 2004). Planty (2004) reported substantial changes in the characterization of the high-risk victim groups if series incidents were counted. When series victimizations are excluded, demographic groups traditionally thought of as high-risk groups emerge with the highest rates (e.g., Blacks 35 compared with Whites 27 and Hispanics 29 per 100,000; males 32 versus

TABLE 6.2. *Total number of victimizations, by series counting scheme and year; 1993–2002*

Year	Series = 0	Series = 1	Series = Mode	Series = Median	Series = Victim Estimate	Series = Only[a]
1993	11,365,078	12,147,707	16,060,852	19,191,369	27,375,186	782,629
1994	11,349,638	12,072,381	15,686,096	18,577,067	26,167,771	722,743
1995	9,969,943	10,592,290	13,704,025	16,193,414	26,151,056	622,347
1996	9,332,823	9,885,279	12,647,560	14,857,385	25,546,326	522,456
1997	8,864,863	9,352,187	11,788,811	13,738,109	19,737,470	487,324
1998	8,340,624	8,799,113	11,091,858	12,926,014	19,178,576	458,539
1999	7,330,214	7,710,968	9,614,736	11,899,260	16,297,193	380,754
2000	6,240,418	6,448,330	7,487,888	7,695,799	10,135,979	207,912
2001	5,775,173	6,019,460	7,240,896	8,218,044	9,444,176	244,287
2002	5,355,549	5,595,442	6,794,907	7,754,479	9,088,361	239,893
Percent change 1993–2002	−52.9	−53.9	−57.7	−59.6	−66.8	−69.3

[a] Series incidents counted as one victimization.

females 24 per 100,000). If series are counted as the victim's estimate, the demographic makeup of the high-risk group changes dramatically. Hispanics (77 per 100,000) would have higher rates than Blacks (47 per 100,000) and Whites (39 per 100,000), and no substantive difference would be detected between males and females (both at 45 per 100,000 residents). The inclusion of series incidents substantially changes not only the level of victimization but also the characterization of victimization. The divergence between the NCVS and UCR for certain crime types may be explained, in part, by this bias.

As stated earlier, there is some concern and suspicion about the accuracy of the series incident estimates. For example, counting series incidents as reported by the victim would result in a 225 percent change in the 1993 annual estimates for rape and sexual assault (Planty, 2004). This increase is driven by 21 unweighted series incidents. This amounts to a rise from 485,300 victimizations to about 1,721,300. Such dramatic shifts in crime rates and counts suggest these numbers are too unstable and that a more reasonable solution would be to include series victimizations as something other than the victim's estimate to avoid this instability. Clearly both counting extremes of all or nothing produce substantial error that is not easy to manage. Reasonable solutions are to include series incidents as either as the mode or median number of victimizations. Unlike the mean, these estimates are not subject to the impact of the very large and rare outliers.

The analysis that follows assesses the impact that series incidents have on the quantitative differences between the UCR and NCVS estimates for aggravated assaults, for the reasons stated earlier.[3] The research question is as follows: What is the impact of series counting schemes on the annual number and rate of violent victimizations in comparison to the UCR? Three counting procedures – counting series incidents as zero, the mode (six), and the median – are compared for aggravated assaults reported to the police. A second research question is warranted by the attention attracted by the "overlap" of the UCR trends with those of crimes reported to the police in the NCVS. The question is whether this "overlap" is largely due to the counting rules applied to high-volume repeat victimization. I attempt to answer this

---

[3] See the discussion on page 157 of this chapter.

question by assessing how variation in counting rules affects the trend in aggravated assaults reported to the police in the NCVS.

ANALYSIS

Using data from the 1993–2002 NCVS, rates for aggravated assault are generated using the three series incident counting schemes and compared with the UCR arrest rates. This study used individual-level data of all household members aged 12 and older to construct these estimates, and the few incidents that occurred outside of the United States were excluded from the analysis. Annual incidence rates are reported. The incidence rate takes into account the population at risk to adjust for exposure and is included in annual reports on victimization in the United States published each year by the U.S. government. The incidence rate is simply the weighted number of victimizations reported in the NCVS each year, over the weighted number of persons in a particular population for that year. This estimate is represented in the context of some common base, in this case, out of 1,000 persons.

The first stage of the analysis quantifies the impact of the series counting procedures for the aggravated assaults in the UCR and compares these with the NCVS counting schemes for 1993 through 2002. Series incidents are counted as zero victimizations (0), as the mode (6 incidents), and as the median (approximately 10 incidents every year). Counts and rates for these estimates are compared with the UCR estimates for aggravated assault.

In the second stage, only NCVS aggravated assaults for which the police were notified are used in the analysis to make it more comparable to the UCR estimates. Police notification occurs in about half of all violent crime and about 58 percent of all aggravated assaults reported in the NCVS (Hart and Rennison, 2003).

The NCVS is not a simple random sample, so it is necessary to control for the complexity of the sampling design when generating variance estimations. To do this, the analysis used weighted data and the complex sampling design variables (primary sampling units, stratum) to ensure the correct variance estimates are generated for significance testing. In many cases, small sample sizes render many of these estimates unreliable.

SERIES INCIDENTS AND AGGRAVATED ASSAULTS

Table 6.3 presents descriptive statistics for series incidents classified as aggravated assaults. Similar to all violence, series incidents make up about 4 percent of all aggravated assaults reported in the NCVS from 1993 to 2002. When counted as one victimization series, incidents add, on average, 76,000 aggravated assaults to the annual estimates. Counting each as the mode or six victimizations increases the aggravated assault annual count about 25 percent, on average (Table 6.4). The percent change in NCVS counts when series incidents are excluded as opposed to being counted as the mode of six fluctuates from a high of about 35 percent in 1996 to a low of 11 percent in 2000. Clearly, counting series as reported will increase any existing divergence between the UCR and NCVS estimates, and, as expected, the two NCVS counting schemes have a substantial impact on the magnitude of the aggravated assault rates (Figure 6.1).

As with total victimization (Table 6.2), the rate of decline for series aggravated assaults is faster than the decline in nonseries aggravated assaults over the 1993–2002 time period (73 percent vs. 60 percent; Table 6.4). Both have declined faster than the UCR aggravated assault rate (21 percent decline).

Compared with the UCR, there is a greater divergence in the early years (1993–1994) than the later years 2000–2002 regardless of the series treatment (Figure 6.2). With series excluded from the aggravated assault counts, the percent difference between the NCVS and UCR is about 175 percent in 1993, declining to roughly 50 percent for the later years (2000–2002). When series incidents are counted as the mode, the percent difference runs from about 250 percent to a low of about 70 percent in 2002. Counting series incidents as the median, the percent difference from the UCR is higher than the mode in the early years (about 316 percent), but about the same in 2002 (about 70 percent). Including series incidents increases the magnitude of the divergence but not the general pattern of divergence over time.

When the NCVS is restricted further by limiting the aggravated assaults to only victimizations where the police were notified, a number of patterns emerge. First, there is an overlap between the UCR and NCVS counts that occurs in 1995 and from 1998 through 2002

TABLE 6.3. *Descriptive statistics for the number of aggravated assault victimizations (AAVs) reported in a series incident (SI), by year, 1993–2002*

Year	Percentage AAVs[a]	Mean no. AAVs per SI	Mode no. AAVs per SI	Median no. AAVs per SI	Maximum reported incidents per AA Series[b]	No. unweighted series AAIs	No. unweighted AA Incidents	No. weighted AA Incidents[a]
1993	4.5	24	6	11	350	46	966	119,425
1994	4.7	20	6	10	104	49	1014	121,686
1995	5.1	26	6	10	180	39	754	100,881
1996	5.5	50	6	12	750	43	737	112,147
1997	4.9	24	6	10	120	31	644	95,129
1998	4.0	31	6	9	300	24	559	67,495
1999	3.1	25	6	12	136	17	494	49,168
2000	1.7	16	6	7	75	8	397	21,044
2001	3.2	16	6	9	75	14	388	38,034
2002	3.1	26	6	7	160	8	310	32,118
Annual average	4.0	28	6	10	225	28	626	75,713

[a] Series incidents counted as one victimization.
[b] Minimum number reported in a series incident is six victimizations, which is also the mode for each year.

TABLE 6.4. *Number of aggravated assaults, by Uniform Crime Reports (UCR) and National Crime Victimization Survey (NCVS) counting schemes for series incidents, 1993–2002*

Year	UCR	Series = 0	Series = 1	Series = Mode	Series = Median	Series = Only[a]
1993	1,135,607	2,562,857	2,682,282	3,279,405	3,876,530	119,425
1994	1,113,179	2,478,149	2,599,835	3,208,266	3,695,009	121,686
1995	1,099,207	1,882,806	1,983,687	2,488,091	2,891,614	100,881
1996	1,037,049	1,943,847	2,055,994	2,616,730	3,289,612	112,147
1997	1,023,201	1,842,217	1,937,346	2,412,990	2,793,506	95,129
1998	976,583	1,631,369	1,698,864	2,036,339	2,238,824	67,495
1999	911,740	1,517,411	1,566,579	1,812,417	2,107,425	49,168
2000	911,706	1,185,663	1,206,708	1,311,929	1,332,973	21,045
2001	909,023	1,165,966	1,204,000	1,394,171	1,508,273	38,034
2002	894,348	1,015,257	1,047,375	1,207,965	1,240,083	32,118
Percent change						
1993–2002	−21.2	−60.4	−61.0	−63.2	−68.0	−73.1

[a] Series incidents counted as one victimization.

(Figure 6.3). Overlap is when estimates from the UCR are larger than estimates from the NCVS. The overlap from 2000 to 2002 occurs regardless of the series incident counting scheme.

Once these counts are translated into rates, the overlap between the two collections is limited to 2000–2002, and only when series is excluded (Figure 6.4). There is no overlap once series incidents are counted as the mode or median number of victimizations. More important, when aggravated assaults are limited to police-reported cases, the divergence between the two collections is much less (Figure 6.5). Where the percent difference between the UCR and NCVS for all aggravated assaults ranges from 316 to 50 percent (depending on the series counting procedure), the percent difference for police-reported aggravated assaults ranges from a high of 125 percent to about −20 percent (the overlap). When series are excluded for police-reported victimizations, the percent differences range from about 45 percent to −20 percent with the overlap occurring in 2000–2002. When series incidents are included as the mode, the percent difference ranges from about 90 percent in 1993 to about 5 percent in 2002 with no overlap. Using the median, the percent difference between the NCVS and UCR for police-reported aggravated assaults ranges from 127 in 1993 to about 8 percent in 2003, again with no overlap being observed. A reasonable inclusion of series incidents for police-reported aggravated assaults shows a general pattern of convergence between the two systems. Again, the convergence is primarily due to a faster decline in the NCVS rate over the 10-year period.

DISCUSSION

NCVS counting procedures can have a significant impact on the national cross-sectional victimization rates. Currently, the counting rules exclude reports of victimizations from the high-volume, repeat victim. If the number of victimizations reported in these series incidents is accurate, annual estimates published by the government are severely underestimated. The NCVS measurement error associated with counting series incidents certainly cannot explain the divergence between UCR and NCVS estimates because the inclusion of series incidents will only serve to increase the already larger NCVS estimate.

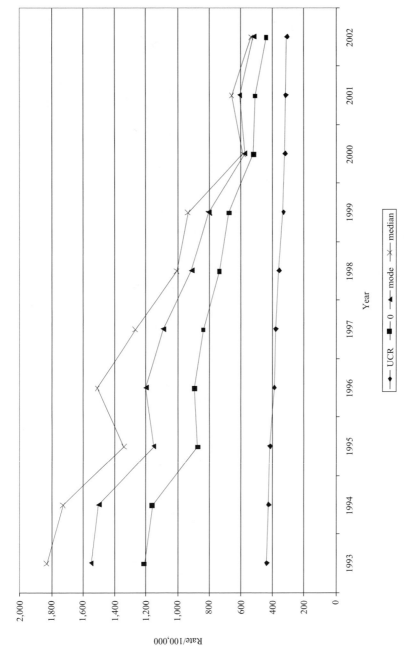

Figure 6.1. Aggravated assault rate per 100,000 persons, by Uniform Crime Reports (UCR) and National Crime Victimization Survey (NCVS) series counting schemes, 1993–2002.

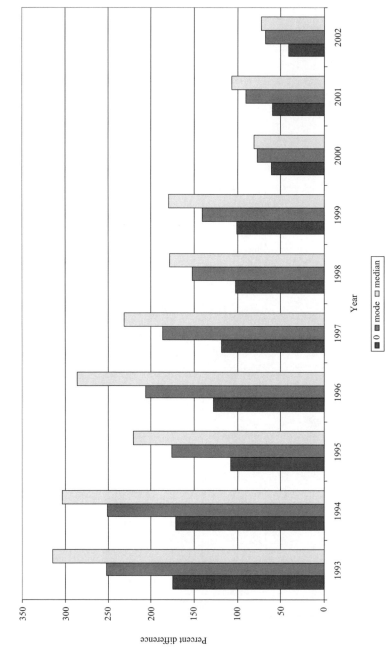

Figure 6.2. Percent difference between National Crime Victimization Survey (NCVS) victimization rates and Uniform Crime Reports (UCR) rates, by NCVS series counting schemes, 1993–2002.

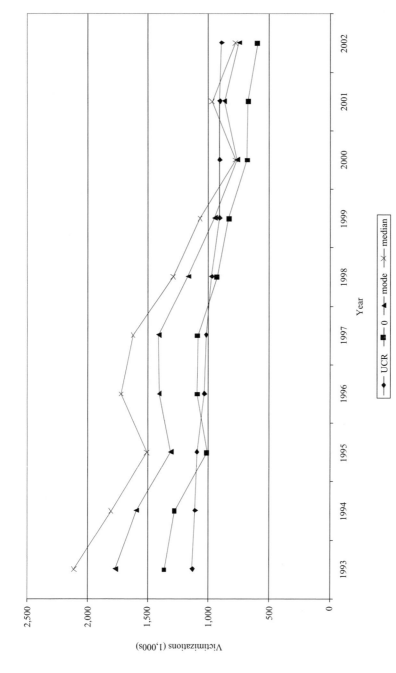

Figure 6.3. Number of aggravated assault victimizations reported to police, by Uniform Crime Reports (UCR) and National Crime Victimization Survey (NCVS) series counting schemes, 1993–2002.

175

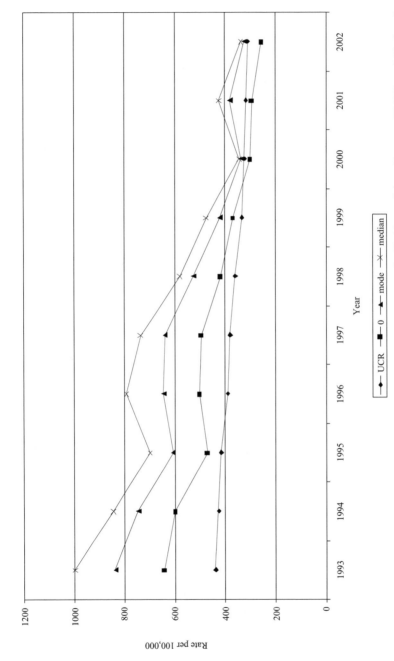

Figure 6.4. Police-reported aggravated assault rate per 100,000 persons, by Uniform Crime Reports (UCR) and National Crime Victimization Survey (NCVS) series counting schemes, 1993–2002.

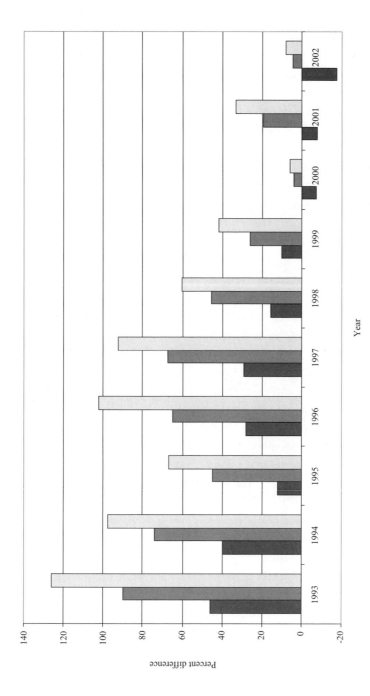

Figure 6.5. Percent difference of police-reported National Crime Victimization Survey (NCVS) aggravated assault rates and Uniform Crime Reports (UCR) rates, by NCVS series counting schemes, 1993–2002.

177

This is precisely what we see when we take reasonable steps to include series incidents. The percent difference between the UCR and NCVS rates increases from about 170 percent to about 250 percent, when series incidents are counted as the modal value (six victimizations) in 1993. By 2002, the difference between the NCVS and UCR is about 50 percent. Regardless of the counting scheme employed, however, the UCR and NCVS follow a similar trajectory over this time period, suggesting some level of convergence. This tendency toward convergence is attributed to the victimization rate declining faster than the UCR rate (see percent change in Table 6.4). It is not clear whether the steep decline in series incidents is attributable to a methodological artifact, is representative of a substantive decline in repeat victims over this period, or both.

It is also important to note that the percent change in series incidents is different from the percent change in nonseries incidents over the period. From 1993 to 2002, series incidents declined 73 percent, whereas nonseries incidents declined only 60 percent. This suggests that it may not be appropriate to assume that the exclusion of series does not affect change estimates in the NCVS.

Once the NCVS is limited to only police-reported victimizations in an attempt to make it more comparable to the UCR estimates, we notice an overlap when the UCR estimates are larger than the NCVS estimates. When we factor in the population over time (rates), the overlap is limited to 2000–2002. Three general patterns emerge. First, like the overall aggravated assault trends, both the NCVS and UCR estimates decline over time, with the NCVS declining at a faster rate. Second, once series incidents are introduced, the UCR overlap is not evident. There is, however, a fair level of convergence compared with the previous years regardless of the series counting procedure. In 1993 and 1994, police-reported aggravated assaults from the NCVS were about 40 percent higher than UCR aggravated assault rates. By 2000–2002, the percent difference fluctuated between 5 and 20 percent. Finally, when series incidents are included, both the magnitude of level and annual change estimates are affected, but not the overall trend.

A number of limitations must be considered when interpreting and assessing the contribution of these findings. First, although the NCVS employs similar definitions to the UCR, the NCVS uses a taxonomy to classify victimizations as aggravated assaults that is not refined by the presence of evidence or witnesses. As with victimization rates in general, there is a basic need to overgeneralize the similarities of incidents to facilitate comparisons between groups because of reasons related to statistical power. When a person reports multiple aggravated assaults, he or she is defined as a repeat victim regardless of the connectivity of the events. One should recognize the assumption of homogeneity when interpreting the estimates presented here.

Second, we do not know how much repeat victimization is captured in the UCR. Although adjusting the NCVS causes an increase in divergence between the two systems, it is quite possible that the UCR severely underestimates repeat victimization as well. In other words, although series incidents are a significant measurement error in terms of the magnitude and distribution of the victimization rate, it may not be such an important factor in understanding the divergence between the UCR and NCVS. Police research suggests that many crimes are never reported to the police and remain unfounded and subsequently not recorded (Buzawa and Austin, 1993; Farrell and Pease, 2003; Hart and Rennison, 2003; Skogan, 1976). Other bureaucratic policies and procedures limit the ability to link events and victims. This type of underestimation may be a wash with the series exclusion rule employed in annual estimates from the NCVS. In other words, both systems may do a poor job of capturing repeat victims. Any subsequent adjustment has a limited impact on the divergence or convergence patterns over time.

References

Anderson, D., Chenery, S., & Pease, K. (1995). *Biting back: Tackling repeat burglary and car crime* (Crime Detection and Prevention Series, Paper 58). London: Home Office.

Biderman, A. D. (1980). "Notes on measurement by crime victimization surveys." In S. E. Fienberg & A. J. Reiss, Jr. (Eds.), *Indicators of crime and criminal justice: Quantitative studies* (NCJ-62349). Washington, DC: Bureau of Justice Statistics, U.S. Department of Justice, pp. 29–32.

Biderman, A. D., Johnson, L. A., McIntyre, J., & Weir, A. W. (1967). *Report on a pilot study in the District of Columbia on victimization and attitudes toward law enforcement, President's Commission on Law Enforcement and Administration of Justice* (Field Surveys I). Washington, DC: U.S. Government Printing Office.

Biderman, A. D., & Lynch, J. (1991). *Understanding crime incidence statistics: Why the UCR diverges from the NCS.* New York: Springer-Verlag.

Biderman, A. D., & Reiss, A. J. (1967). "On exploring the 'dark figure' of crime." *Annals of the American Academy of Political and Social Science* 374:1–15.

Bridgeman, C., & Hobbs, L. (1997). *Preventing repeat victimisation: The police officer's guide.* London: Home Office.

Buzawa, E., & Austin, T. (1993). "Determining police response to domestic violence victims: The role of victim preference." *American Behavioral Scientist* 36:610–623.

Chenery, S., Ellingworth, D., Tseloni, A., & Pease, K. (1996). "Crimes which repeat: Undigested evidence from the British Crime Survey 1992." *International Journal of Risk, Security & Crime Prevention* 1:207–216.

Chu, A., Eisenhower, D., Hay, M., Morganstein, D., Neter, J., & Waksberg, J. (1992). "Measuring the recall error in self-reported fishing and hunting activities." *Journal of Official Statistics* 8:19–39.

Czaja, R., Blair, J., Bickart, B., & Eastman, E. (1994). "Respondent strategies for recall of crime victimization incidents." *Journal of Official Statistics* 10:257–276.

Dodge, R. W. (1984). "Series victimization – what is to be done?" In R. G. Lehnen & W. G. Skogan (Eds.), *National Crime Survey: Working papers, volume II: Methodological studies* (NCJ-90307). Washington, DC: Bureau of Justice Statistics, U.S. Department of Justice.

Dodge, R. W. (1987). *Series crimes: Report of a field test* (Bureau of Justice Statistics Technical Report). Washington, DC: U.S. Department of Justice.

Ellingworth, D., Farrell, G., & Pease, K. (1995). "A victim is a victim: Chronic victimisation in four sweeps of the British Crime Survey." *British Journal of Criminology* 35:360–365.

Farrell, G. (1995). "Preventing repeat victimization." In M. Tonry & D. P. Farrington (Eds.), *Crime and justice: Building a safer society* (Vol. 19, 469–534). Chicago: University of Chicago Press.

Farrell, G., & Pease, K. (1993). *Once bitten, twice bitten: Repeat victimisation and its implications for crime prevention* (Home Office Crime Prevention Unit Series, No. 46). London: Her Majesty's Stationary Office.

Farrell, G., & Pease, K. (2003). "Measuring and interpreting repeat victimization using police data: A study of burglaries in Charlotte, North Carolina." *Crime Prevention Studies* 16:269–285.

Farrell, G., & Sousa, W. (2001). "Repeat victimization and 'hot spots': The overlap and its implications for crime prevention and problem-oriented policing." *Crime Prevention Studies* 12:221–240.

Farrell, G., Tseloni, A., & Pease, K. (2005). "Repeat victimization in the ICVS and NCVS." *Crime Prevention and Community Safety: An International Journal* 7:7–18.

Fienberg, S. E., & Reiss, A. J. (1980). *Indicators of crime and criminal justice: Quantitative studies* (NCJ-62349). Washington, DC: Bureau of Justice Statistics, U.S. Department of Justice.

Gondolf, E., & McFerron, R. (1989). "Handling battering men: Police action in wife abuse cases." *Criminal Justice and Behavior*, 16:429–439.

Hart, T., & Rennison, C. (2003, March). *Reporting crime to the police, 1992–2000.* Washington, DC: Bureau of Justice Statistics, U.S. Department of Justice.

Mathiowetz, N. (2000, October). "The effects of length of recall on the quality of survey data." Invited paper, Fourth Conference on Methodological Issues in Official Statistics, Stockholm, Sweden.

Pease, K. (1998). *Repeat victimisation: Taking stock* (Crime Prevention and Detection Paper 90). London: Home Office.

Pease, K., & Laycock, G. (1996). *Reducing the heat on hot victims.* Washington, DC: Bureau of Justice Statistics, Department of Justice.

Penick, B., & Owens, M. (1976). *Surveying crime.* Washington, DC: National Academy of Sciences.

Planty, M. (2004). *The role of repeat victimization in the production of national annual estimates of violence.* Unpublished manuscript prepared for the American Statistical Association and Bureau of Justice Statistics Research Grants Program.

Reiss, A. J. (1986). "Official and survey crime statistics." In E. A. Fattah (Ed.), *From crime policy to victim policy: Reorienting the justice system* (pp. 53–79). New York: MacMillian Press.

Rennison, C. (2002). *Criminal victimization 2001: Changes 2000–2001 with trends 1993–2001.* Washington, DC: Bureau of Justice Statistics, U.S. Department of Justice.

Shenk, F., & McInerney, W. (1981). "Analytic limitations of the National Crime Survey." In R. G. Lehnen & W. G. Skogan, *The National Crime Survey: Working papers, volume I: Current and historical perspectives* (NCJ-75374). Washington, DC: Bureau of Justice Statistics, U.S. Department of Justice.

Sherman, L., Gartin, P., & Buerger, M. (1989). "Hot spots of predatory crime: Routine activities and the criminology of place." *Criminology* 27:27–56.

Sherman, L., & Rogan, D. (1995). "Gun violence: 'Hot spots' patrol in Kansas City." *Justice Quarterly* 12:673–694.

Sherman, L., & Weisburd, D. (1995). "General deterrent effects of police patrol in crime hot spots: A randomized controlled trial." *Justice Quarterly* 12:625–648.

Skogan, W. (1976). "Citizen reporting of crime: Some national panel data." *Criminology* 13:535–549.

Skogan, W. (1981). *Issues in the measurement of victimization.* Washington, DC: U.S. Department of Justice.

Trickett, A., Osborn, D., Seymour, J., & Pease, K. (1992). "What is different about high crime areas?" *British Journal of Criminology* 32:81–89.

CHAPTER SEVEN

Exploring Differences in Estimates of Visits to Emergency Rooms for Injuries from Assaults Using the NCVS and NHAMCS

Jacqueline Cohen and James P. Lynch

Researchers seeking to provide a better understanding of crime statistics tend to compare survey-based statistics such as the National Crime Victimization Survey (NCVS) with data from police administrative series like the Uniform Crime Reports (UCR). Because these two types of data collections systems are so different, simple direct comparisons are of little value regarding limitations inherent to a particular data collection system (McDowall and Loftin, this volume). This chapter explores the NCVS data using a different perspective that compares data from the national crime survey of population with those from a national survey of establishments – the National Hospital Ambulatory Care Survey (NHAMCS). This comparison provides an understanding of how the design, instrumentation, and procedures of the NCVS may influence estimates of interpersonal violence, particularly that component of violence resulting in injuries treated in hospital emergency rooms.

The estimates of emergency room visits for injuries due to violence obtained from the NCVS are considerably smaller than those from the NHAMCS. The analyses include a series of adjustments to these estimates that explore the role of features specific to each survey in the observed differences. The household sampling frame employed in the NCVS receives special attention as a potential source of the observed differences. Investigating this source of divergence is particularly important because many of our major social indicators on the economy and participation in government programs depend upon household surveys. If some population groups are underrepresented in the household sampling frame used in Census surveys and this undercoverage results in underestimates of violence, this finding could have implications for the use of the household frame to estimate the magnitude of other problems that disproportionately affect marginal populations, such as unemployment, poverty, drug abuse, and poor health status.

The first section that follows describes the two surveys, but principally the NHAMCS because the NCVS is described extensively in Chapter 2. The second section presents the unadjusted estimates of the rate of emergency room visits due to violent crime from the two surveys. The third section outlines a series of potential explanations for the observed rate differences, and the last section includes a series of adjustments to the rates designed to test the plausibility of the various explanations.

THE NHAMCS AND THE NCVS

The National Center for Health Statistics annually fields a family of surveys designed to measure utilization of health care services in a variety of provider settings. The NHAMCS estimates the level and type of outpatient medical services provided in hospital emergency departments (EDs) and outpatient departments (OPDs) nationally. Fielded for the first time in 1992, the NHAMCS supplements data on ambulatory medical care services provided in physicians' offices collected since 1973 in the National Ambulatory Medical Care Survey. Patients treated in hospital-based ambulatory care settings differ in certain demographic and medical characteristics from patients treated in physicians' offices, and the NHAMCS provides data on this important segment of ambulatory care services (http://www.cdc.gov/nchs/about/major/ahcd/nhamcsds.htm).

NHAMCS relies on a national probability sample of EDs and OPDs in general (medical and surgical), short-stay (average length of stay less than 30 days) hospitals (excluding federal, military, and Veterans Administration hospitals) located in the 50 states and the District of Columbia. A four-stage probability design samples in the following order from: (1) geographic-based primary sampling units (PSUs consisting of counties, county equivalents, or metropolitan statistical areas [MSAs]), (2) hospitals in the selected PSUs, (3) EDs and OPDs in these hospitals, and (4) patient visits to these departments.

The NHAMCS PSUs are the probability subsample of PSUs used in the 1985–1994 National Health Interview Surveys. About 1,900 PSUs were stratified by socioeconomic and demographic variables within four geographic regions by MSA or non-MSA status. The selection probability was proportional to PSU size. The final sample includes a fixed panel of 600 hospitals (drawn from about 5,600 hospitals nationally) located in 112 PSUs across the country. A target number of 50 visits to each sampled ED were selected systematically – every nth visit based on the expected number of patients who will be seen in each ED – over a randomly selected four-week reporting period during the survey year. The data used here include the samples of about 23,000 visits to hospital EDs in each year from 1995 to 1998.

Specially trained hospital staff members implement the visit sampling process and extract the information from the sampled records onto data collection forms. Census field representatives collect these forms, check them for completeness, and perform various edit checks on the forms and keyed data. Sampling weights and nonresponse adjustments are applied to produce population estimates of total ED visits in the nation. The ED data include variables to identify injury visits; whether the injury was unintentional, intentionally inflicted in an assault, or self-inflicted; and mechanism (weapon type) producing the injury. These variables are the basis for estimating total ED visits for assault injuries.

In contrast, the NCVS is based on a probability sample of households residing in housing units contained in the address lists emerging from the United States decennial census. Addresses are selected from the list in a multistage process described in detail in Chapter 2. The households selected from the lists are visited by Census interviewers, and all members of the household 12 years of age and older are interviewed about their violence and theft crime victimization experiences. Interviews are highly structured; all respondents answer the same screener questions, and computer-assisted interviewing is employed in some circumstances. Respondents who mention that they were actually attacked in an incident of interpersonal violence are asked about any injuries they sustained and any medical care they received, including whether the individual was treated in a hospital emergency room or an emergency clinic.

If all things were equal between the NCVS and NHAMCS, both surveys would provide similar estimates of the number of assault victims who were treated in hospital EDs. There are some important differences in survey methodology, however, and the estimates from the two surveys differ substantially, with almost fivefold more assaults treated in hospital EDs estimated from NHAMCS than from NCVS. Because adjustments can be made to the data to take account of some of the design differences, we can calibrate the contribution of specific methodological differences in the observed disparity in estimates. A series of adjustments that rely on information available in existing data reduce the divergence ratio in half to about 2.5.

COMPARING ESTIMATES FROM THE SURVEYS

Figure 7.1 displays national estimates of the number of assault injuries detected by the two annual surveys of crime victims and hospital emergency departments during the period 1995–1998. An average annual total of 3.8 million violent injuries were detected by the NCVS and NHAMCS surveys.

NCVS injuries are partitioned by whether police are informed and whether victims sought medical care in hospital emergency departments. The annual average count of assault injuries reported to the NCVS by victims was more than 2.3 million. Victims indicate that police were informed about just over half of these injuries (1.25 million), and victims injured in violent attacks sought care in emergency departments for 376,000 violent injuries. Not surprisingly, police were more likely to be informed about an assault injury when the victim sought medical care (78 percent vs. 49 percent, respectively, among ED and non-ED injuries reported to the NCVS; odds ratio = 3.68 with 95 percent confidence interval [2.95, 4.59] is significant).

Estimates of the number of violent injuries that are treated in hospital EDs are substantially different in the NCVS and the NHAMCS (Figure 7.1). The estimate from victim reports to the NCVS is under 400,000 violent injuries treated in EDs annually from 1995 to 1998.

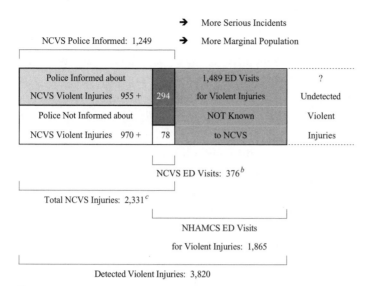

Figure 7.1. Detected violent injuries in the National Crime Victimization Survey (NCVS) and National Hospital Ambulatory Care Survey (NHAMCS): Annual averages for the United States, 1995–1998 (000s).[a]
Notes: [a]National Crime Victimization Survey (NCVS) estimates come from semi-annual surveys of crime victimization experiences during years 1995–1998. Violent incidents include crime types 1 to 15 and 17. Estimates for the total resident population of United States apply person weights to sample data. National Hospital Ambulatary Care Survey (NHAMCS) estimates come from annual surveys of hospital emergency departments about patient visits during the same years 1995–1998. "External cause of injury" codes (i.e., e-codes) identify visits for treatment of violent injuries. Total population estimates apply patient-visit weights to sample data. [b]Total National Crime Victimization Survey (NCVS) violent injuries treated in emergency departments include an additional 4,000 visits with unknown police status. [c]Total National Crime Victimization Survey (NCVS) violent injuries include an additional 34,000 visits with unknown police status.

Estimates from NHAMCS data for the same period are nearly 5 times higher at 1.865 million violent injuries treated in EDs annually. If the NHAMCS estimates are taken at face value, the crime victimization survey failed to detect 80 percent – or nearly 1.5 million – of the violent injuries seen in hospital emergency departments.

These results are consistent with other estimates that find large numbers of violent injuries are missing from crime victimization surveys. Relying on several estimates of the expected ratio of nonfatal-to-fatal gunshot injuries, Cook (1985) estimated that from 1973 to 1979, the

National Crime Survey underestimated nonfatal gunshot injuries by
threefold. More recently, Rand (1997) compared 1994 NCVS violent
injury data with data from a special Study of Injured Victims of Violence (SIVV) fielded as part of the annual National Electronic Injury
Surveillance System (NEISS) of injuries treated in hospital emergency
departments during the same time period. Rand's study found the
SIVV estimated that 1.34 million distinct violent injuries were treated
nationally compared with 0.54 million injuries treated in EDs estimated from violent victimizations using the NCVS data – a ratio of 2.5
between SIVV and NCVS estimates. The more recent data from 1995
to 1998 presented in Figure 7.1 show a substantially higher fivefold
difference between estimates from the NHAMCS health care establishment survey and the NCVS crime victimization survey.[1]

All of these findings suggest that the NCVS substantially under-
counts victims of violence who incur injuries that result in treatment in
hospital emergency rooms or freestanding emergency clinics. An alternate view is that some of the difference is attributable to the NHAMCS
overcounting injuries attributable to violence. This view has some support from data in the UCR and Rand's (1997) SIVV study.

Although annual national police data are available from the UCR,
these data typically do not distinguish between injuries and noninjuries
among violent crimes recorded by police. The Bureau of Justice Statistics (BJS, 2001), however, contrasts police- and NCVS-based estimates
of serious violent crimes known to police. The vast majority of these
crimes are aggravated assaults that by definition involve weapon use or
injury. Figure 7.2 displays these alternative annual estimates from 1973
to 2000. The two estimates diverge substantially early in the period –
NCVS counts of violent offenses known to police are 2.6 times larger
than similar UCR counts in 1973 – but steadily converge to be virtually
identical at 1.25 million serious violent crimes by 2000.[2] During the

---

[1] The discrepancy increases when inpatient hospital stay data are examined. In 1997,
the National Hospital Discharge Survey estimated a total of 280,265 hospital stays
for violent injuries (from author analysis: counts present assault on any of seven
diagnoses) and the NCVS estimated 44,449 such stays – a sevenfold undercount of
violent injuries that result in inpatient hospital stays.

[2] This convergence is not due to changes in victim reporting to police. Annual rates of
victims reporting violent victimizations to police remained relatively stable in a range
from 50 percent to 60 percent for almost 30 years in NCVS data. The increase in
UCR counts of serious violent crimes seems to be associated with an increase in police

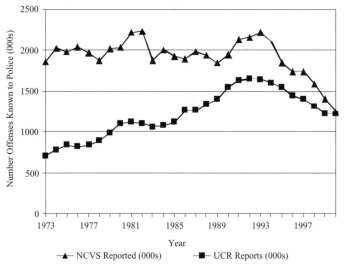

Figure 7.2. National Crime Victimization Survey (NCVS) and Uniform Crime Reports (UCR) serious violent crimes known to police: United States, 1973–2000. Data are from Bureau of Justice Statistics (2001).

period 1995–1998, NCVS counts of serious violent crimes reported to police agreed substantially with UCR data, with NCVS counts just 1.2 times the corresponding police counts in UCR data. The increasing correspondence between NCVS and UCR data for a subset of similar violent incidents that are found in both data series lends some credibility to NCVS estimates more generally.

The SIVV study was based on a supplement to NEISS, which employs a sample of hospital emergency rooms (Rand, 1997). Hospitals are asked to complete forms requesting information from patient records on all injuries that present at emergency rooms during a given period. As noted earlier, this ED data for year 1994 estimates 1.34 million ED-treated assault injuries nationally compared with an estimated 0.54 million violent injuries treated in emergency care facilities estimated from NCVS data for the same year. Although these results

recording of victim reports in their count of "founded" crimes reported to the UCR. The proportion of victim-reported serious violent crimes that show up in police data increased steadily from a low of 40 percent in 1973 to nearly 100 percent recorded in 2000. One factor contributing to convergence may be declining tendencies by police to treat violent and potentially violent incidents between family, intimates, and acquaintances as private matters that are resolved informally and do not enter official police counts of violent incidents.

support the argument that the NCVS underestimates these violent injuries, the fact that similar data drawn from hospital records produce different estimates (1.34 million vs. 1.865 million violent injuries treated in hospital emergency rooms) also supports a conclusion that NHAMCS may overestimate ED-treated violent injuries by a modest amount (NHAMCS/SIVV = 1.29 compared with a ratio of 4.95 between NHAMCS and NCVS).

Relying only on comparisons of estimated total counts, it is impossible to determine which data series produces the most accurate estimates. The divergence among estimates may be attributable to an underestimate in the NCVS, an overestimate in the NHAMCS, or both. This chapter now turns to the question of why the NHAMCS and NCVS estimates differ and how can this knowledge inform us about divergence between the NCVS and UCR.

SOURCES OF DIVERGENCE BETWEEN NCVS AND NHAMCS

The most likely sources of divergence in the two surveys arise from differences in sample design, survey instrumentation and procedures, as well as the interaction of these differences with changes in the society. Differences in sample design refer to differences in the population of interest, the sampling frame, and the method of selection. Instrumentation refers to the questions asked of respondents and the mode by which these questions are conveyed. Procedures include rules governing the interview and the estimation process, for example, rules on respondent selection or the number of callbacks. Rules governing the weighting of data or the treatment of missing data are examples of rules affecting the estimation process.

Interactions between survey designs and societal changes occur when the survey procedures are the same, but society changes in ways that alter the components of emergency treatment of violent injuries that surveys capture. If, for example, more and more schools and workplaces have their own clinics and equivalents of emergency rooms, then the NHAMCS sampling frame will exclude these alternative treatment facilities and exclude any visits to these facilities. If respondents to the NCVS regard these facilities as emergency rooms, however, the treated injuries will be counted in the NCVS. Although the survey procedures remained constant, the societal changes would contribute to divergence between the two survey estimates.

Sample Design

One of the major differences between the NCVS and NHAMCS is the sample design. The population that the ED component of NHAMCS seeks to describe is visits to emergency rooms in noninstitutional, short-stay hospitals. The NCVS is designed to represent the population of criminal victimization incidents experienced by the noninstitutionalized residential population of the United States. To produce estimates for the relevant population, the NHAMCS uses a list of hospitals and clinics in the United States. In the first stage of selection, PSUs are chosen randomly. Hospitals are selected randomly within these PSUs, and EDs are chosen within the hospitals. Finally, patient visits are sampled systematically (every nth visit) from the ED records at these sites. The NCVS is also a multistage cluster sample, except the sampling frame is households residing in housing units included in the master address list from the decennial census. PSUs are sampled first followed by enumeration districts, census tracts, and segments of housing units. The final unit of selection is the household.

These differences in sample design can affect estimates of visits to emergency rooms for treatment of assault injuries when the design results in differential inclusion of these visits. If the household frame, for example, omits marginal populations who have no permanent residence, and if this population is more prone to injuries from assaults, then the NCVS will underestimate ED visits due to assaults.

Instrumentation

The NCVS gathers information in an interview with the respondent in which questions are asked about the respondent's victimization experiences and the consequences of those victimizations, including emergency room visits. The NHAMCS, in contrast, uses data collection forms that are completed by hospital staff based on information recorded at the time of the ED visit. These are very different data collection processes that can substantially affect the resulting data. NCVS interviews inquire directly about the victimization experiences and include a number of cuing prompts to remind respondents about potential incidents. ED records, by contrast, primarily reflect concerns about diagnosis and treatment, and so medical practitioners may not inquire about how the patient incurred the injury; even when they do, the medical record may not include the patient's response. Cause of injury is an important public health concern, however, and increasingly widespread requirements to use cause-of-injury e-codes in cases involving injuries increase the salience of cause of injury as an important component of the medical record.

For an emergency room visit to be included in the NCVS, the respondent must report being a victim of a crime in which they were attacked and injured. Moreover, they must also indicate that they sought treatment for that injury and that the treatment was administered in a hospital emergency room or a freestanding emergency clinic. If any of these screening events are not reported, then the visit will not be identified in the NCVS.

Perhaps the most difficult determination to be made in the NCVS is that a criminal victimization has occurred. Many events that satisfy the legal definition of an assault are not reported in the survey because they are not stereotypic crimes. Assaults by intimates or siblings, for example, are often considered "private matters" rather than crimes, and they are not reported to the NCVS (Fisher and Cullen, 2000). Similarly, assaults in which the respondent was the initial aggressor may result in an emergency room visit but not be mentioned as a crime in the NCVS. The status of injuries to bystanders who intervene may also be ambiguous. Because these injuries are collateral to victim injuries, some individuals who are injured during a crime may not consider themselves as victims because they were not the initial focus of the assault. All of these circumstances would lead the NCVS to underestimate the number of violence-related injuries treated in the ED.

Another difference is that the NCVS relies on the respondent to identify the type of facility where the victim sought treatment, and this definition may not be consistent with the definition used in the NHAMCS. Because this level of precision is not central to the mission of the NCVS, little cuing or data checks are performed to ensure that the facility type is accurate. It is not clear whether this feature of the NCVS would over- or underestimate the number of visits. Respondents might mistake doctor's offices for emergency rooms or emergency clinics and vice versa.

The NHAMCS instrument also can be a source of estimation discrepancy. The NHAMCS relies almost entirely on the quality of the original hospital records. If the required information was not entered into the medical record at the time of the patient visit, it will not be included in the data. Because contextual features of an injury are generally not essential to medical diagnosis or treatment, information about the circumstances surrounding the injury will often be missing from medical records. The problems with relying on medical records are evident in the large amount of missing data for some variables. For example, the NHAMCS data collection form for 1995 and 1996 includes a variable for relationship between victims and offenders in an assault, but is missing in 50 percent of assault injuries those years. This variable was dropped from the data collection form in 1997–1998. Other relevant variables are also missing from NHAMCS data for all study years 1995–1998, including the place where injury occurred (missing in 44 percent of assault injuries) and injury type (missing in 29 percent of assault injuries).[3]

Assault injuries in NHAMCS data are identified by external cause of injury "e-codes" derived from information in the medical record. Since 1992, providers who seek reimbursement for medical services from publicly funded Medicare and Medicaid programs have been required to supply e-codes for all treated injuries, and these codes are rapidly becoming a standard part of medical records. These codes identify intent or manner of injury (accident, self-inflicted, intentional assault) and mechanism (e.g., firearm, cutting, unarmed brawl) in injury cases. E-codes are well recorded in NHAMCS data for the study years 1995–1998 – only 11.2 percent of injury visits to emergency rooms either fail to include any e-codes (0.6 percent) or use e-codes that do not identify intent (10.6 percent).[4]

---

3 Place where an injury occurred refers to type of location and includes categories such as inside a residence, at school, or on a street/highway. Injury type includes categories such as penetrating injury, internal injury, spinal chord or nerve damage, orthopedic injuries, and superficial injuries.
4 NHAMCS data include another variable that designates intent for the 0.6 percent of injury visits that do not include specific e-codes.

Although information is not readily available to quantitatively assess the accuracy of intent coding in the available e-codes, this coding follows well-defined protocols. Cause of injury is coded using the *Supplementary Classification of External Causes of Injury and Poisoning* (e-codes) from the *International Classification of Diseases, 9th Revision, Clinical Modification* (ICD-9-CM). The documentation from the Public Health Service and Health Care Financing Administration provides clear protocols for how the hospital staff determines whether an injury was the result of an assault. Hospital staff members routinely use this coding protocol as part of the medical record.

The criteria for assault in NHAMCS may differ from those used in the NCVS. If the hospital staff members who abstract the data do not distinguish between thwarted offenders and victims among patients or between intended and unintended injuries, the NHAMCS data will overstate visits due to assault victimizations. On the other hand, if the staff uses a more stringent definition of assault, then this might understate these events. Coding practices of the NHAMCS suggest a reluctance to inappropriately designate an injury as intentional when there is inadequate information in the record. In 1995 and 1996, injuries with undetermined intent were coded as accidents, and in 1997 a new explicit code for undetermined intent was introduced. These injuries of undetermined intent potentially include uncounted assault injuries that would contribute to underestimates of assault visits to EDs in NHAMCS data.

Other differences in instrumentation across the two surveys also can contribute to divergence. The NCVS, for example, employs a special procedure for "series" incidents that involve high-volume, repeat victimization. Specifically, when a respondent reports six or more crimes that cannot be dated separately and are similar in their details, the interviewer can treat them as a series incident. Detailed information is collected only for the most recent incident in a series, rather than for all of them, and the total number of incidents in the series is recorded (Planty, Chapter 6, this volume). These incidents are excluded from official counts of victimization published by BJS because of concerns about the accuracy of the number of events in the series. Public use data files include these series incidents but as Planty demonstrates, it is difficult to determine the number of incidents in the series. Treating series victimizations as single incidents or excluding them from victimization counts will clearly lead to an underestimate of emergency room visits for injuries resulting from interpersonal violence in the NCVS relative to the NHAMCS.

It is also possible that some injured victims visit an ED more than once for the same injury. These multiple visits per injury will be counted in NHAMCS data but not in NCVS data. The victim survey only collects information on the prevalence of emergency room visits per crime and not their incidence.

The skip pattern employed by the NCVS can also contribute to divergence in the estimates of ED visits. NCVS respondents are asked about injuries to themselves and others at two places in the survey – when the respondent reports being attacked and later if respondents say that they or someone else took actions to protect themselves. Other injuries that are incurred during assaults – for example, by victims falling down without being attacked or by wounded bystanders – will not be detected in the NCVS if there is no report of an offender attack or protective action during an incident. These exclusions will lead the NCVS to underestimate the number of visits arising from injuries sustained during assaults relative to NHAMCS estimates.

Procedures
Although collected from different sources, the field procedures used in the two surveys are similar in some respects. Census employees collect the NCVS data, whereas hospital staff trained and supervised by Census field representatives collect NHAMCS data. NHAMCS field representatives do not actually collect the data from patient medical records, but they review the emergency department logs used for visit sampling to determine whether cases are missing and edit the forms completed by hospital staff for missing data. When data are missing, efforts are made to complete the data by consulting with hospital staff or reviewing relevant medical records. Quality control over NCVS data collection includes reinterviewing 10 percent of the respondents and employing centralized computer-assisted telephone interviewing (CATI). Quality control for the NHAMCS involves a similar 10 percent

independent coding and verification procedure. Coding discrepancies and illegible items are reviewed and adjudicated at the National Center for Health Statistics.[5]

Estimation procedures in the two surveys are also similar – sample counts are weighted up to obtain population counts, but the units of count differ. The unit of count in the NHAMCS is a distinct patient visit to the ED. The NCVS has several possible units of count including crime incidents, distinct victims regardless of the number of incidents they incur, and victimizations experienced by persons and households.[6] The NCVS units most comparable to NHAMCS visits are personal victimizations that count all violent crimes experienced by all victims in an incident. Violent victimization counts are obtained by weighting reported incidents by the person weight. Incident counts are obtained by dividing the victimization weight for each incident by the number of victims in the incident and multiplying sample counts by this new weight. This is done to prevent double counts of incidents because all victims in the incident have a chance of being in the NCVS sample. To the extent that assault incidents involve more than one injured victim, using incident counts would underrepresent ED visits in the NCVS compared with the NHAMCS.

In sum, the divergence in estimates from the NCVS and the NHAMCS could be due to the substantial differences between the two surveys in their sample design, instrumentation, and estimation procedures. Data collection and quality control procedures are generally similar and not likely to be a major factor in the divergent estimates. Among the methodological differences, one likely source of divergence is the fact that the NCVS sampling frame excludes marginal populations that have a tenuous and fluid relationship to households

---

[5] Documentation of the NHAMCS is available from the Internet. Data collection procedures are described at http://www.cdc.gov/nchs/about/major/ahcd/imputham.htm. Users can also download full documentation in ftp files named "docyy.exe" (where $yy = 95, 96, 97,$ or 98 for each data year) from ftp://ftp.cdc.gov/pub/Health_Statistics/NCHS/Dataset_Documentation/NHAMCS/. Data collection procedures are described in the file named "DESCRIPT" obtained by executing "docyy.exe."

[6] Incidents are counts of distinct criminal events without regard to the number of victims. Victimizations separately count the crime for every distinct victim in an incident.

and the NHAMCS does not. Survey nonresponse – where individuals at high risk of victimization are included in the sampling frame but do not respond to the survey – will also affect the capacity of the NCVS to detect victimization experiences. Another likely source of divergence comes from differences in instrumentation; differences in the definitions of victimization, emergency rooms, and injury as well as differences in counting rules can produce different estimates of injuries due to violence. In the next section, we make some adjustments to the NCVS and NHAMCS counts to estimate the size of the contribution to divergence that is attributable to quantifiable instrumentation differences.

ESTIMATING EFFECTS OF DIFFERENCES IN SURVEY METHODS

Although much information is unavailable to test fully the effects of survey differences on divergence between the NCVS and NHAMCS, we are able to explore some of the effects of some of the most likely sources. The plausibility of the hypothesis that divergence is due to the exclusion of marginal populations can be explored by assessing the relative magnitude of the divergence across population groups that are differentially affected by census undercoverage. If the divergence is greater for groups known to be underrepresented in the NCVS than for those groups that are not, this finding would lend support to the idea that underrepresentation of marginal groups contributes to divergence. The plausibility of instrumentation differences accounting for the divergence can be tested by comparing divergence across events that are of varying degrees of ambiguity as a crime event. If we can assume that stereotypic crime events will be less affected by discretionary judgments and differences in definitions than more ambiguous crime events, then seeing greater divergence among ambiguous crimes would support the contention that divergence is due to differences in instrumentation.[7]

---

[7] This is not dissimilar to the assumption made by Rosenfeld in Chapter 9 in which he assesses the effects of changes in the handling of domestic violence on the UCR and NCVS aggravated assault trends.

Adjusting for Observable Differences in Instrumentation

Before we begin comparing divergence across groups and types of events, we first begin by assessing the impact of making the data series as comparable as possible by adjusting for sources of divergence whenever we can. Specifically, the NHAMCS rates can be adjusted by eliminating visits to EDs by persons younger than 12 years. Similarly, we can adjust the NCVS rates by (1) using person weights instead of incident weights to estimate distinct persons who are victims, (2) including series incidents, (3) estimating the number of multiple ED visits for a single assault injury, (4) including certain collateral injuries sustained by bystanders or persons who intervened in the victimization incident, and (5) adjusting for the NCVS skip pattern. These adjustments do not exhaust all the differences in instrumentation between the two surveys, but they are adjustments that can be made most readily.

Excluding Visits by Persons Under 12 Years. NHAMCS visits to EDs for assault injuries to persons younger than 12 years are outside the scope of the NCVS estimate. These ED visits by young children represented 8.35 percent of total NHAMCS visits to EDs for treatment of assault injuries in the period 1995–1998. The estimated NHAMCS counts in Figure 7.1 and Table 7.2 are already adjusted to exclude these ED visits by young children.

Using Person Weights of Victims Instead of Incident Weights. When estimating assault injuries treated in EDs, the relevant units are persons. Rather than counting distinct assault incidents that involve injuries, we are interested in counting all injured persons in those incidents. This is accomplished by using the patient weight in the NHAMCS and the person weight in the NCVS. Using person weights instead of incident weights resulted in an increase of 12.5 percent in the NCVS counts of assault injuries that are treated in emergency rooms as a result of incidents that occurred in the period 1995–1998. This adjustment is already reflected in the estimates shown in Figure 7.1 and Table 7.2.

Adjusting for Series Incidents. For the period 1993–2002, about 5.1 percent of all violent victimizations in the NCVS were reported as a series incident. Although information is not available in public use NCVS files, a recent analysis of private NCVS data reports annual estimates for the number of victimizations in series incidents as follows: the mean was 22.1, the median was 9.9, the mode was 6.0, and the average annual maximum was 324.2 incidents in a series (Planty, Chapter 6, this volume). It is obvious that the manner in which one includes series incidents makes a difference in NCVS estimates of the level of crime and crime-related injury. Just including the series as one event will produce lower estimates than using the mode, median, or mean. The mean would typically be used to provide the most accurate estimate of the total volume of victimizations in all series incidents, but in this case, the mean is the most unstable measure because its magnitude is affected by a small number of extremely high values. Using either the mode (6.0) or the median (9.9) will produce less volatile estimates of the number of crimes (and possible injuries) per series incident.

Only 3 percent of NCVS injuries treated in hospital EDs are series incidents. Assuming that the typical series includes between 6.0 and 9.9 incidents, and the same rates of injury and treatment outcomes among all series incidents, the adjusted number of injuries and ED visits would increase by a ratio of 1.15 to 1.27. The new estimate of total violent victimizations is obtained by adding the contribution of separate incidents in each series ($N * 0.03 * 6.0$ or 9.9) to that from single incidents ($N * 0.97 * 1.0$) for $N =$ the total number of violent victimizations before the adjustment. The adjustment factor for violent injuries treated in hospital EDs is obtained from the ratio of adjusted victimizations to unadjusted victimizations and represents between 15 and 27 percent increases in the NCVS estimates of ED visits for assault injuries.

Adjusting for Multiple Visits per Crime. Some victims will make more than one ED visit for the same assault injury. These multiple visits are included in the NHAMCS estimate but not in the NCVS estimate. Several studies using local area data provide estimates of short-term return rates following discharge from hospital EDs. All indications are that these revisit rates are low – about 3 percent of all visits are returns within three days after initial discharge – and revisit rates are highest for chronic conditions such as asthma and lower for injuries (Gordon et al., 1998; Keith et al., 1989; Lucas and Sanford, 1998;

Pierce et al., 1990). A national estimate of the multiple visit rate can be obtained from total injury visits to EDs (including initial and return visits) available from NHAMCS and total injuries (initial visit only) treated in EDs available from NEISS-AIP data.[8] Based on national estimates from these two sources for year 2000, the average number of ED visits per injury during that year was 1.315 (40,447,000 total injury visits from NHAMCS/30,747,000 total injuries from NEISS-AIP; Centers for Disease Control [CDC], 2001; McCaig and Ly, 2002).[9] For physical assaults the same average is 1.351 visits per assault injury (2,172,000 NHAMCS assault injury visits/1,608,000 NEISS-AIP assault injuries) (CDC, 2002; McCaig and Ly, 2002).[10]

Adjusting for Collateral Injuries to Others. For NCVS respondents to report an emergency room visit resulting from interpersonal violence, they must first report being a victim of an attack in a violent crime that resulted in injury. As described previously, there are a number of ways that violence may not be viewed as a crime by NCVS respondents but may be included in NHAMCS data of injuries sustained

---

[8] Beginning in July 2000, the U.S. Product Safety Commission in collaboration with the National Center for Injury Prevention and Control at CDC expanded the National Electronic Injury Surveillance System – All Injury Program (NEISS-AIP) to include injuries from all causes including violent assaults and self-inflicted harms. NEISS-AIP collects data on all nonfatal injuries treated in hospital EDs from a nationally representative sample of about 65 hospitals. The very large sample of about 500,000 injuries annually includes about 30,000 assault injuries – the largest collection of this type of injury available in a national sample. Public use NEISS-AIP data are available for download from the Internet at the Interuniversity Consortium for Political and Social Research at the University of Michigan: http://webapp.icpsr.umich.edu/cocoon/NACJD-SERIES/00198.xml.

[9] The focus by NEISS-AIP on treated injuries rather than all ED visits makes NEISS-AIP data more directly comparable to counts from the NCVS. They are not used throughout the current study because they were not available for enough years to support the analyses in this chapter. Multiple years of data are preferred because the NCVS sample of ED visits is small in any single year (annual average is 131 over the four-year period from 1995 to 1998), and multiple years of data will produce more precise (lower variance) NCVS estimates. Published results from NEISS-AIP partial-year data for injuries in 2000 first appeared in 2001.

[10] The estimate of total injuries from NEISS-AIP in the denominator is probably inflated somewhat because it annualizes data collected for summer months from July to September 2000 when injuries are likely to be higher than during other times of the year. The estimate of physical assault injuries from NEISS-AIP is less inflated because it annualizes data collected for the period July to December 2000.

during an assault. The violent injuries seen in EDs in NHAMCS data, for example, might also include perpetrators, law enforcement officers, and bystanders who suffer collateral injuries during crime incidents. These other injuries are included in person-weighted estimates from the NCVS only if respondents who suffer collateral injuries identify themselves as crime victims. These events may not be reported as crimes, however, because the other parties present during an assault incident were not themselves the specific focus of the original crime.

Even if collaterally injured parties fail to report these injuries as crime incidents, the volume of violent injuries that is missed is likely to be small because collateral injuries are so rare. The NCVS survey inquires about other injured parties as part of a series of questions about actions taken by victims and bystanders during crime incidents. An estimated 29,476 incidents per year (2.57 percent) involved detected injuries to other persons during an annual average of 1,148,711 violent incidents where protective actions made the situation worse. Even if each of these incidents involved an average of two collaterally injured persons who are not already estimated among NCVS victims, the resulting collateral injuries to others would increase NCVS estimates of total violent injuries treated in EDs by only 2.5 percent. At a rate of two persons collaterally injured per incident, 58,952 injuries would be added to the current NCVS estimate of 2,330,872 persons injured annually in violent incidents. Assuming that these injured persons seek care in EDs at the same 16.16 percent rate as reported by injured NCVS respondents, 9,527 injuries would be added to the current NCVS estimate of 376,633 violent injuries treated in hospital EDs.

Adjusting for the Skip Pattern. The skip pattern of items in the NCVS survey also contributes to some undercount of violent injuries. Only those respondents who report that they are victims of an actual attack are asked the additional questions about injuries they sustained during a violent incident and whether they received medical treatment. A small annual number of 18,926 ancillary injuries to respondents are elicited by questions that are asked only of the 736,401 annual victims who report that they or someone else took protective actions that made the situation worse during an incident and the victims did not already report the injuries that they sustained. If these 2.57 percent victims seek ED treatment at the same 16.16 percent rate as other injured respondents, the annual NCVS count of ED visits for assault injuries to respondents increases by only 3,058 (0.8 percent above the current estimate of 376,633 ED visits annually).

Questions about ancillary injuries to victims and to other persons are asked only if respondents report that the victim or someone else present at an incident took protective actions that made the situation worse. Persons who might be injured during a crime and show up in EDs – for example, by falling down without being attacked or as wounded bystanders – will not be detected in the NCVS if there are no reports of offender attacks or of protective actions that made the incident worse. The rates of ancillary injuries that are detected when protective actions do worsen the victimization incident provide a basis for estimating how many injuries might be missed by the survey skip patterns, however.

Ancillary injuries of respondents and other participants each occur at a 2.57 percent rate among violent incidents in which protective actions worsen outcomes. If violent injuries to victims that are missed by the survey skip patterns occur at the same 2.57 percent rate, the number of respondent violent injuries would increase by 92,586 annually and ED visits by 14,962, a 4.0 percent increase from the already reported level of 376,633 ED visits. This adjustment of 4 percent was computed by assuming that the candidates for undetected respondent injuries include violent victimizations that do not already involve both reported respondent injuries and reports of protective actions that worsen outcomes. There was an average of 3,602,554 such victimizations annually from 1995 to 1998. Applying a 2.57 percent rate of ancillary respondent injuries to these victimizations yields expected increments of 92,586 respondent injuries and 14,962 ED visits (92,586 ∗ 0.1616). The combined annual increase to ED visits from ancillary assault injuries to respondents is 4.8 percent (3,058 + 14,962) added to the current annual average of 376,633 ED visits.

Similarly, we can estimate the number of undetected ancillary injuries to others in violent incidents that do not involve actions that worsen outcomes. The estimated annual increase is 126,024

more incidents with injuries to others and 20,365 more ED visits –
a 5.4 percent increase from the currently reported annual estimate of
376,633 ED visits. This adjustment was computed by assuming that violent incidents that do not already involve reports of protective actions
that worsen outcomes are candidates for undetected injuries to others.
There was an average of 4,903,664 such incidents annually from 1995
to 1998. Applying a 2.57 percent rate of ancillary injuries of others to
these incidents yields an expected annual increment of 126,024 incidents with injuries of others and 20,365 of these incidents with ED
visits (126,024 ∗ 0.1616).

Combining the Adjustments. The combined effects of the proposed
adjustments to NCVS estimates for series crime, multiple ED visits
for the same injury, collateral injuries to other parties, and ancillary
injuries missed by the survey skip pattern are as follows:

Series crimes	Multiple visits	Collateral injuries to others	Ancillary injuries to respondents	Ancillary injuries to others	Total adjustments
1.27	∗ 1.351	∗ 1.025	∗ 1.048	∗ 1.054	= 1.94

When these adjustments are made to the NCVS estimate, the count of
ED visits for injuries sustained during assaults almost doubles. The
combined adjustment ratio of 1.94 does not include the 8.35 percent reduction in the NHAMCS estimate from excluding the under
age 12 population or the 12.5 percent increase in the NCVS estimate
from using person weights rather than incident weights. Because these
adjustments are so straightforward, whereas others are less so, they are
not belabored here and are simply included in the base ED visit estimates reported for the NCVS and NHAMCS in Figure 7.1 and in all
subsequent analyses.

The near doubling of the NCVS estimate reduces the ratio of
NHAMCS-to-NCVS assault injury visits from 5.0 down to about 2.5.
This increase in the NCVS estimate of ED visits is achieved by capturing more injuries among crime incidents that victims already report
to the NCVS. These adjustments do not include any of the effects of
crime events that may not be reported as such by respondents in the

crime survey. The adjustments made here are those that are easiest to make using information that can be obtained from existing data.

Estimating the Effects of Differences in Sample Design and Other Survey Features

Other potential sources of substantial divergence between the two data series are: (1) problems in the NCVS sampling frame that dispropor- tionately exclude potential victims at higher rates than nonvictims, (2) higher nonresponse rates from failure to participate in the NCVS by victims included in the sample, and (3) the failure of the NCVS to elicit reports about certain incidents as crimes. The magnitude of these sources of divergence cannot be addressed with straightforward quantitative adjustments like those explored in the previous section. Rather, we infer their effects in an indirect manner by examining those respondents who are differentially affected by these features of survey design and by assessing differences in impact across various types of events. In the case of differences in sample design, their contribution to divergence is estimated by comparing estimates across groups dif- ferentially affected by undercoverage and nonresponse. The effects of nonreporting of crime events are evaluated by comparing events known to be differentially affected by reporting differences across surveys.

Comparing Divergence Across Marginal Populations to Assess the Effects of Underrepresentation of Marginal Groups in Household Surveys. The underrepresentation of marginal populations in household surveys comes in part from undercoverage in the census address-list sampling frame and in part from nonresponse. If these marginal populations are not as well represented in household surveys as other groups and if these excluded populations have higher rates of emergency room vis- its for assault injuries, this would make the NCVS estimates low relative to those from the NHAMCS.

Undercoverage in the NCVS. The NCVS, like many other population sur- veys, relies on the Census Bureau's Master Address File of housing units developed from the decennial census and annually updated with data on newly constructed housing to generate nationally representative samples of persons residing in households and certain group quarters. By design, the sampling frame excludes persons living in correctional and health care institutions and those residing in military vessels or barracks. For purposes of comparison with NHAMCS, the greater consequence is the exclusion of nonmilitary, noninstitutional populations who do not reside in households. This excluded population includes homeless persons who do not reside in any conventional form of living quarters (including group quarters like boarding houses and transient hotels). It also excludes other transient populations who may stay temporarily in a variety of housing units but would not be designated as household members in any of these housing units.

Unconventional and fluid living arrangements make it difficult to capture some persons in residential-based sampling frames. Populations that are difficult to sample pose an especially significant problem for NCVS crime measures because they come disproportionately from subpopulations at higher risk of violent crime victimization, most notably Black males. If the ratio of NHAMCS to NCVS estimates is greater for groups known to be underrepresented in the census address frame, then this would support the contention that undercoverage is a source of divergence in these estimates.

The Census Bureau estimates the undercount using a demographic analysis procedure that relies on estimates of births, deaths, and migration derived independently from census counts. The result is an estimate of the expected population in various demographic subgroups that can be compared with census counts. The accuracy of the resulting undercount rates depends on the accuracy of the estimates of the various population components. The procedure and estimates for 1990 and 2000 are described in Robinson et al. (1993) and Robinson and Adlakha (2002). Census estimates of undercoverage indicate that in the period 1990–2000, an average of 0.9 percent of the population was excluded from the census address list. Undercoverage is greater for some groups compared with others, with 4.15 percent of Blacks excluded, 6.65 percent of Black males, and 9.85 percent of young Black males (see Table 7.1). The undercoverage rate in the address frame is greater for more marginal populations like young Black males than it is for groups in more traditional housing arrangements.

TABLE 7.1. *Estimated undercount rate in decennial census of U.S. population from 1940 to 2000[a]*

Year	Total population	Black population	Black males	Adult black males
1940[a]	5.6	10.3	–	–
1950[b]	4.4	9.6	–	–
1960[b]	3.3	8.3	–	–
1970[b]	2.9	8.0	–	(14.0)[d]
1980[b]	1.4	5.9	–	(11.0)[d]
1990[c]	1.7	5.5	8.1	11.3
2000[c]	0.1	2.8	5.2	8.4

[a] The undercount rate is calculated from $100 * (DA - C) / DA$, where DA is the population estimated from a demographic analysis procedure and C is the count from the decennial census.

[b] Undercount rates from 1940 to 1980 censuses are from Fay et al. (1988) republished in Anderson and Fienberg (1999, table 4.1).

[c] Undercount estimates for 1990 and 2000 rely on "revised" demographic analysis results (released October 2001). These address concerns about underestimation of immigration in earlier DA estimates. Rates for Black males are from Robinson and Adlakha (2002, table 3). Rates for total population and Black men aged 20–64 are from Robinson et al. (2002, table 7).

[d] The rates for Black men in 1970 and 1980 are approximations based on graphed values over age presented in Robinson et al. (1993, figure 4a).

Table 7.2 presents evidence relevant to the effects of differential undercoverage rates on NCVS–NHAMCS divergence. Percentages by attribute reveal differences in relative composition of different demographic groups in the two surveys. The NHAMCS–NCVS ratio addresses differences in the magnitude of estimated counts. There is no difference between NCVS and NHAMCS estimates of gender composition, with about 60 percent males among assault victims treated in hospital EDs. Adults aged 21 to 49 are slightly more likely in NHAMCS data, but the differences are not statistically significant. Both data sets also find 85 percent urban area residents among assault victims treated in EDs. Results for victim race are distinctive: Blacks, and especially Black males, are significantly more likely to be found in NHAMCS data of ED visits. Although Black males comprise 10 percent of NCVS assault victims treated in a hospital ED, they are 20 percent of NHAMCS assault injuries.

TABLE 7.2. *National Crime Victimization Survey (NCVS) and National Hospital Ambulatory Care Survey (NHAMCS) estimates of violent injuries treated in hospital emergency departments: variation by attributes of violent incidents: annual averages in United States, 1995–1998*[a]

Victim and incident attributes	NCVS Population estimate	NCVS Sample	NHAMCS Population estimate	NHAMCS Sample	Percent by attribute NCVS	Percent by attribute NHAMCS	NHAMCS-to-NCVS ratio
Total (90% Confidence Interval)	376,633 (301,279 451,987)	(524)	1,865,297 (1,591,412 2,139,182)	(1,823)	100.0	100.0	4.95
Victims							
Males	226,431	(304)	1,148,991	(1,142)	60.1	61.6	5.07
Females	150,202	(220)	716,306	(681)	39.9	38.4	4.77
Age 12–20	121,525	(162)	442,968	(428)	32.3	23.7	3.65
21–29	96,264	(124)	542,094	(511)	25.6	29.1	5.63
30–49	133,128	(198)	762,822	(759)	35.3	40.9	5.73
50+	25,716	(40)	117,412	(125)	6.8	6.3	4.57
Black	79,586	(97)	595,532	(636)	21.1	31.9*	**7.48**
White	281,841	(407)	1,213,628	(1,121)	74.8	65.1*	**4.31**
Black, Females	42,639	(55)	232,124	(240)	11.3	12.4	5.44
White, Females	103,965	(160)	455,276	(411)	27.6	24.4	4.38
Black, Males	36,947	(42)	363,408	(396)	9.8	19.5**	**9.84**
White, Males	177,876	(247)	758,352	(710)	47.2	40.7	4.26
Incidents:							
Weapon[b]	112,966	(157)	393,246	(407)	30.0	21.1	3.48
No Weapon	241,664	(336)	1,388,087	(1,346)	64.2	74.4*	**5.74**
Missing	22,003	(31)	83,964	(70)	5.8	4.5	NA
Urban Area	319,311	(448)	1,580,472	(1,635)	84.8	84.7	4.95
Not Urban	57,322	(76)	285,149	(188)	15.2	15.3	4.97

(*continued*)

TABLE 7.2 (continued)

Victim and incident attributes	NCVS		NHAMCS		Percent by attribute		NHAMCS-to-NCVS ratio
	Population estimate	Sample	Population estimate	Sample	NCVS	NHAMCS	
Relationship[c]							
Stranger	167,534	(124)	286,860	(144)	44.8	28.2**	**1.71**
Not Stranger	206,281	(151)	730,676	(329)	55.2	71.8**	**3.54**
Missing[d]	57,322	(7)	1,021,602	(498)	NA	NA	NA
Place of Injury							
Residence	140,719	(200)	429,473	(379)	37.4	40.6	3.05
Street	122,755	(168)	302,558	(331)	32.6	28.6	2.46
Other	113,160	(156)	325,112	(311)	30.0	30.8	2.87
Missing[e]	0	(0)	808,154	(802)	NA	NA	NA

[a] Data are from annual National Crime Victimization Surveys (NCVS) and National Hospital Ambulatory Care Surveys (NHAMCS) for years 1995 to 1998. NCVS data are weighted by person weights to reflect national estimates of the number of injured victims, rather than the number of incidents that involve injuries usually reported for NCVS data. NHAMCS data are weighted by patient visit weights to reflect national estimates of total patient visits to hospital emergency departments. For comparability with NCVS data, NHAMCS estimates exclude visits by children under age 12.

[b] Weapons in both surveys include firearms, knives, other sharp instruments, and blunt objects.

[c] NHAMCS collected data on offender–victim relationship in 1995–1996 and dropped the variable in 1997–1998. For comparability, the NCVS data for the offender relationship are restricted to the same years. The average annual counts are 384,489 in the NCVS and 2,039,138 in the NHAMCS for years 1995–1996.

[d] Offender relationship and place where the incident occurred are missing in substantial numbers of emergency department visits for assault injuries in the NHAMCS (50 percent missing relationship and 44 percent missing place). For greater comparability between the NCVS and NHAMCS, the percentages for these variables are renormalized to exclude missing cases. There is no similar adjustment for missing data in the counts, and the large share of NHAMCS visits with missing data lowers the NHAMCS-to-NCVS ratios for these variables uniformly below the overall ratio of 4.95.

[e] Tests for significant differences contrast NCVS and NHAMCS estimates of population proportions of each attribute among violent injuries treated in hospital emergency departments. Estimates of standard errors rely on procedures recommended by each survey (pp. xlv–liv of NCVS codebook available from Interuniversity Consortium for Political and Social Research, and RSE files of relative standard errors in annual documentation files provided with NHAMCS). The significance levels for differences in proportions in a two-tailed test are *p < .05 and **p < .01.

The same pattern is evident in the ratio of estimates of ED visits from the NHAMCS to those from the NCVS.[11] The ratios of visits for females (4.77) and for males (5.07) are similar to the overall ratio of 4.95. With an NHAMCS-to-NCVS ratio of 9.8, however, the apparent NCVS undercount for Black male victims is twice the fivefold ratio found overall.[12] Thus, the NCVS undercount is considerably greater for groups with higher census undercoverage rates than for those with lower undercoverage rates.

Just as Black males contribute disproportionately to the undercount in decennial censuses, they are also difficult to capture in household-based samples. The estimated overall undercount rate has declined in every census since 1940, reaching a level of only 0.1 percent in 2000 (Table 7.1). Although also declining, Black males – especially adult Black males – continue to suffer from the highest undercount rates of any demographic subgroup (Robinson et al., 2002, table 7). Revised estimates of the undercount rate suggest that nearly 10 percent of adult Black males were not counted in the 2000 Census. The independent data from hospital administrative records indicating that large numbers of Black males are treated for assault injuries in hospital EDs but go undetected in NCVS household surveys provide further indirect confirmation of the difficulties in accurately accounting for this subpopulation.

The NCVS (and most other household surveys) addresses the general problem of census undercoverage through poststratification adjustments to the weights used to develop the national estimates. The adjustments increase weights to account for the differential undercoverage across population subgroups. They do not capture any distinctive victimization risks faced by the undercovered population, however.

---

[11] The results from the two measures need not be similar. For example, the magnitude of count estimates for a demographic group could be similar in the two surveys, whereas their relative composition varies with differences in the estimated total population of ED visits.

[12] It is not advisable to apply the single overall adjustment factor of 1.94 to individual population groups because it is reasonable to expect differences across population groups in rates of series crimes, multiple ED visits per injury, corollary and ancillary injuries to respondents, and other participants. The differences among victims that lead to sharp departures from an overall ratio of 4.95 are likely to have similarly varying effects on the adjustment factors for individual population groups.

The adjustment among adult Black males, for example, scales up from the victimization experiences of those Black males who do respond to the NCVS. If respondents from this population subgroup are less vulnerable to violent victimization than Black males who are excluded from the original sampling frame, the adjusted national estimate of assault victims will still underestimate Black male assault victims. Unfortunately, there is no easy and direct way to test the assumption that the victimization, injury, and ED visit rate for those included in the sample frame are the same as those who are not.

One way to estimate whether undercoverage could produce the observed differences in the estimates of emergency room visits across the two surveys is to see how high a visit rate would be required for the undercovered population to account for these differences. If this number is reasonable, then this would support arguments that this is the source of divergence in the estimates. If the number is implausibly high or low, then the household sampling frame becomes a less plausible source of divergence.

The imputation procedures used by the Census to correct for undercoverage assume that persons responding to the survey are like those who are undercovered with respect to their victimization, injury, and use of EDs. Given this assumption, the contribution of covered and uncovered populations should be in proportion to their size. So, for example, between 1990 and 2000 approximately 93.5 percent of the total Black male population was in the census sample frame used by the NCVS, and they produced an estimated 34,545 assaults treated in EDs annually. Under current imputation procedures, the approximately 6.5 percent of Black males who were undercovered in the sampling frame contribute about 2,402 incidents, for a total of 36,947 ED visits. With an NHAMCS estimate of 363,408 ED visits by Black males, this leaves a total of 326,461 ED visits missing from the NCVS estimate

The NCVS undercount ratio of 9.84 for Black males is about twice the overall ratio of 4.95. It is not unreasonable to assume that Black males are similarly twice as vulnerable to series incidents, multiple visits to EDs, and injuries to other participants as the overall population. Greater involvement in risky behaviors such as alcohol and drug consumption, illicit drug markets, gang activities, gun carrying, and gun use by young Black males are all likely to increase their experiences of repeated series victimizations, more serious injuries that require multiple visits for treatment, and multiple offenders or victims in violent incidents (Browning and Huizinga, 1999; Elliott et al., 1989; Huizinga and Jacob-Chien, 1998; Lizotte and Shepherd, 2001; Loeber et al., 1999, 2001; Thornberry et al., 2003). A doubling increases the adjustment ratio for these factors from the overall ratio of 1.94 to 3.88 for Black males, and the adjusted NCVS ED visits become 134,035 and 9,320, respectively, for a total of 143,355. The increase of 106,408 ED visits from instrumentation adjustments for Black males represents 33 percent of the 326,461 missing ED visits.

When the 143,355 incidents are subtracted out from the 363,408 total missing visits, this leaves 220,053 ED visits that must be accounted for by the 6.5 percent of Black males who are undercovered in the sampling frame. When we divide this balance of missing NHAMCS visits by the estimated 9,320 ED visits contributed by undercovered Black males, the resulting ratio is 24. This means that the visit rate for the undercovered Black males would need to be 24 times that of the Black male population covered in the NCVS sample to explain the differences in visit counts estimated for the NCVS and NHAMCS surveys. Such an annual rate of visits to EDs for assault injuries is implausibly high even for individuals who are very prone to assault injuries.

In looking for an alternative estimate of the differences in ED visit rates between the more and less marginal populations, it may not be unreasonable to use the ratio of the Black male homicide rate to the White male homicide rate. This estimate is not the product of a household survey and should not be affected by census undercoverage. In the period 1990–2000, the Black male homicide rate was about seven times that of White males (Fox and Zawitz, 2005). If we multiply this factor of seven times the adjusted NCVS estimate of 9,320 ED visits by undercovered Black males, the estimate of NCVS ED visits attributable to this group increases by 55,920 to 65,240, accounting for 17 percent of the 326,461 NHAMCS visits that are missing from the NCVS. Thus, when reasonable assumptions are made about the differential experience of undercovered groups with respect to victimization, injury, and ED visits, the effect of undercoverage on divergence in a highly undercounted population group is about one-half the 33 percent change obtained from survey instrumentation adjustments.

It is worth noting, however, that the differences between the NCVS and NHAMCS estimates of visits are very large even for nonmarginal groups. The estimate of visits in the NHAMCS for White women, for example, is 4.5 times that of estimates from the NCVS, yet less than 0.1 percent of the White female population is omitted from the census address frame. Furthermore, the increment of 55,920 ED visits for undercovered Black males is only a small 4 percent share of 1,488,664 total missing ED visits overall (1,865,297 – 376,633). Although demographic groups with higher proportions of undercoverage in the census address frame also have high divergence ratios of NHAMCS to NCVS estimates of ED visits, it is unlikely that undercoverage accounts for a great deal of this difference.

Assessing the Effects of Nonresponse. Nonresponse differs from undercoverage in that the potential respondent is known to live in a sampled unit and the potential respondent is known to be eligible for inclusion in the survey, but the interviewer cannot make contact with this individual during the prescribed field period or the respondent refuses to participate. Nonresponse in the NCVS is generally quite low by current survey standards, with a household response rate of 95 percent and the individual response rate of 89 percent (Simon and Mercy, 2001). This response rate varies across demographic and survey treatment groups. Table 7.3 summarizes the nonresponse rates (expressed as a percentage) for these groups in survey year 1999.

The most notable result is not in the table: 31 percent of sampled Black men aged 24 to 34 who are not reference persons failed to respond.[13] As with undercoverage, nonresponse is highest among those population groups who are traditionally considered to be most marginalized. And in the case of young Black males, nonresponders are also most likely to be at risk of violent victimization and presumably

---

[13] Reference persons are the persons in a household relative to whom all other persons' relationships are determined (e.g., son, spouse, sibling). The Census tries to interview at least one person in a household so as to maintain their household response rate. If only one person in the household is contacted, that person will be the reference person. As a result, nonreference persons have much higher nonresponse rate than reference persons.

TABLE 7.3. *Person nonresponse rates in the
National Crime Victimization Surveys by respondent
characteristics (collection year 1999)*[a]

Respondent attributes	Nonresponse rate (percent)
Respondent Status	
Reference Person	7.5
Other	19.8
Race	
Black	13.2
Non-Black	10.4
Age	
12–34	14.3
35–49	10.1
50–64	9.0
65+	5.2
Race and Age	
Black, 12–34	17.4
Non-Black, 12–34	13.9
Black, 35–49	12.1
Non-Black, 35–49	9.3
Black, 50–64	9.1
Non-Black, 50–64	9.8
Black, 65+	6.5
Non-Black, 65+	5.1
Race and Gender	
Black, Males	17.4
Black, Females	10.2
Non-Black, Males	12.9
Non-Black, Females	8.1

[a] Rates calculated from data provided in Peterson (1999).

contribute at very high rates to emergency room visits for assault
injuries. One crucial difference between undercoverage and nonresponse is the fact that nonresponse in these marginal groups is 2 to
3 times as large as undercoverage – 9.85 percent undercoverage for
young Black males in the 2000 Census versus 31 percent nonresponse
to the NCVS in survey year 1999. For Black males, the figures are
generally similar – 5.2 percent compared with 17.4 percent.

Like undercoverage, weighting takes account of nonresponse to some extent in the NCVS, so that groups like male adolescents who have relatively high nonresponse rates will have adjustments to their basic weights to compensate for nonresponse.[14] As in the case of undercoverage, the adequacy of these weights requires the assumption that persons who respond to the survey are like those who do not, at least in terms of their victimization, risk of injury, and use of EDs. Some support for this assumption is offered by Biderman and Cantor (1984) in their study of bounding in the NCS. They monitored the reporting of persons over time in the survey and found that persons interviewed in two consecutive six-month periods in the NCS did not differ in their victimization rates from persons who were nonrespondents in Time 1 and respondents in Time 2. The only exception was the first interview, which always produced higher reporting rates than in subsequent interviews.

This study does not include respondents who never return to the survey, but episodic nonrespondents should be closer to complete nonrespondents than to complete respondents. Bates and Creighton (2000) attempted to test the similarity of respondents and nonrespondents by comparing respondents interviewed in the normal field period with those "late responders" who are interviewed late in the field period after several attempts to contact. Although late responders differ from early responders on some demographic characteristics (late responders tended to have a higher income, were younger, and were more likely to be Black), their victimization rates are not that different.

When we use the same sensitivity analysis with nonresponse that we did with undercoverage, we see that nonresponse also cannot account for the large differences in ED visits between the two surveys, but it can account for more of the difference than undercoverage. The nonresponse rate of Black males is 17.4 percent, and under the assumption that nonrespondents have the same victimization, injury, and ED visit rates, the nonrespondents should account for 6,429 of the total estimated 36,947 visits by Black males in the NCVS. Applying the same assumptions used in the case of undercoverage, we assume

---

[14] In some cases proxy interviews are used to deal with nonresponse. For example, respondents who do not speak common languages or are away from home during the interview period can be interviewed by proxy.

the instrumentation adjustment for series crimes, multiple visits, and injuries to others is twice the overall ratio of 1.94. At 3.88, this adjustment increases the Black male nonrespondent count of NCVS ED visits to 24,945 and the total count for Black males to 143,355 ED visits. The total increment of 106,408 ED visits by Black males from the instrumentation adjustment is 33 percent of the 326,641 missing NHAMCS ED visits by Black males.

As before, the difference between NHAMCS counts and the adjusted NCVS counts is 220,053 ED visits that must be accounted for by the 17.4 percent of sampled Black males who fail to respond to the NCVS. When we divide this balance of missing NHAMCS visits by the estimated 24,945 ED visits already contributed by nonrespondent Black males, the visit rate for assault injuries by Black male nonrespondents would have to be 9 times the visit rate of Black male respondents. This is within a reasonable range. For example, when we assume that the rate of ED visits for assault injuries by Black male nonresponders is 7 times that of responders, then nonresponse accounts for an additional 149,670 ED visits by this population group. This increment represents 46 percent of the total observed difference of 326,461 ED visits for assault injuries by Black males estimated by the NHAMCS and NCVS. This is a considerable effect on the divergence of the two estimates within this category of high nonresponders. Furthermore, the potential contribution by Black male nonresponders would account for 10 percent of total missing ED visits across all population groups.

Summary. Although the adjustments made here are ad hoc and somewhat imprecise, they provide a rough estimate of the potential importance of underrepresentation of marginal populations in the NCVS for estimating victimizations, assault injuries, and ED visits for these injuries in those population groups. Nonresponse seems to be more consequential for these estimates than undercoverage. The effects of these sources of underrepresentation on national estimates for the entire population will not be as large because these marginal populations are a relatively small component of the overall population.

Comparing Divergence Across Clear and Ambiguous Crime Events. The previous section examined factors that affect the composition of respondent samples. These sample design issues are not likely to explain fully the discrepancy between NHAMCS and NCVS counts of assault injury visits to EDs. We next consider the contribution of victimizations, injuries, and ED visits that are missed by the NCVS when respondents fail to report all their victimization experiences.

Respondent Nonreporting of Crime Victimization. Rand (1997) discussed the potential role of respondent nonreporting as a factor in the 2.5-fold difference in ED visits estimated from 1994 NCVS data and SIVV data for the same year. Rand noted that violent injuries that show up in hospital ED data will be missed by the NCVS if respondents do not regard some violent encounters as crimes. This tendency by victims to view some violence as falling outside the scope of crimes reported to the NCVS was an important motivation for the NCVS survey redesign implemented in 1992. The changes, designed to better elicit reports about especially sensitive incidents involving sexual assaults and crimes by intimates and family members, were successful in increasing the numbers of reported interpersonal violent incidents by 49 percent and household property crimes by 23 percent (Kindermann et al., 1997). Furthermore, larger increases were observed for less serious forms of crime. Among violent crimes, these included crimes involving non-strangers, attempts rather than completed crimes, crimes not reported to police, and assaults that did not involve weapons or injuries.

The continuing large differences between violent injuries detected by the NHAMCS and by the redesigned NCVS suggest that nonreporting by some victims continues to contribute to an undercount of violent injuries in NCVS data. If we assume, as Rosenfeld does in Chapter 9 (this volume), that less serious and less stereotypic crime events will be more affected by differences in the respective data collection systems, then we should see smaller differences between the two systems in estimated visits for more serious events.

One indicator of the seriousness of a violent event is whether a weapon is used in the assault that leads to injury. Events involving weapons should be reported more completely in both series because there is less likely to be ambiguity with regard to the determination that this is a crime event. The results in Table 7.2 indicate that compared with NHAMCS data, NCVS data contain a significantly lower percentage of ED visits that do not involve weapons and a corresponding higher percentage of visits that involve weapons. Likewise, the undercount ratio of NHAMCS ED visits to NCVS visits is higher (5.7) for events that do not involve weapons and lower (3.5) for events involving weapons.

Involvement of offenders who are known to victims might also introduce ambiguity for victims about whether these incidents are crimes and result in lower reporting of these events to the NCVS. Compared with NHAMCS data, the percentage of ED visits for assault injuries by strangers is significantly higher in NCVS data and the percentage for assault injuries inflicted by offenders who are known to victims is lower in NCVS data. The NHAMCS-to-NCVS undercount ratios for stranger and nonstranger assault injuries are uniformly lower than the fivefold ratio observed over all ED visits for assault injuries. This anomaly is due to the large share of missing relationship data in 50 percent of NHAMCS ED visits for assault injuries. The relative size of the ratios is as expected among the events that do include information about relationship, however: The NCVS undercount is larger in incidents that do not involve strangers than in those involving strangers.

These findings are compatible with concerns about varying levels of discretion and differences in instrumentation that contribute to reporting differences across the surveys. The greater divergence among ambiguous crimes and lower divergence among stereotypic crimes is consistent with a pattern of greater discretionary judgments and differences in definitions about what types of events are crimes that favor failure to report some events in the NCVS, less restrictive standards for defining events as crimes in EDs, or both. Unfortunately, the available data will not allow us to distinguish between the relative contributions of underestimates in the NCVS and overestimates in the NHAMCS.

CONCLUSION

The NHAMCS offers an opportunity to learn more about how the design of the NCVS can affect the data from that survey. Specifically, the fact that the NCVS is a household sample and the NHACMS is based on a sample of hospital emergency departments provides the opportunity to assess the effects of undercoverage in the household frame and nonresponse by sampled entities on estimates of serious violence in the NCVS. Through a series of rough adjustments for differences between the two surveys and simple simulations, we were able to see that the undercoverage is not a major factor in explaining the differences in estimates of ED visits for assault injuries. With reasonable assumptions about the victimization experience of undercovered population groups, underrepresentation of marginal populations in the household frame has only a small impact on estimates of ED visits. Nonresponse in highly victimized groups is likely to have a more sizable effect on estimates than undercoverage.

It is more difficult to assess the effects of differences in instrumentation and procedures on the divergence of estimates from the two surveys. The influence of some of these differences, such as the exclusion of persons under 12 years or the use of incident weights (rather than victim weights), is relatively easy to estimate, but these differences do not account for the differences in the size of the estimates. Adjustments for other design differences, such as the exclusion of series incidents in the NCVS or the fact that it does not collect data on multiple visits for a single assault injury, are more speculative, but they suggest that these differences are more consequential in explaining differences in the estimates.

The fact that the estimates from the two surveys are most similar for more serious events, that is, injuries involving weapons or offenders who are strangers, and least similar for less serious events is intriguing and open to a number of interpretations. One implication is that statistical series dealing with crime and its consequences will produce more similar results when the crime events are serious and unambiguous. This is what Rosenfeld (Chapter 9, this volume) found in his comparisons of the NCVS and the UCR. There is simply less opportunity for discretion in the definitions and procedures of the data collection systems to affect the resulting data. This is somewhat reassuring.

Another interpretation is that the large differences between the NHAMCS and NCVS estimates of visits for less serious events are due to the underrepresentation of less serious and less stereotypic crime events in the NCVS. The controversies about surveying rape and domestic violence certainly indicate that victims are less likely to consider these events "crimes" because they are committed by familiars rather than strangers or there is ambiguity regarding provocation and consent (Fisher and Cullen, 2000). Surveys that define themselves as "health" surveys are much more likely to elicit these events because patients do not filter out "noncrime" incidents. The work surrounding the NCVS redesign also showed that additional cuing and explicitly soliciting these gray area events substantially increased the reporting of more minor events in the survey (Cantor and Lynch, 2000, 2005).

The results also support the contention that modest amounts of the difference in estimates of ED visits are due to underrepresentation in the NCVS of collateral injuries to perpetrators, bystanders, and police officers, as well as collateral injuries to respondents that do not require an offender attack. It is also possible that hospital staff members are not filtering out intentional injuries that are not crimes. Sorting this out requires more information on the criteria used by hospital personnel to determine whether an injury was the result of a criminal act and how reliably these criteria are applied for variables that are peripheral to medical concerns with diagnosis and treatment of the physical and mental health consequences of an injury.

References

Anderson, M. J., & Fienberg, S. E. (1999). *Who counts? The politics of census-taking in contemporary America.* New York: Russell Sage Foundation.

Bates, N., & Creighton, K. (2000). "The last ten percent: What can we learn from late interviews?" *Proceedings of the American Statistical Association, Section on Governmental Statistics.* Alexandria, VA: American Statistical Association.

Biderman, A., & Cantor, D. (1984). "A longitudinal analysis of bounding, respondent conditioning and mobility as a source of panel bias in the National Crime Survey." *Proceedings of the American Statistical Association, Social Statistics Section.* Philadelphia, PA: American Statistical Association.

Browning, K., & Huizinga, D. (1999). *Highlights of findings from the Denver youth survey* (OJJDP Fact Sheet). Washington, DC: U.S. Department of Justice, Office of Juvenile Justice and Delinquency Prevention.

Bureau of Justice Statistics. (2001). *Four measures of serious violent crime.* Washington, DC: U.S. Department of Justice, Office of Justice Programs.

October 27, 2003 version of the data retrieved from http://www.ojp. usdoj.gov/bjs/glance/tables/4meastab.htm.

Cantor, D., & Lynch, J. P. (2000). "Self-report surveys as measures of crime and criminal justice." In *Criminal justice 2000: Measurement and analysis of crime and justice* (Vol. IV, pp. 85–138). Washington, DC: U.S. Department of Justice.

Cantor, D., & Lynch, J. P. (2005). "Exploring the effects of changes in design on the analytical uses of the NCVS data." *Journal of Quantitative Criminology* 3:23.

Centers for Disease Control and Prevention. (2001). "National estimates of nonfatal injuries treated in hospital emergency departments – United States, 2000." *MMWR* 50(17):340–346. Retrieved December 26, 2005 from http://www.cdc.gov/mmwr/PDF/mm5017.pdf.

Centers for Disease Control and Prevention. (2002). "Nonfatal physical assault-related injuries treated in hospital emergency departments – United States, 2000." *MMWR* 51(21):460–63. Retrieved December 25, 2005 from http://www.cdc.gov/mmwr/PDF/mm5121.pdf.

Cook, P. J. (1985). "The case of the missing victims: Gunshot woundings in the National Crime Survey." *Journal of Quantitative Criminology* 1:91–102.

Elliott, D. S., Huizinga, D., & Menard, S. (1989). *Multiple problem youth: Delinquency, drugs and mental health problems.* New York: Springer-Verlag.

Fay, R. E., Passel, J. S., Robinson, J. G., & Cowan, C. D. (1988). *The coverage of the population in the 1980 Census.* Washington, DC: U.S. Government Printing Office.

Fisher, B. S., & Cullen, F. T. (2000). "Measuring the sexual victimization of women: Evolution, current controversies and future research." In *Criminal justice 2000: Measurement and analysis of crime and justice* (Vol. IV, pp. 317–390). Washington, DC: U.S. Department of Justice.

Fox, J., & Zawitz, M. (2005). *Homicide trends in the United States.* Washington, DC: Bureau of Justice Statistics.

Gordon, J. A., An, L. C., Hayward, R. A., & Williams, B. C. (1998). "Initial emergency department diagnosis and return visits: Risk versus perception." *Annals of Emergency Medicine* 32:569–573.

Huizinga, D., & Jacob-Chien, C. (1998). "The contemporaneous co-occurrence of serious and violent juvenile offending and other problem behaviors." In R. Loeber & D. P. Farrington (Eds.), *Serious and violent juvenile offenders: Risk factors and successful interventions* (pp. 47–67). Thousand Oaks, CA: Sage.

Keith, K. D., Bocka, J. J., Kobernick, M. S., Krome, R. L., & Ross, M. A. (1989). "Emergency department visits." *Annals of Emergency Medicine* 18:964–968.

Kindermann, C., Lynch, J., & Cantor, D. (1997). *Effects of the redesign on victimization estimates* (NCJ-164381). Washington, DC: Office of Justice Programs, Bureau of Justice Statistics, U.S. Department of Justice.

Lizotte, A. J., & Shepherd, D. (2001). "Gun use by male juveniles: Research and prevention." *Juvenile Justice Bulletin.* Washington, DC: Office of Juvenile Justice and Delinquency Prevention, U.S. Department of Justice.

Loeber, R., DeLamatre, M., Tita, G., Cohen, J., Stouthamer-Loeber, M., & Farrington, D. P. (1999). "Gun injury and mortality: The delinquent backgrounds of juvenile victims." *Violence and Victims* 14:339–352.

Loeber, R., Kalb, L., & Huizinga, D. (2001). "Juvenile delinquency and serious injury victimization." *Juvenile Justice Bulletin.* Washington, DC: Office of Juvenile Justice and Delinquency Prevention, U.S. Department of Justice.

Lucas, R. H., & Sanford, S. M. (1998). "An analysis of frequent users of emergency care at an urban university hospital." *Annals of Emergency Medicine* 32:563–568.

McCaig, L. F., & Ly, N. (2002, April 22). "National Hospital Ambulatory Medical Care Survey: 2000 – Emergency department summary." *Advance Data from Vital and Health Statistics,* No. 326. Hyattsville, MD: National Center for Health Statistics. Retrieved December 26, 2005 from http://www.cdc.gov/nchs/data/ad/ad326.pdf.

Peterson, A. (1999, August 17). "Person non-response trends for the National Crime Victimization Survey." Memorandum to Documentation. Washington, DC: Demographic Statistical Methods Division, United States Census Bureau.

Pierce, J. M., Kellerman, A. L., & Oster, C. (1990). "'Bounces': An analysis of short-term return visits to a public hospital emergency department." *Annals of Emergency Medicine* 19:752–757.

Rand, M. (1997). *Violence-related injuries treated in hospital emergency departments.* Washington, DC: Bureau of Justice Statistics.

Robinson, J. G., & Adlakha, A. (2002, December 31). "Comparison of A.C.E. Revison II results with demographic analysis." *DSSD A.C.E. Revision II* (Memorandum Series #PP-41). Washington, DC: United States Department of Commerce, U.S. Census Bureau. Retrieved January 15, 2004 from http://www.census.gov/dmd/www/pdf/pp-41r.pdf.

Robinson, J. Gregory, Adlakha, A., & West, K. K. (2002, May). *Coverage of population in Census 2000: Results from demographic analysis.* Paper presented at the 2002 Annual meeting of the Population Association of America, Atlanta, GA.

Robinson, J. G., Ahmed, B., Gupta, P. D., & Woodrow, K. A. (1993). "Estimation of population coverage in the 1990 United States Census based on demographic analysis." *Journal of the American Statistical Association* 88:1061–1071.

Simon, T., & Mercy, J. (2001). *Injuries from violent crime 1992–2000*. Washington, DC: Bureau of Justice Statistics.

Thornberry, T. P., Krohn, M. D., Lizotte, A. J., Smith, C. A., & Tobin, K. (2003). *Gangs and delinquency in developmental perspective*. Cambridge, England: Cambridge University Press.

SOURCES OF DIVERGENCE
IN THE UCR

Using NIBRS to Study Methodological Sources of Divergence Between the UCR and NCVS

Lynn A. Addington

INTRODUCTION

This chapter examines the contribution of methodological differences to divergence when comparing crimes reported to the Uniform Crime Reporting System (UCR) and National Crime Victimization Survey (NCVS). This study focuses on differences in population coverage and crime counting rules between the two series. Population coverage differences concern the UCR's inclusion of commercial and nonindividual victims and its inclusion of individual victims of all ages. Crime counting rule variations include the application of the UCR's Hierarchy Rule and the UCR's consideration of robberies as property offenses as opposed to crimes against a person. Understanding the extent to which these differences play a role in divergence between the UCR and NCVS is important to better ascertain whether this divergence is an artifact of methodologies or the result of substantive issues.

Although the methodological differences between the UCR and NCVS are easy to identify, they are much more difficult to quantify. As a result, little is known about the extent, if any, to which these differences contribute to divergence. Researchers have attempted to adjust each series to account for these differences (see Chapter 4, this volume, for a summary). These adjustments, however, are only approximations. The UCR's traditional summary reporting system does not collect the incident details necessary to measure these differences accurately and inform about potential sources of divergence. Currently the UCR is in the process of a substantial conversion from its aggregate system ("the summary system") to the National Incident-Based Reporting System

(NIBRS), which, as its name suggests, collects incident-level data. For the study of divergence between the UCR and NCVS, incident-based reporting of police statistics begins to supply the detailed information necessary to measure noncorresponding aspects of the UCR and NCVS. As such, NIBRS presents the first opportunity to assess the contribution of design differences to divergence.

This chapter uses NIBRS data to assess the degree to which methodological differences between the UCR and NCVS contribute to divergence. To do so, this chapter is organized in the following manner: The first section explains the methodological differences between the two series and summarizes the ways in which previous researchers have attempted to quantify these differences. The next section provides a general overview of NIBRS with a focus on how NIBRS can inform the methodological contribution to divergence. The third section uses NIBRS data to analyze the extent to which methodological differences contribute to divergence. The fourth section extends this analysis of NIBRS data to evaluate the validity of prior adjustments to the summary system in an effort to remove sources of divergence and to compare the two systems more effectively. This chapter concludes with a discussion of these analyses and an assessment of the extent to which methodological differences contribute to divergence.

METHODOLOGICAL DIFFERENCES DEFINED

Although the UCR and NCVS both collect crime data, each does so in a slightly different manner. This chapter focuses on four of the UCR's data collection methodologies and contrasts them with the NCVS. These four methodologies concern (1) the UCR's inclusion of commercial and nonindividual victims, (2) the UCR's inclusion of individual victims of all ages, (3) the application of the UCR's Hierarchy Rule,[1] and (4) the UCR's inclusion of robberies as property offenses

---

[1] As discussed further later in the chapter, the Hierarchy Rule is only used in the UCR's summary system; it is no longer employed by NIBRS. This chapter includes an examination of the Hierarchy Rule because the summary system data are still being reported by the Federal Bureau of Investigation (FBI) in their annual crime estimates and publications such as *Crime in the United States* (FBI, 1999). The other three data collection methodologies are still used by NIBRS (see Table 8.1).

TABLE 8.1. *Overview of methodological differences between the UCR and NCVS*

Methodology	UCR		NCVS
	Summary system	NIBRS	
Population Coverage			
Inclusion of nonindividual victims	Yes	Yes (but identified)	No
Inclusion of victims under 12	Yes	Yes (but identified)	No
Counting Rules			
Use of Hierarchy Rule	Yes	No (includes up to 10 offenses per incident)	Yes (but allows for researcher options)
Use of property counting rule for robberies	Yes	Yes (but allows for researcher options)	No

as opposed to crimes against a person for counting purposes. The first two concern differences in the population covered and the last two relate to how crimes are counted. Table 8.1 lists these differences and compares the UCR summary system, NIBRS, and the NCVS. Because of previous coverage of these issues (see Chapters 2 and 3, this volume), the following discussion provides a brief description of these methodologies and predicts how these differences might contribute to divergence. In this discussion, it is important to keep in mind that these data collection strategies do not occur in a vacuum and a crime can be subject to (and affected by) more than one methodology. At this point, these factors are discussed singly for ease of explanation. In quantifying the methodological differences, the third section of this chapter examines possible cumulative effects of these differences.

Population Coverage Differences

Inclusion of Nonindividual Victims. Unlike the NCVS, which only collects information from individuals, the UCR Program includes crime victims of all types such as commercial enterprises and other nonindividuals like government and religious entities (Federal Bureau of

TABLE 8.2. *Predicted contribution to divergence of methodological differences*

Methodology	Predicted contribution to divergence (UCR vs. NCVS)
Population Coverage	
Inclusion of nonindividual victims	Increase UCR crime rate (increase crimes reported – numerator effect; may vary by crime)
Inclusion of victims under 12	Decrease UCR crime rate (increase population – denominator effect; may vary by crime)
Counting Rules	
Use of Hierarchy Rule	May decrease UCR crime rate for those crimes lowest on the hierarchy scale (decrease crimes reported – numerator effect)
Use of property counting rule for robberies	Decrease UCR robbery rate (decrease robberies reported – numerator effect)

Note: Predicted effects are based on examining methodologies singly rather than cumulatively.

Investigation [FBI], 1992). For purposes of studying divergence, the inclusion of these nonindividual victims affects the overall UCR crime rate by increasing the numerator, or the number of crimes reported, compared with the NCVS. Table 8.2 summarizes the *overall* effect of each methodological difference on divergence between the UCR and NCVS. It should be noted, however, that the inclusion of commercial and other nonindividual victims does not affect all crimes. For example, forcible rape and aggravated assault by definition can involve only individual victims (FBI, 1992). Comparisons of these offenses in the UCR and NCVS would not be affected by this methodological difference.

Inclusion of Victims Under Age 12. With regard to individual victims, the UCR includes crime victims of all ages. This is in contrast with the NCVS, where household members must be at least 12 to be eligible to participate in the survey (Bureau of Justice Statistics [BJS], 2002). As a result, the overall UCR crime rate would be lower than that reported by the NCVS, especially if those under 12 are victimized disproportionately less than those over 12. The inclusion of victims under 12 in the UCR affects the crime rate in this manner because the

UCR has a larger population denominator than the NCVS. As with non-individual victims, the contribution to divergence likely varies across crime types because some crimes, such as motor vehicle theft, are less likely to have victims under 12.

Counting Rules

Use of the Hierarchy Rule. The UCR's summary system only counts the most serious Index offense[2] in those situations where more than one crime occurred in a single incident. This practice is referred to as the Hierarchy Rule (FBI, 1984). The NCVS also uses a comparable scheme referred to as the "seriousness hierarchy" to classify a victimization involving more than one crime in official reports of NCVS incident rates (BJS, 2002). Unlike the UCR, however, the NCVS collects and preserves information for each crime occurring in the incident, which enables researchers to create their own classification scheme (BJS, 2002). Another difference between the UCR and NCVS hierarchy classifications is that the NCVS places all crimes against a person above property crimes. The effect of this classification difference can be seen with simple assaults, which are the most common violent crimes reported to the NCVS (Rand and Rennison, 2002). In the NCVS, simple assaults are considered to be more serious than burglaries or other property offenses. In the UCR, simple assaults are not Index offenses and are not included in the hierarchy. For an incident involving a burglary and a simple assault, the UCR would report the burglary, whereas the NCVS would not. This practice could result in divergence with regard to burglary or other property offenses.

The UCR's Hierarchy Rule could contribute to divergence if there are a large number of incidents that involve more than one offense. The Hierarchy Rule in the summary system would affect the UCR crime rates by decreasing the number of crimes in the numerator. The Hierarchy Rule does not affect all crimes equally. For comparisons with the NCVS, the crimes least affected are rape and aggravated assault. Only murder is more serious than rape, and murders

---

[2] The Index offenses in order of most to least serious on the hierarchy are murder, forcible rape, robbery, aggravated assault, burglary, larceny-theft, and motor vehicle theft (FBI, 1984). For example, if a victim is raped and robbed in a single incident, only the rape would be counted because it is more serious on the UCR hierarchy. For purposes of this chapter, murder is not included in these comparisons because it is outside the scope of the NCVS.

are outside the scope of the NCVS. For aggravated assault, the more serious offenses are murder, rape, and robbery. Because all of these offenses include assaultive violence, the aggravated assault would be considered a lesser included offense rather than a separate crime in that incident and would not be affected by the Hierarchy Rule. For purposes of comparisons with the NCVS, aggravated assaults would not be affected by the Hierarchy Rule.

Counting Robberies as Property Offenses. Both the UCR and NCVS count personal crimes differently than property crimes. The UCR counts crimes against a person (such as forcible rape or aggravated assault) as one offense for each victim of the crime (FBI, 1984). For example, if two people are assaulted and seriously injured outside of a nightclub, the UCR would count two aggravated assaults. The NCVS employs a similar counting rule for personal victimizations. For crimes against property, the UCR counts one offense for each incident or "operation" (FBI, 1984). For example, if a home is burglarized, it is counted as one burglary even though four individuals living in the home had items stolen. The NCVS has a similar rule and attributes property crimes to one victim (the household). Where the two series differ is with regard to designating property crimes. The UCR considers robbery to be a property offense while the NCVS considers it to be a personal victimization. In an incident where two victims are robbed, the UCR would count this as one robbery and the NCVS as two. In its incident counts, the NCVS attempts to make its counts more comparable to the UCR by adjusting this number to account for the fact that two victims were robbed in the same incident (BJS, 2002). The NCVS adjustment is not perfect. This adjustment is dependent on the respondent recalling and informing the interviewer about any additional victims. In addition, if one of the victims is a nonindividual (such as a business), the NCVS does not make such an adjustment. As a result, even with the NCVS's adjustment, this counting rule could contribute to divergence by decreasing the number of robberies counted by the UCR.

Prior Attempts to Measure These Differences

Previous researchers interested in studying sources of divergence could only approximate these methodological disparities based on additional information provided in the summary UCR Program as well as external data sources (e.g., Biderman and Lynch, 1991; Rand and Rennison, 2002; see also discussion in Chapter 4, this volume). This additional information allowed researchers to make some informed approximations in an attempt to remove victims under 12 and nonindividual victims from the UCR. Researchers have been less successful with regard to adjusting for the counting rule differences. As a result, most adjustments concern the population coverage issues; however, the accuracy of these adjustments is unknown. The following discussion summarizes these attempts and indicates the limitations with the techniques used.

Researchers employ a simple adjustment for the inclusion of victims under age 12 in the UCR by using a population base of individuals aged 12 or older (rather than the entire U.S. population) to calculate the UCR crime rates for comparison with the NCVS. This adjustment assumes that only a small number of victims under 12 are included in the overall crimes reported by the UCR (Biderman and Lynch, 1991, p. 33).

With regard to the UCR's inclusion of commercial or nonindividual victims, the adjustments become slightly more complex. Here researchers use additional aggregate data from the summary UCR Program collected in the Supplement to Return A (e.g., Biderman and Lynch, 1991). The Supplement to Return A collects details about robberies, burglaries, larceny-thefts, and motor vehicle thefts. These details provide some guidance as to the type of victim involved. For example, the Supplement to Return A categorizes larceny-thefts by type. Some of these thefts are clearly commercial (such as shoplifting); others are clearly personal (pocket picking); and others are ambivalent (theft from a building). Although the Supplement to Return A provides details to allow educated guesses as to the number of nonindividual victims, the accuracy of these adjustments is unknown. The fourth section of this chapter provides a more detailed description of the adjustments used by Biderman and Lynch as well as a discussion assessing the validity of these adjustments.

Researchers have not been successful in finding proxy measures to adjust for the differences in counting rules. This often results in no adjustments being made (e.g., Rand and Rennison, 2002). The summary UCR does not give the number of other crimes that occurred in the incident, so it is impossible to adjust for the Hierarchy Rule. No additional information collected by the summary system (such as the number of victims) is available to help with adjusting the count of robberies. As a result, Biderman and Lynch (1991, p. 59) concluded that the entire "UCR Robbery class [was] suspect with regard to the comparability of its scope to that of NCS robbery category."

Previous researchers have made the most of what little information they had at their disposal. The preceding discussion indicates the difficulty and imprecision in adjusting the UCR and NCVS to minimize the methodological differences between the two systems. The previous limitations highlight the role NIBRS can play in ascertaining the degree to which methodological differences contribute to divergence because NIBRS eliminates the need to engage in these elaborate calculations and provides more direct measures. The next section describes those unique features of NIBRS data.

NIBRS AND LIMITS OF THESE DATA

NIBRS Overview

This section provides a brief description of NIBRS with a focus on those attributes relevant to examining methodological differences and divergence. Readers interested in more extensive discussions of NIBRS including the conversion process can refer to other sources such as Addington (2004), BJS (1997, 2000), FBI (1992), and Maxfield (1999).

NIBRS is a significant departure from the UCR's summary reporting system. The summary system collects only aggregate-level information for eight Index offenses (see Chapter 3, this volume). NIBRS collects incident-level details for 46 Group A offenses, which include the eight former Index offenses.[3] This information includes details on the offenses, victims, and offenders. Of relevance for this chapter, NIBRS provides information necessary to identify the differences in population coverage between the UCR and NCVS. NIBRS identifies

---

[3] Group A offenses in NIBRS increase the number of crimes that can be compared with the NCVS, most notably simple assaults.

the victim type, which is categorized as individual, business, financial institution, government, religious organization, society, other, or unknown. NIBRS also collects demographic information about individual victims, including their age. With regard to the differences in the counting rules, NIBRS eliminates the need for the Hierarchy Rule because it includes information for up to 10 offenses in one incident. NIBRS also provides information regarding the number of victims involved in an incident, which allows researchers to select level of analysis and study the effect of employing the summary UCR system's property counting rules for robberies.[4]

NIBRS Data Used in This Chapter

The descriptive analyses presented in the following paragraphs use data from the 2001 NIBRS because these constitute one of the most recent years of public use data (FBI, 2004). These data are available through the National Archive of Criminal Justice Data. The data used here are disaggregated by crime type to allow for comparisons across crimes. The crimes examined are those six crimes comparable to the former Index offenses and the NCVS: forcible rape,[5] robbery, aggravated assault, burglary, larceny-theft,[6] and motor vehicle theft. The unit of analysis is at the victim level.[7] NIBRS allows researchers great flexibility in electing what level of analysis to use. The victim level is used with all crimes, even property offenses, which results in some

---

[4] Official UCR statistics published by the FBI still use the property counting rule for robberies.

[5] For this discussion, forcible rape includes the NIBRS crimes of forcible rape, forcible sodomy, and sexual assault with an object to make it most comparable to the NCVS crime of rape. This decision expands the definition of rape used in the summary system and was made to remove possible divergence due to different definitions used in the UCR and NCVS. One difference in particular concerned the summary UCR system's including only female victims in its definition of rape, whereas the NCVS included both male and female victims.

[6] Larceny-thefts here include the NIBRS offenses of pocket picking, purse snatching, shoplifting, theft from a building, theft from a coin-operated machine or device, theft from a motor vehicle, theft of motor vehicle parts or accessories, and all other larcenies. This is done to make the larceny-thefts most comparable to the summary system and NCVS.

[7] Because analysis is at the victim level, it is possible that the victim reported more than one crime during the incident.

imprecision because property crimes are typically counted at the operation or incident level as opposed to the victim level. This decision
was made for the following three reasons: First, analysis at the victim
level is required to examine the number of nonindividual victims as
well as the effect of counting robberies as property offenses. Second,
switching the level of analysis for other comparisons became an overly
difficult and confusing undertaking. The benefit of NIBRS data is the
tremendous amount of detail; however, this also results in comparable
increase in complexity for manipulating the files. Using only one level
of analysis vastly reduces this complexity. Finally, although this decision may result in some slippage in the analysis of property offenses,
the errors likely result in a more conservative count.[8]

Limitations on NIBRS Data

One caveat in using NIBRS data is its limited coverage. NIBRS is a
substantial departure in crime data collection for law enforcement
agencies and requires a lengthy certification process. As a result, conversion to NIBRS has been gradual. NIBRS agencies covered only 17%
of the U.S. population in 2001 (BJS, 2004). Because participation in
NIBRS is voluntary, these agencies do not constitute a random sample
of U.S. law enforcement agencies. In 2001, only 21 states were NIBRS-
certified.[9] Within these 21 states, not all agencies submit data in NIBRS
format. Only 7 states fully report in NIBRS; the other 14 states have less
than full participation in NIBRS. Law enforcement agencies that participate in NIBRS tend to represent smaller populations areas. In 2001,
no agency covering a population of more than 1 million participated
in NIBRS.[10]

---

[8] Only a small percentage of property offenses involve more than one victim and would
be subject to this counting rule. Nine percent of burglaries, 5% of thefts, and 2%
of motor vehicle thefts involved more than one victim. Robberies had the largest
percentage of multiple victims (24%). This issue with robberies is addressed later as
one of the four methodological differences between the UCR and NCVS.

[9] In addition, three agencies from Kentucky and one from the District of Columbia also
submitted NIBRS data in 2001. In the District of Columbia, only the Metro Transit
Police report NIBRS data (BJS, 2004). One reason for this situation is the fact that
a few states do not have a state-level UCR program (Maltz, 1999). In these cases and
under special circumstances, the FBI certifies individual agencies (BJS, 1997).

[10] For example, in NIBRS-certified states such as Massachusetts and Michigan, departments serving larger communities such as Boston and Detroit do not submit NIBRS

These factors result in a large case selection bias in which smaller population areas are overrepresented (Addington et al., 2001). It is possible that UCR data from smaller agencies may differ from larger agencies in the crime patterns examined here. This nonrepresentativeness of NIBRS suggests exercising some caution when interpreting the results and generalizing beyond the NIBRS-participating agencies included in this study. Given this caveat, NIBRS data nonetheless do provide a unique opportunity to quantify and begin a dialogue of how these design differences might contribute to divergence in the two series. In a similar light, Biderman and Lynch (1991, pp. 64–65) believed researchers could "reap the benefits" of NIBRS even before it was fully implemented nationwide because "data from one or several large states would provide some estimates of the importance of some sources of discrepancies that we could only guess at."

EXAMINING METHODOLOGICAL DIFFERENCES BY CRIME TYPE

The following discussion focuses on each crime type as opposed to the overall effect on the UCR rates for two reasons. First, not all crimes are equally affected by these methodological issues (see Table 8.2; Biderman and Lynch, 1991; Rand and Rennison, 2002). Second, researchers tend to disaggregate the UCR data at some level such as examining just aggravated assaults or only violent crime.

Table 8.3 summarizes the UCR methodologies that affect each crime and as a result may contribute to divergence when comparing the UCR and NCVS for a particular offense. The crimes are discussed in greater detail in this section and are addressed in order of least to most affected by the number of methodological differences. As Table 8.3 indicates, rapes and aggravated assaults are affected by only one difference in methodology. These crimes are discussed first. The property offenses of burglary, larceny-theft, and motor vehicle theft are examined next. These crimes are viewed as being affected by three methodological

data (Addington et al., 2001). The Fairfax County (Virginia) Police Department is the largest NIBRS-reporting agency (covering a population of 948,050; Justice Research Statistics Association, 2005).

TABLE 8.3. *Applicability of UCR methodologies on different crimes*

	Type of UCR methodology			
Offense	Inclusion of victims under 12?	Inclusion of nonindividual victims?	Likely effect of Hierarchy Rule?	Use of property counting rule?
Forcible rape	Yes	No	None	No
Robbery	Yes	Yes	Little	Yes
Aggravated assault	Yes	No	None	No
Burglary	Yes	Yes	Some	Yes*
Larceny theft	Yes	Yes	Some	Yes*
Motor vehicle theft	Yes	Yes	Some	Yes*

* The NCVS employs a comparable rule.

differences because the NCVS employs a similar property counting rule. Robbery is discussed last because robberies are affected by all four differences.

Tables 8.4 to 8.8 summarize the effect of each methodological difference by crime. The tables report the effects separately but also build on each other cumulatively. For example, nonindividual victims are removed from Tables 8.5 to 8.8 and victims under 12 are removed from Tables 8.6 to 8.8. This is an attempt to reflect more accurately the fact that these data collection methodologies occur simultaneously.

TABLE 8.4. *Inclusion of nonindividual victims: Victim type by crime type, 2001 NIBRS (full victim file)*

	Crime type					
Victim type	Rape	Robbery	Aggravated assault	Burglary	Theft	Motor vehicle theft
Individual	23,171 (100%)	45,398 (82%)	134,270 (100%)	240,724 (71%)	768,736 (64%)	126,866 (84%)
Nonindividual	0 (0%)	10,171 (18%)	0 (0%)	76,144 (23%)	369,562 (31%)	16,767 (11%)
Unknown	0 (0%)	48 (0.1%)	0 (0%)	19,932 (6%)	55,982 (5%)	7,684 (5%)
Total	23,171	55,617	134,270	336,800	1,194,280	151,317

TABLE 8.5. *Inclusion of individual victims under 12: Victim age by crime type, 2001 NIBRS (individual victims only)*

	Crime type					
Age	Rape	Robbery	Aggravated assault	Burglary	Theft	Motor vehicle theft
Under 12	5,265 (23%)	690 (2%)	6,050 (5%)	656 (0.3%)	5,742 (1%)	139 (0.1%)
12 or older	17,591 (76%)	43,727 (96%)	123,222 (92%)	228,505 (95%)	722,867 (94%)	120,018 (95%)
Unknown	315 (1%)	981 (2%)	4,998 (4%)	11,563 (5%)	40,127 (5%)	6,709 (5%)
Total	23,171	45,398	134,270	240,724	768,736	126,866

Note: Percentages may not equal 100% due to rounding.

Because of the complexity in maintaining this framework, the counting rules are not cumulatively applied in Tables 8.7 and 8.8.

Forcible Rape and Aggravated Assault

Forcible rape and aggravated assault are discussed together because each one is affected by the same methodological difference in comparing these crimes between the UCR and NCVS – the inclusion of victims under 12 years of age. Both rape and aggravated assault involve individual victims by definition, and the counting rule is the same in the UCR and NCVS. As discussed earlier, rape is not affected by the Hierarchy Rule for purposes of comparisons with the NCVS because only

TABLE 8.6. *Application of the Hierarchy Rule: Number of offenses per crime incident by crime type, 2001 NIBRS (individual victims 12 or older)*

	Rape	Robbery	Aggravated assault	Burglary	Theft	Motor vehicle theft
Only offense	16,049 (91%)	41,102 (94%)	115,482 (94%)	177,405 (78%)	625,869 (87%)	109,132 (91%)
More than one offense*	1,542 (9%)	2,625 (6%)	7,740 (6%)	51,100 (22%)	96,998 (13%)	10,886 (9%)
Total	17,591	43,727	123,222	228,505	722,867	120,018

* This number includes crimes that would be lower on the hierarchy as well as crimes that would not have been Return A Offenses and therefore not subject to the Hierarchy Rule.

TABLE 8.7. *Application of the Hierarchy Rule: Number of crimes more serious on hierarchy scale by crime type, 2001 NIBRS (individual victims 12 or older)*

				Additional criminal offense occurring in same incident			
Crime	Rape	Robbery	Aggravated assault	Burglary	Theft	Motor vehicle theft	Total
Rape	x	x	x	x	x	x	0 (0%)
Robbery	191 (0.4%)	x	x	x	x	x	191 (0.4%)
Aggravated assault	0 (0%)	0 (0%)	x	x	x	x	0 (0%)
Burglary	362 (0.2%)	1,089 (0.5%)	1,706 (0.7%)	x	x	x	3,157 (1%)
Theft	97 (0%)	0 (0%)	847 (0.1%)	22,380 (3%)	x	x	23,324 (3%)
Motor vehicle theft	2 7 (0%)	0 (0%)	241 (0.2%)	1,605 (1%)	5,036 (4%)	x	6,909 (6%)

x = additional criminal offense not subject to Hierarchy Rule.

homicides are more serious than rapes in the UCR hierarchy scale, and homicides are outside the scope of the NCVS. Similarly, the Hierarchy Rule has little effect on aggravated assault because it is a lesser included offenses of all the more serious crimes on the UCR hierarchy.

Table 8.5 reports the number of victims under 12 included in the count of aggravated assaults and rapes. For aggravated assaults, these numbers illustrate how the inclusion of victims under age 12 may contribute to divergence by decreasing the UCR aggravated assault rate. The UCR rate would be calculated using a disproportionately large denominator because the percentage of victims who are under

TABLE 8.8. *Application of the property counting rule: Number of robbery incidents involving more than one victim, 2001 NIBRS (individual victims 12 or older)*

	Robbery
More than one victim in incident	10,574 (24%)
Total	43,727

12 (5%) is much smaller than the percentage of those under 12 in the U.S. population.[11] For rapes, this information demonstrates how adjusting for the population difference itself may contribute to divergence. Typically researchers simply use a denominator based on the over-12 population to adjust for the population difference between the UCR and NCVS. In this situation, the under-12 population contributes 23% of the rape victimizations. If the under-12 population is removed from the denominator and no adjustments are made to the numerator, this adjustment would overestimate the rape rate reported by the UCR.[12]

Burglary

With comparisons of UCR and NCVS burglary data, three methodological differences can contribute to divergence: the two population coverage issues and application of the Hierarchy Rule. With regard to the population coverage, 71% of the burglary victims reported to the 2001 NIBRS are individuals and 23% are nonindividuals (Table 8.4). The inclusion of nonindividual victims is the biggest methodological source of divergence for burglaries. Of the individual victims, 95% of the burglary victims are 12 years old or older, and only a handful are under 12 (Table 8.5). The fact that any victims of burglary are under age 12 is somewhat surprising. These numbers may be due to the inclusion of all family members as victims of a burglary or due to data entry errors.

With regard to the counting rules, the Hierarchy Rule could affect the number of burglaries reported in the UCR because rape, robbery, and aggravated assault rank as more serious crimes on the hierarchy scale. As shown in Table 8.6, 78% of the burglaries involve only one offense. As such, 22% of burglaries could be affected by the Hierarchy

[11] For example, 21% of the U.S. population was under age 14 as measured by the 2000 Census (U.S. Department of Commerce, 2001).

[12] It should be reiterated that this study included the NIBRS crimes of forcible rape, forcible sodomy, and sexual assault with an object in its definition of rape to make the definition most comparable to the NCVS definition. This definition is broader than the UCR definition, which does not include forcible sodomy. The percentage of victims under age 12 for each of the crimes included in the definition of rape are forcible rape (14%), forcible sodomy (49%), and sexual assault with an object (39%).

Rule in the summary system. It is important to note that NIBRS collects information on crimes not included in the old Hierarchy Rule as well as crimes that are less serious on the hierarchy scale. A closer examination of these additional offenses shows that only 1% of all burglaries would not have been counted in the summary system because these included burglaries that involved a forcible rape, robbery, or aggravated assault (Table 8.7). It is important to reiterate that for the discussion of burglaries (as well as the following discussions of larceny-theft and motor vehicle theft), analysis is conducted at the victim level, which is a slightly different count than the "operation" or incident level used in the UCR. As a result, the percentages reported in Table 8.7 represent the greatest number of offenses that could be affected by the Hierarchy Rule.

As noted earlier, burglaries might be affected by a "reverse" Hierarchy Rule for those incidents when a burglary occurs in conjunction with a simple assault. In these incidents, the NCVS data reported by BJS would not include the burglary and instead would just count the simple assault. As a result, the official NCVS figures would report fewer burglaries. Using NIBRS data (in analyses not presented here), about 1% of the NIBRS burglaries that included at least one other crime involved a simple assault. This would result in UCR reporting a slightly larger number of burglaries than the NCVS; however, it is unlikely the inclusion of these burglaries makes much of a contribution to divergence.

Larceny-Theft

Larceny-theft also is affected by population coverage issues and application of the Hierarchy Rule. With regard to population coverage issues, 64% of the larceny-theft victims reported to the 2001 NIBRS are individuals and 31% are nonindividuals (Table 8.4). Larceny-theft has the largest percentage of nonindividual victims of all the crimes examined here. For larceny-thefts (as with burglaries), the inclusion of nonindividual victims is the biggest methodological source of divergence. Among the individual victims, 94% are aged 12 years or older, 1% are under 12, and the remaining victims were of an unknown age (Table 8.5).

The application of the Hierarchy Rule likely has some effect on larceny-theft because it is the next to last crime on the hierarchy scale.

As discussed earlier, the contribution to divergence depends on how many offenses involve more than one crime. As shown in Table 8.6, 87% of the larceny-thefts involve only one offense. At most, 13% of the larceny-thefts would have been affected by the Hierarchy Rule in the summary system; however, not all of these additional crimes are more serious Index offenses. Only 3% of all larceny-thefts would not have been counted in the summary system because they occurred with a more serious offense on the hierarchy scale (Table 8.7).

Motor Vehicle Theft

As with burglary and larceny-theft, motor vehicle theft is affected by three methodological differences: the two population coverage issues and application of the Hierarchy Rule. With regard to victim type, 84% of the motor vehicle theft victims reported to the 2001 NIBRS are individuals, and 11% are nonindividuals (Table 8.4). For the individual victims, 95% of the motor vehicle theft victims are 12 years old or older, 5% are of an unknown age, and a handful are under 12 (Table 8.5). As with burglaries, the fact that any victims of motor vehicle theft are under 12 is surprising. Because this number is so small, it is most likely due to data entry errors in reporting victim age.

With regard to the counting rules, the Hierarchy Rule would be predicted to have the greatest effect on motor vehicle theft because it is the lowest on the hierarchy scale. As shown in Table 8.6, 91% of the motor vehicle thefts involve only one offense. At most, 9% would have been affected by the Hierarchy Rule in the summary system. As discussed previously, NIBRS collects information on crimes not included in the old Hierarchy Rule. Six percent of all motor vehicle thefts would not have been counted in the summary system. As indicated in Table 8.7, motor vehicle theft is most affected by application of the Hierarchy Rule of all of the UCR–NCVS offenses. Both the inclusion of nonindividual victims and the effect of the Hierarchy Rule contribute to divergence for motor vehicles thefts.

Robbery

Unlike the preceding five crimes, robbery is affected by all four methodological differences, which make robberies the most difficult to compare between the UCR and NCVS and the most susceptible to methodological sources of divergence. With regard to population coverage issues, UCR robberies include all victim types and ages. As Table 8.4 shows, 82% of robbery victims reported to the 2001 NIBRS are individuals, and 18% are nonindividuals. As with the three other property-related crimes, the inclusion of nonindividual victims is one of the biggest contributors to divergence for robberies. For the individual victims, 96% of the robbery victims are aged 12 years or older, about 2% are under 12, and the remaining victims are of an unknown age (Table 8.5).

With regard to the counting rules, the Hierarchy Rule likely has the smallest effect of all the crimes examined with regard to comparing UCR and NCVS robberies because only forcible rape is more serious on the hierarchy scale. As shown in Table 8.6, 94% of the robberies involve only one offense. At most, 6% would have been affected by the Hierarchy Rule in the summary system. Further exploration of these crimes indicates that less than 0.5% of all robberies would not have been counted in the summary system (Table 8.7).

In trying to compare those reported in the UCR with those in the NCVS, the unique problem encountered with robberies is the fact that the UCR counts robberies as property crimes. As discussed earlier, an incident that involves a robbery is counted as one robbery no matter how many victims. The NCVS counts robbery as a personal crime or one incident for each victim or person. Table 8.8 shows that this counting rule could have a fairly large effect because 24% of robberies involve more than one victim. It is difficult to say how many of these are not counted and create divergence with the NCVS because (1) it is possible that not all of the victims in the incident were victims of the robbery and (2) there may be commercial or nonindividual entities that were the additional victim. Because of limitations with the NIBRS data, the exact percentage of robberies that would not be counted and would contribute to divergence cannot be determined. Viewing this figure most crudely as being overinclusive, up to a quarter of the robberies known to police might not be counted in the UCR. Although the NCVS does adjust for multiple victims of robbery, this difference could contribute to divergence especially if the other victim is a non-individual entity. So while the contribution of this counting rule to divergence may not be one-quarter of all robberies, it is likely this rule contributes to divergence. Although NIBRS cannot readily pinpoint the exact contribution to divergence, using NIBRS data can minimize this problem and provide greater comparability because NIBRS allows researchers the option of selecting the level of analysis.

ASSESSING THE VALIDITY OF PROXY MEASURES OF NONINDIVIDUAL VICTIMS

Of the methodological differences discussed in this chapter, the inclusion of nonindividual victims contributes the most to divergence between the UCR and NCVS for the four property-related crimes. This section assesses the validity of prior attempts to measure and adjust for the number of commercial victims in the UCR. Although NIBRS eliminates the need to approximate victim type, examining the validity of the adjustments used with the summary UCR data remains an important exercise for two reasons. One is that the UCR data continue to be reported in summary format during the conversion period. Because NIBRS agencies only cover 17% of the U.S. population (BJS, 2004), the FBI converts NIBRS data into summary format for its annual crime estimates and official reports (FBI, 1999). This practice is done to maintain a consistent time series of crime data and is likely to continue for the foreseeable future. A second reason is that decades of UCR data are in summary format. To the extent these approximations are valid, this knowledge would give researchers greater confidence when studying divergence and trying to minimize that proportion due to methodological differences between the UCR and NCVS.

With the summary system, the actual number of commercial victims could not be ascertained because of the aggregate nature of the data collection. Additional UCR data collected by the Supplement to Return A allows for approximations and adjustments. Although the Supplement to Return A provides information to identify those robberies, burglaries, and thefts that might involve nonindividual victims, it does not give a specific count of nonindividual victims. To assess the validity of these approximations, the adjustments used by Biderman and Lynch (1991) are replicated because these are the best documented and most extensive. The 2001 NIBRS data are used to recreate these measures. This replication is possible because NIBRS collects information comparable to the Supplement to Return A. These replicated Supplement to Return A measures are compared with the actual percentage of nonindividual victims specifically identified in the NIBRS data. The analyses that follow are conducted at the victim level in order to obtain the clearest comparison of the type of victim and the accuracy of the adjustment. The four UCR-NCVS crimes affected by the inclusion of commercial victims are discussed separately because different approximations are used to estimate the number of nonindividual victims for robbery, burglary, larceny-theft, and motor vehicle theft.

Robbery

For robberies, information from the Supplement to Return A gives seven breakdowns of robbery based on the location where it occurred. The seven locations are: highway, commercial house, gas/service station, convenience store, residence, bank, and miscellaneous. For comparisons with the crime survey, Biderman and Lynch (1991, pp. 114–115) used only residential robberies because they found no means to disentangle individual and nonindividual victims from the robberies occurring in nonresidential locations. When they excluded these nonresidential categories of robberies, Biderman and Lynch also adjusted the National Crime Survey data to remove robberies occurring in commercial locations.

NIBRS data can replicate the Supplement to Return A classifications. NIBRS provides greater details regarding the location of the crime, so it was necessary to collapse the categories to correspond with the Supplement to Return A information. The locations were combined as follows: highway (included NIBRS location of highway/road/alley); commercial house (included NIBRS locations of bar/nightclub, commercial/office building, department/discount store, grocery/supermarket, hotel/motel, liquor store, restaurant, specialty store); residence (included NIBRS location of residence/home); bank (included NIBRS location of bank/savings and loan); and miscellaneous (included NIBRS locations of air/bus/train terminal, church/synagogue/temple, construction site, drug store/doctors office/hospital, field/woods, government/public building, jail/prison, lake/waterway, parking lot/garage, rental storage facility, school/college, and other/unknown). The results for this analysis are presented in Table 8.9.

TABLE 8.9. *Percentage of nonindividuals in robbery categories, 2001 NIBRS (victim-level, victim type known)*

Robbery locations from Supplement to Return A	Percentage of nonindividual victims
Highway	2%
Commercial house	38%
Gas/service station	44%
Convenience store	45%
Residence	2%
Bank	50%
Miscellaneous	9%

$N = 55,567$.

Nonindividual victims appear in every location, even residences, although nonindividuals account for only 2% of these victims (Table 8.9). The small percentage of nonindividual victims in highway robberies is of note because, as Biderman and Lynch (1991, p. 114) hypothesized but were unable to confirm with additional data, "some appreciable proportion" of these robberies would involve nonindividual victims. Beyond the small percentage of nonindividual victims in the residential and highway robbery cases, nonindividual and individual victims are highly commingled in the remaining location categories.

Burglary

Biderman and Lynch (1991) used information from the Supplement to Return A to approximate those burglaries involving nonindividual victims. The Supplement to Return A classifies burglaries by location: residence versus nonresidence. Biderman and Lynch assumed most residential burglaries would involve individual victims and that high comparability would exist between UCR residential burglaries and those reported to the crime survey. The location information in NIBRS can replicate these categories. Here home locations are compared with all other locations. As shown in Table 8.10, residential location provides a good approximation of burglaries involving individual victims; however, one-third of the nonresidential burglaries involve individual victims.

TABLE 8.10. *Percentage of nonindividuals in burglary*
categories, 2001 NIBRS (victim-level, victim type known)

Burglary locations from Supplement to Return A	Percentage of nonindividual victims
Residential	3%
Nonresidential	63%

$N = 316,868$.

Larceny-Theft

For thefts, the Supplement to Return A provides information on the nature of these thefts. These subcategories include pocket picking, purse snatching, shoplifting, theft from motor vehicles, theft of bicycles,[13] theft from a building, theft from any coin-operated machines, and all others. Biderman and Lynch (1991) used this information to distinguish thefts that clearly would involve an individual compared with a nonindividual victim. For example, pocket picking suggests an individual victim and shoplifting suggests a commercial (nonindividual) victim. Other categories are less clear, such as theft from a building, which could involve either an individual or commercial victim. To make the UCR and NCS most comparable, Biderman and Lynch removed from the UCR those thefts that were "clearly" commercial (shoplifting and theft from coin-operated machine) but included the other types.

NIBRS provides comparable categories that allow replication of the Supplement to Return A. As Table 8.11 shows, pocket picking and purse snatching are the thefts most likely to involve individual victims (although a small percentage of nonindividual victims is reported) and shoplifting is most likely to involve nonindividual victims (although here as well a small percentage of individual victims is seen). Individual and nonindividual victims are mixed throughout categories such as theft of motor vehicle parts, theft from a coin-operated machine (despite Biderman and Lynch's assumption), and other thefts.

Motor Vehicle Theft

Unlike the preceding three crimes, the Supplement to Return A provides no information regarding motor vehicle thefts that might assist

---

[13] NIBRS does not collect information regarding theft of bicycles.

TABLE 8.11. *Percentage of nonindividuals in larceny-theft categories, 2001 NIBRS (victim-level, victim type known)*

Larceny-theft categories in Supplement to Return A	Percentage of nonindividual victims
Pocket picking	5%
Purse snatching	2%
Shoplifting	98%
Theft from building	27%
Theft from coin-operated machine	87%
Theft from motor vehicle	6%
Theft of motor vehicle parts/access	10%
All other larceny	32%

$N = 1,138,298.$

in identifying possible nonindividual victims. Biderman and Lynch (1991) attempted to measure these victims by using an elaborate system of type of vehicle and the proportion of those types of vehicles owned by businesses to tease out the number of commercial vehicles. No simple method exists to estimate the number of commercial victims of motor vehicle theft in the summary system.

To summarize, the Supplement to Return A allows researchers to make some educated adjustments to better compare the summary UCR system and the NCVS. The adjustments are not perfect. Less than perfect adjustments fail to remove the methodological component of divergence. As a result, nonindividual victims remain in comparisons with the NCVS and may contribute to divergence. Moreover, as Biderman and Lynch (1991) described in their work, adjusting the UCR could contribute to divergence if comparable adjustments are not made to the NCVS data, such as the removing robberies occurring in commercial locations from the UCR but not from the NCVS data.

DISCUSSION AND CONCLUSIONS

Even before NIBRS was implemented, Biderman and Lynch (1991) anticipated the benefits of this new form of UCR data collection with regard to the study of divergence. They recognized that NIBRS would "extend considerably our ability to identify the degree to which the

TABLE 8.12. *Contribution of various UCR methodologies to divergence for UCR–NCVS crimes*

Offense	Nonindividual victims	Victims under 12	Effect of Hierarchy Rule	Property counting rule
Rape	None 0%	*Some 23%	None 0%	None
Robbery	Some 18%	Few 2%	Very little 0.4%	*Most affected (up to 24%)
Aggravated assault	None 0%	Few 5%	None 0%	None
Burglary	Some 23%	Very few 0.3%	Little 1%	None (same rule as NCVS)
Larceny-theft	*Some 31%	Very few 1%	Little 3%	None (same rule as NCVS)
Motor vehicle theft	Some 11%	Very few 0.1%	*Little 6%	None (same rule as NCVS)

* = Most affected of UCR crimes for this particular methodology.

UCR is or is not counting equivalently the same phenomenon as the [NCVS]" because of its collection of incident-based data (Biderman and Lynch, pp. 60–61). This prediction was correct. NIBRS allows researchers for the first time to quantify the methodological differences between the UCR and NCVS. Understanding these methodological contributions to divergence remains an important issue because the UCR data continue to be reported in summary format.

Table 8.12 summarizes the effect of the four methodological differences for each type of UCR-NCVS crime. These differences all contribute to divergence when comparing crimes between the two data systems. The effect of these methodological differences is not uniform across type of crime. Looking across the rows of the table, robberies are the crime most affected by all the methodological differences and aggravated assaults the least. Rapes and larceny-thefts are greatly affected by a single methodological difference: for rapes, it is the inclusion of victims under age 12, and for larceny-thefts, it is the inclusion of nonindividual victims. In addition to varying across type of crime, each methodological difference makes a different contribution to divergence. Looking down the columns of the table, the inclusion of nonindividual victims contributes the most to divergence and the Hierarchy and property counting rules the least.

NIBRS can greatly inform the study of divergence both by quantifying the differences and by adjusting the UCR data to make the two series more comparable methodologically. NIBRS, however, does not eliminate all of the problems that may play a role in divergence. The UCR remains a collection of crimes known to the police. NIBRS does not ameliorate the problem of the "dark figure" of unreported crime. The UCR also relies on crime classification by the responding officer, which can lead to misclassification and divergence. For example, it is possible that police identify a victim as an individual (as opposed to a business) when it was actually the company's property that was stolen. How a crime is classified also depends on the officer's determination, which may change over time (see Chapter 9, this volume). The police recording could differ from how the NCVS would categorize that crime because the NCVS relies on attribute coding. Because of these issues, researchers should be mindful to other sources of divergence when comparing crimes such as aggravated assaults that appear to be very comparable to the NCVS from a methodological standpoint.

Finally, it should be reiterated that the NIBRS data relied on in this chapter have a small agency bias, and it will be necessary to reevaluate these analyses as larger jurisdictions begin reporting NIBRS data. Based on the foregoing analysis, it appears that methodological differences between the UCR and NCVS do contribute to divergence; however, this contribution provides only part of the story, and other sources of divergence must be considered.

References

Addington, L. A. (2004). "The effect of NIBRS reporting on item missing data in murder cases." *Homicide Studies* 8:193–213.

Addington, L. A., Loftin, C., & McDowall, D. (2001, November). *The quality of NIBRS murder data.* Paper presented at the Annual Meeting of the American Society of Criminology, Atlanta, GA.

Biderman, A. D., & Lynch, J. P. (1991). *Understanding crime incidence statistics: Why the UCR diverges from the NCS.* New York: Springer-Verlag.

Bureau of Justice Statistics. (1997). *Implementing the National Incident-Based Reporting System: A project status report.* Retrieved December 18, 2002, from http://www.ojp.usdoj.gov/bjs/pub/pdf/inibrs.pdf.

Bureau of Justice Statistics. (2000). *Effects of NIBRS on crime statistics.* Retrieved December 18, 2002, from http://www.ojp.usdoj.gov/bjs/pub/pdf/enibrscs.pdf.

Bureau of Justice Statistics. (2002). *National Crime Victimization Survey, 1992–2001* (codebook). Compiled by the U.S. Department of Commerce, Bureau of the Census. Ann Arbor, MI: Inter-university Consortium for Political and Social Research. (Available from National Archive of Criminal Justice Data, http://www.icpsr.umich.edu/NACJD.)

Bureau of Justice Statistics. (2004). *Level of participation by states as of December, 2002.* Retrieved April 30, 2004, from http://www.ojp.usdoj.gov/bjs/nibrsstatus.htm.

Federal Bureau of Investigation. (1984). *Uniform Crime Reporting handbook.* Washington, DC: U.S. Government Printing Office.

Federal Bureau of Investigation. (1992). *Uniform Crime Reporting handbook, National Incident-Based Reporting System edition.* Washington, DC: U.S. Government Printing Office.

Federal Bureau of Investigation. (1999). *Conversion of NIBRS data to summary data.* Washington, DC: U.S. Department of Justice. (Available from http://www.fbi.gov/ucr/nibrs/manuals/conversion.pdf.)

Federal Bureau of Investigation. (2004). *National Incident-Based Reporting System, 2001* [Data file]. Compiled by the U.S. Department of Justice, Federal Bureau of Investigation. Ann Arbor, MI: Inter-university Consortium for Political and Social Research. (Available from National Archive of Criminal Justice Data, http://www.icpsr.umich.edu/NACJD.)

Justice Research and Statistics Association. (2005). *50 largest NIBRS agencies.* IBR Resource Center. Retrieved March 31, 2005, http://www.jrsa.org/ibrrc/index.html.

Maltz, M. D. (1999). *Bridging gaps in police crime data: A discussion paper from the BJS Fellows Program.* Washington, DC: Bureau of Justice Statistics.

Maxfield, M. G. (1999). "The National Incident-Based Reporting System: Research and policy applications." *Journal of Quantitative Criminology* 15:119–149.

Rand, M. R., & Rennison, C. M. (2002). "True crime stories? Accounting for differences in our national crime indicators." *Chance* 15:47–51.

U.S. Department of Commerce. (2001). *Profiles of general demographic characteristics 2000: 2000 Census of population and housing.* Washington, DC: U.S. Department of Commerce. (Available at http://www.census.gov/prod/census2000/dp1/2hkoo.pdf.)

CHAPTER NINE

Explaining the Divergence Between UCR and NCVS Aggravated Assault Trends

Richard Rosenfeld

Trends in aggravated assaults recorded by the police and those reported in victim surveys diverge over time in the United States. Police-recorded assaults trend upward during the 1980s and flatten in the 1990s, whereas survey-estimated assaults are flat during the 1980s and decline during the 1990s. Previous research has attributed the divergence between the police and survey trends to changes in police recording practices, independent of the underlying rate of victimization (Blumstein, 1998; O'Brien, 1996). This study adds to that research by comparing police and survey trends in firearm and nonfirearm aggravated assaults, on the assumption that police recording practices are more likely to affect the latter than the former. Consistent with this assumption, the results show much less divergence in gun than nongun assault time trends. Together with previous research, this study offers strong, albeit circumstantial, evidence that changes in police recording of assaults explain much of the divergence in aggravated assault trends derived from police records and victim surveys. It also appears that the NCVS redesign has helped to reduce the divergence between UCR and NCVS aggravated assault trends in recent years.

BACKGROUND AND SIGNIFICANCE

Although the United States' two major crime indicators, the FBI's Uniform Crime Reports (UCR) and the Bureau of Justice Statistics' National Crime Victimization Survey (NCVS), are based on distinct methods of obtaining information about the number and nature of criminal events, they should tell essentially the same story about

changes in crime rates over time. Confidence in the integrity of the
nation's crime statistics depends to a large degree on what researchers'
refer to as their "convergent validity," that is, whether different measures of the same phenomenon yield similar results (see Chapter 4,
this volume). Simply put, a definitive answer to the critical policy and
research question of whether crime is going up or down over time
requires that the two major crime indicators produce similar estimates
of crime trends.

Prior research has shown divergent time trends in UCR and NCVS
violent crime rates (Blumstein et al., 1991; Menard and Covey, 1988;
Messner, 1984; O'Brien, 1985, 1990, 1996). It has long been known
that the UCR crime statistics exclude a substantial number of crimes
that victims, for whatever reason, choose not to report to the police.
The impetus for the creation of a parallel national crime indicator
to the UCR was in large part to evaluate this so-called dark figure of
crimes unknown to the police. The NCVS, begun in 1973 (and until
1992 called the National Crime Survey [NCS]), surveys a nationally
representative sample of households in the United States and asks
respondents who indicate they were the victim of a crime whether
they reported the crime to the police. Sizeable fractions of victims tell
interviewers they did not report the crime to the police. For example,
51% of violent crime victims in 2002 did not report the incident to the
police (Rennison and Rand, 2003). Assuming no other differences,
then, the UCR's tally of police-recorded crimes missed roughly one-
half of all violent crimes (excluding homicides) in 2002.

In principle, the dark figure of crimes not known to the police has
a known relationship to both the NCVS and UCR crime counts. To
reconcile the two measures of crime, one need only reduce the NCVS
crimes by the number of crimes victims reported to the police or scale
up the UCR crimes by the number they did not report to the police. Of
course, other differences between the two crime measures also must be
accounted for. The crime classifications used in the two series differ in
some important respects. For example, the UCR rape count excludes
rapes of male victims, and the NCVS robbery count excludes commercial victimizations. Such differences are reasonably transparent,
however, and when appropriate adjustments are made, the two measures yield similar, if not identical, estimates of the number of crimes

that occur in the United States at a given point in time (Biderman and Lynch, 1991).[1]

The "dark figure" of crimes not known to the police helps to explain the divergence in crime *levels* measured in the UCR and NCVS, but not in crime *trends*. Even when adjusted for crimes victims say they reported to the police, UCR and NCVS crime rates continue to diverge over time. O'Brien (1996) has shown that UCR and NCVS violent crime rates were negatively correlated with one another between 1973 and 1992, even when comparisons are limited to NCVS incidents reported to the police. The only exception is robbery, for which the bivariate correlation is positive but small ($r = .20$) and nonsignificant. In general, the UCR violent crime rates trended upward over the 25-year period, and the NCVS rates declined.

When the UCR and NCVS violent crime series are detrended through first-differencing, the pattern of negative correlations disappears. All of the correlations become positive, and those for two of the violent crimes (robbery and aggravated assault with injury) are statistically significant (O'Brien, 1996, pp. 189–193). This result suggests that the two crime series converge, if modestly in some cases, in their year-to-year differences but diverge in their multiyear trends. O'Brien (1996) argued that the best explanation for the contrasting trends in UCR and NCVS violent crimes is heightened "police productivity" over time (see also Blumstein et al., 1991, 1992; Jencks, 1991).

According to the productivity hypothesis, with the widespread adoption of the 911 emergency system, increased computerization of patrol dispatch and crime records, and greater sensitivity to violence against women, the police record more crimes than in the past. Importantly, to account for the contrasting trends in the UCR and NCVS series, increased police efficiency in crime recording must have occurred independently of both the *incidence* of criminal victimization and the *reporting* of crimes to the police. This implies that the police have not only become more aware of putative crimes over time but also are less

---

[1]   The two measures will never yield identical crime estimates, because the UCR counts all crimes known to the police, regardless of the victim's age, whereas the NCVS count is restricted to victims aged 12 and older. Moreover, Addington (Chapter 8, this volume) shows the limits of our current ability to identify commercial crimes in the UCR.

likely to "unfound" reports of criminal incidents and exclude them from official crime counts.

Direct evidence that changes in police crime recording explain the divergence in UCR and NCVS national crime trends would require investigation of the records of a representative sample of police departments over a lengthy time period – a daunting research challenge. Even then, such a study would miss "unfounded" events for which no record exists. Because founding an event as a crime typically initiates the creation of a criminal incident report, the number of missing cases very likely would be large and would vary according to departmental procedures for documenting calls for service that do not result in an incident report.

The founding of reports as criminal incidents is part of a broader crime classification process in which all law enforcement agencies engage. Once they determine an event qualifies as criminal, the police then must classify it as a particular crime type, a process that necessarily involves discretion. The UCR program provides standard crime classification guidelines to reporting agencies, but this does not guarantee reliability in the way different agencies, or a single agency over time, classify crimes, even the serious Part I offenses that comprise the UCR's Crime Index. The Part I offense that arguably is subject to the greatest discretion is the heterogeneous category of "aggravated assault" (see Blumstein, 1998, p. 949). The UCR defines aggravated assault as "an unlawful attack by one person upon another for the purpose of inflicting severe or aggravated bodily injury. This type of assault usually is accompanied by the use of a weapon or by means likely to produce death or great bodily harm. Simple assaults are excluded." The UCR goes on to define simple assault, a Part II offense, as "assaults and attempted assaults which are not of an aggravated nature and do not result in serious injury to the victim" (http://www.fbi.gov/ucr/cius_03/pdf/03sec7.pdf).

It is not difficult to see how such definitions, even when applied by trained analysts, may result in different classifications of the same event. Some departments may choose to limit the category of aggravated assaults to only those cases involving a weapon or relegate all attempted assaults to the category of simple assault. Reasonable differences may exist over what degree of force is required to produce actually or potentially "severe" injury or "great bodily harm." More pertinent to the issue of how classification procedures may affect crime trends, agencies may "upgrade" the classification of particular crimes over time, such that events that had been routinely classified in a less serious category (e.g., simple assault) are classified in a more serious category (e.g., aggravated assault). The "downgrading" of incidents from more to less serious crime categories also may occur.

O'Brien's (1996) police productivity hypothesis is consistent with the upgrading of violent crimes by the police over time. Given the amount of police discretion in the classification of assaults and increased attention to assaults involving female victims, we might expect to observe especially steep upgrading in UCR assaults from the category of "simple" to "aggravated." As the police have gotten tougher on domestic assaults through mandatory or pro-arrest policies and specialized victim assistance units, more events that law enforcement agencies would not have founded as crimes in the past are likely to be classified as criminal assaults and a greater proportion of them classified as aggravated rather than simple assaults. As Walker (1985, p. 31) has observed, "get-tough" movements primarily affect how the police handle *less* serious events, because they presumably have been tough on serious crime all along (for evidence on the handling of domestic disturbances, see Lanza-Kaduce et al., 1995). Therefore, the growth over time in the UCR aggravated assaults would be expected to occur among less serious cases, perhaps especially those not involving weapons.

Importantly, we would not expect to observe as much upgrading in the NCVS assaults, primarily because NCVS interview and computerized coding procedures are more systematic and standardized than the crime classification practices of the thousands of police agencies that report to state or the national UCR program. The NCVS definitions of aggravated and simple assault are very similar to the UCR definitions.[2] The NCVS underwent a significant redesign in 1992, however,

---

[2] One difference is that the NCVS definition of aggravated assault explicitly includes attempted assaults, whereas the corresponding UCR definition does not. Both definitions include weapon use as an aggravating circumstance. For the NCVS definition of aggravated and simple assaults, see the NCVS criminal victimization glossary at http://www.ojp.usdoj.gov/bjs/pub/ascii/cvus/cvuso2mt.txt.

adding screening questions that did result in increases in estimated assaults as well as other violent crimes (Kindermann et al., 1997). The possible effects of the redesign must be taken into account when comparing UCR and NCVS violent crime trends before and after 1992 (see Chapter 5, this volume).

THE PRESENT STUDY

Extending prior research on the divergence of UCR and NCVS trends in violent crime, this study examines UCR and NCVS aggravated assault trends from 1980 to 2001. After documenting divergence in UCR and NCVS aggravated assault rates over time (with adjustments for effects of the NCVS redesign), I evaluate the hypothesis that the divergence is due to the upgrading of less serious events in the UCR by partitioning both the UCR and NCVS time series into aggravated assaults committed with and without a gun. The more serious UCR and NCVS gun assaults are expected to track one another closely, whereas divergence between the UCR and NCVS should be limited to the less serious nongun incidents, a result consistent with the expectation that changes in police crime recording practices have led to the upgrading of a growing proportion of less serious (i.e., nongun) simple assaults to aggravated assaults.

Specifically, the study examines the following empirical expectations based on the assumption that police agencies have upgraded less serious events over time:

> H_1: *The ratio of nongun to gun aggravated assaults should increase over the 1980–2001 period in the UCR relative to the ratio of nongun to gun events in the NCVS.*
>
> H_2: *UCR and NCVS gun assaults should exhibit similar time trends.*
>
> H_3: *Time trends in UCR and NCVS nongun assaults should diverge, with a greater increase observed in the UCR series.*

Finally, the expected upgrading of assaults by the police should have diminished in recent years as police classification practices stabilize around new conceptions of crime seriousness (cf. O'Brien, 1996, pp. 201–203). In addition, by producing a greater increase in nongun

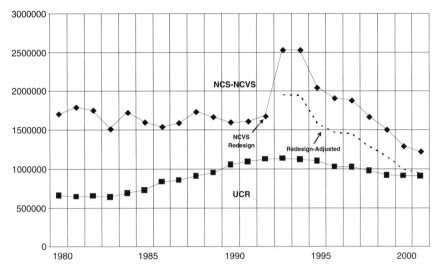

Figure 9.1. Uniform Crime Reports (UCR) and National Crime Survey-National Crime Victimization Survey (NCS-NCVS) aggravated assaults, 1980–2001.

than gun assaults, the NCVS redesign in the early 1990s may have contributed to growing convergence between UCR and NCVS aggravated assaults. Therefore:

> H_4: Both the nongun and total UCR and NCVS aggravated assault series should show diminishing divergence during latter part of the 1980–2001 period.

UCR AND NCVS AGGRAVATED ASSAULT TRENDS

As revealed in prior research, marked divergence exists in the UCR and NCVS aggravated assault trends. Previous studies compare the series only through the early 1990s (Blumstein, 1998; O'Brien, 1996). Figure 9.1 extends the comparison through 2001.

As shown in Figure 9.1, the NCVS series is essentially flat through the 1980s at roughly 1.5–1.7 million estimated aggravated assaults per year, whereas the UCR aggravated assaults trend steadily upward to 1 million events in 1990 from about 0.6 million in 1980, an increase of about two-thirds. Both series decline during the following decade, although a less pronounced drop is evident in the UCR than the NCVS. The correlation between the two series over the entire period is modest and not quite statistically significant at the 0.05 level ($r = .411$, $p = .058$).[3]

It turns out that all of this relationship between the two series is confined to the latter years in the period. If the series are divided at 1992 into pre- and post-redesign subperiods, the correlation between the UCR and NCVS aggravated assaults for the earlier period is actually negative ($r_{80-92} = -.229$) and nonsignificant. By striking contrast, the two series are almost perfectly correlated after the redesign ($r_{93-01} = .969$, $p < .001$). These results match those of prior research on divergence between UCR and NCVS aggravated assault trends and provide some indication of diminishing divergence over time. Before conclusions can be drawn about the temporal relationship between the two indicators, however, it is necessary to account for the possible effects on that relationship of the NCVS redesign.

TAKING ACCOUNT OF THE REDESIGN

Screening questions in the NCS were modified in 1992 to reduce the underreporting of victimizations, especially sex crimes and domestic violence. To assess the effect of the survey revisions on estimated victimization counts, Bureau of Justice Statistics researchers divided the 1992 sample in half. One-half of the respondents received the prior NCS, and the other half received the new NCVS. As expected, the revised survey increased the number of reported victimizations, and the increases were greater, not surprisingly, for less serious incidents. The increase in the number of simple assaults reported by respondents (75%) is more than three times the increase in aggravated assaults (23%) in the redesigned survey (both differences are significant at the .10 level; Kindermann et al., 1997). To be sure, less serious incidents do not account for all of the increase in reported crimes produced by the redesign. The redesign was intended to uncover crimes respondents may not have regarded as "serious" enough to merit reporting under the former screening questions because, for example, they were committed by an acquaintance and not because they were harmless or trivial. Furthermore, only the screening items were changed in the

---

[3]   All p values reported in the text are based on two-tailed tests. The annual NCVS and UCR data summarized in the text are presented in the Appendix.

redesigned survey, not the definitions of the crimes or procedures for classifying and coding them. Still, given the much sharper increase in simple than aggravated assaults after the redesign, it is reasonable to suppose that the redesign in effect produced greater reporting of the less serious aggravated assaults, in this study defined as attacks or threats without a firearm.

To determine the impact of the redesign on the NCVS aggravated assault trend, the NCVS aggravated assault counts for 1993 to 2001 were adjusted downward by a factor of .23, represented by the dashed line in Figure 9.1. Although the redesign produced appreciable growth in NCVS aggravated assaults, they would have increased anyway by about 22% from 1.6 million in 1991 to 1.95 million in 1993. Roughly half of the observed increase in the NCVS over the two years, then, was due to the redesign and the other half to growth in aggravated assaults reported by NCVS respondents.

The observed NCVS aggravated assaults were stationary through 1994 and then dropped sharply over the next seven years. Because the adjusted series is produced by a constant (the same redesign adjustment factor is applied each year), its rate of decline is identical, although it begins from a lower peak. For the same reason, the correlation between the adjusted NCVS and UCR aggravated assaults is the same as that between the observed NCVS and UCR counts after the redesign ($r_{93-01} = .969$).

The redesign did alter somewhat the relationship between the two aggravated assault series over the entire 1980–2001 period, however. Recall that the UCR and the observed NCVS series are moderately correlated ($r = .411$). Even this modest relationship between the two aggravated assault series trends appears to be a consequence of the redesign. When the adjusted values are substituted for the observed NCVS values after 1992, the correlation between the two series for the full period drops to zero ($r = -.01$). One plausible interpretation of this result is that by adding less serious incidents to the NCVS aggravated assault counts, the redesign replicated the effects of the upgrading process in the UCR series, producing a small relationship between the two series whereas, absent the redesign, there would have been none at all.

General conclusions about the divergence between the UCR and NCVS aggravated assault series are largely unaffected by the NCVS redesign. The series exhibit pronounced divergence through the early 1990s and convergence thereafter, some of which may have been due to diminished upgrading in police classification of assaults in recent years and some to the intended effect of the NCVS redesign in reducing respondent underreporting of crimes.

PARTITIONING GUN AND NONGUN ASSAULTS

If upgrading occurred in police-recorded assaults during the 1980s and 1990s, we should observe greater growth over time in less serious incidents. Weapon use, by definition, distinguishes aggravated from simple assaults in both the UCR and NCVS. It is a safe bet that police recording of assaults involving firearms has changed less over the past 25 years than the recording and classification of the more heterogeneous category of nongun assaults, including those involving other weapons such as knives or clubs. To test this assumption, I partitioned the UCR and NCVS yearly aggravated assault series into gun-related and nongun incidents. Upgrading in police recording should be reflected in a rising ratio of nongun to gun incidents in the UCR between 1980 and 2001, whereas the nongun versus gun ratio in the NCVS series should not display similar growth over time – with the possible exception of the post-redesign period. Figure 9.2 shows the ratio of nongun to gun aggravated assaults in the two series.

For the 1980–2001 period as a whole, the ratio of nongun to gun incidents grew in the UCR series, whereas the trend in the NCVS nongun to gun ratio is negative but nonsignificant. This result supports the expectation in H_1 of relative growth in UCR nongun aggravated assaults.

Yet it is apparent from Figure 9.2 that all of this growth has occurred since the early 1990s. Two distinct subperiods characterize both the UCR and NCVS nongun to gun ratios, an earlier period of relatively little change and the more recent period when the ratio rises. If the full 22-year period is divided at the NCVS redesign, and linear time trends are estimated for the nongun to gun ratios during the pre-redesign period, no discernible trend is evident in the UCR ratio ($b_{80-92} = -.008$, $p = .690$), whereas the NCVS nongun to gun ratio exhibits a small, negative trend significant at the .05 level ($b_{80-92} = -.063$, $p = .038$). This result suggests modest divergence consistent with the

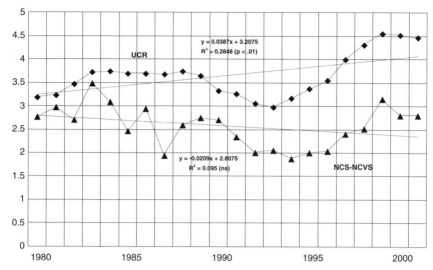

Figure 9.2. Ratio of nongun to gun assaults in the Uniform Crime Reports (UCR) and National Crime Survey-National Crime Victimization Survey (NCS-NCVS), 1980–2001.

upgrading of less serious nongun incidents in police-recorded assaults during the earlier period.

By contrast, relative growth in nongun aggravated assaults characterizes both the UCR and NCVS after the NCVS redesign. Between 1993 and 2001, the nongun to gun ratio rose in both the UCR ($b = .219$, $p < .001$) and the NCVS ($b = .142$, $p = .002$), with roughly 50% greater average growth in the UCR. Taken together, the results for the earlier and more recent periods offer additional evidence of diminished divergence between UCR and NCVS aggravated assaults over time. If the upgrading hypothesis is correct, most of the growing relationship between the UCR and NCVS aggravated assault trends should have occurred in the nongun category, whereas UCR and NCVS gun assaults should be strongly correlated over the entire 1980–2001 period.

Convergence in UCR and NCVS Gun Assaults

Changes in police crime recording and classification practices should have much less effect on trends in gun-related aggravated assaults. Gun assaults in the UCR and NCVS, then, should track one another closely, showing little of the divergence evident in the relationship between

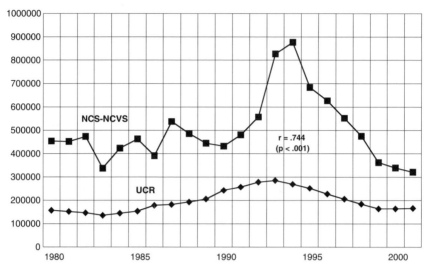

Figure 9.3. Uniform Crime Reports (UCR) and National Crime Survey-National Crime Victimization Survey (NCS-NCVS) gun assaults, 1980–2001.

total UCR and NCVS aggravated assaults. Trends in UCR and NCVS aggravated assaults committed with a gun are displayed in Figure 9.3.

In fact, a relatively strong association exists between the two gun assault trends between 1980 and 2001 ($r = .744$, $p < .001$). Both series trend upward through the early 1990s and then decline. The relationship between the two gun assault trends is far from perfect. Although they share more than 50% common variance, the NCVS series is "noisier" during the 1980s, and they peak a year apart (the UCR in 1993, the NCVS in 1994). They tell essentially the same story, however, about national trends in gun assaults during the past two decades. Existing explanations of the rise and fall of firearm violence in the United States would differ little depending on whether they were based on UCR or NCVS gun assault trends (Blumstein and Wallman, 2000; Rosenfeld, 2004).

Divergence in UCR and NCVS Nongun Assaults

The same cannot be said for the UCR and NCVS nongun assault trends, which are not significantly correlated between 1980 and 2001 ($r = .157$, $p = .486$). As shown in Figure 9.4, UCR nongun assaults increased from 1980 through the early 1990s and decreased slightly thereafter. NCVS

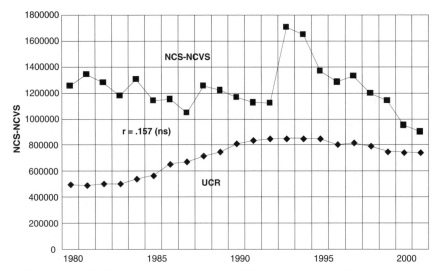

Figure 9.4. Uniform Crime Reports (UCR) and National Crime Survey-National Crime Victimization Survey (NCS-NCVS) nongun assaults, 1980–2001.

nongun assaults decreased somewhat during the 1980s, rose sharply after the 1992 redesign, and then fell through 2001.

It is difficult to determine precisely how much of the increase in the NCVS nongun series is attributable to the redesign, because separate estimates of redesign effects on gun and nongun crimes are unavailable. However, a reasonable assumption is that the increase in NCVS nongun aggravated assaults after the redesign is bounded by that for simple assaults (75%) and total aggravated assaults (23%). If the increase in nongun incidents is situated midway between those two values (49%), and the NCVS nongun assaults after 1992 are scaled down accordingly, the resulting correlation between the two nongun series over the 22-year period is significantly negative ($r = -.590$, $p = .004$). Speculatively, then, it appears that the NCVS redesign may have reduced the divergence between the two nongun aggravated assault trends.

IMPLICATIONS

The present study replicates findings from previous research showing that the UCR and NCVS aggravated assault trends have diverged over time, with the UCR series showing greater growth than the NCVS series. For both research and policy purposes, it is important to understand the reasons for this divergence. A prominent hypothesis is that law enforcement agencies have become more productive in recording crimes with the advent of 911 reporting, increased computerization of crime reports, and greater sensitivity to violence against women (O'Brien, 1996). Because these changes are more likely to have resulted in increases in less serious incidents, I hypothesized that the divergence between the trends in UCR and NCVS aggravated assaults is confined mainly to incidents without a gun and that gun-related assaults in the two series exhibit greater convergence. In addition, I expected to find diminishing divergence over time between the UCR and NCVS time trends, in part due to stabilization in the "upgrading" of crimes by the police and also to the inclusion of less serious incidents in the NCVS aggravated assault series after the 1992 redesign.

The results offer support for each of these expectations. The UCR and NCVS aggravated assault trends display the expected divergence between 1980 and 2001. When gun and nongun aggravated assaults are examined separately, however, greater relative growth is observed in the UCR nongun incidents, and the time trends in gun assaults are more closely related than the trends in nongun assaults. The results also show diminishing divergence over time between the UCR and NCVS aggravated assaults, consistent with the expectation that changes in police crime recording and classification have stabilized. Adjustments for the effects of the NCVS redesign also imply that some of the growing convergence between the two series results from greater growth since 1992 in less serious incidents included in the NCVS aggravated assault category.

The case for crime "upgrading" in the UCR or the NCVS must remain circumstantial until the crime recording and classification practices of representative law enforcement agencies are directly inspected and more precise estimates are available regarding the effects of the NCVS redesign on the growth in less serious crimes. In addition, the present results are limited to the issue of divergence between UCR and NCVS victimization trends and not levels.

Nonetheless, the results are promising in two important respects. First, they offer evidence for the assumption that the nation's two major crime indicators provide similar estimates of change over time in serious crime.[4] Second, they suggest that divergence between crime trends in less serious crimes based on the two indicators has diminished in recent years. If so, and future research confirms the hypothesis of crime upgrading in both the UCR and NCVS, a broader complementarity between the two crime indicators is suggested.

Discussions of the measurement properties of the two indicators generally conclude that UCR crimes are more heavily "filtered" than are criminal victimizations reported to the NCVS (e.g., O'Brien, 1996, p. 189). To become part of the UCR crime count, a victim must decide to report an incident to the police, and the police must decide whether the incident qualifies as a "crime." If the incident is founded as a crime, the police must then determine what type of crime it is, and, finally, must report it to the UCR within the appropriate offense category. Ample room for error or discretion exists at each stage, and measurement error is multiplied across thousands of reporting agencies, which may choose without sanction not to report at all. The major filter, then, between the victim's experience of a crime and its inclusion in the UCR crime statistics is the crime-recording procedures and practices of the police – and that filter is absent from the NCVS.

But it would be incorrect to conclude that (1) the NCVS is "unfiltered" or (2) the effects of filtering on crime trends always or necessarily differ between the UCR and the NCVS. The NCVS also includes a "founding" process in the screening questions and also classifies incidents by offense type. There is little question that crime recording and classification are more reliable in the NCVS than the UCR, but as in the UCR, they are subject to exogenous influences that may be unrelated to "objective" changes in victimization. Funded by Congress and housed in the Department of Justice, the NCVS is hardly immune to political influence. The addition of items on hate crime victimization and crimes against the disabled are two examples of how the crime survey has been modified in response to external stimulus (Lauritsen, 2005). The NCVS redesign is another example.

---

4   Unfortunately, additional evidence of crime seriousness, such as injury, is not available in the UCR, and of course lethal assaults are not included in the NCVS.

Both the UCR and the NCVS have been affected by the "revolution in public attitudes toward domestic violence" (Walker, 1999, p. 105). In both cases, the likely consequence has been crime upgrading producing greater growth over time in less serious incidents, not necessarily limited to domestic assaults. The effect of upgrading on crime trends is time-limited, and so the two series have begun to converge again in the heterogeneous category of aggravated assault. But because, like all social indicators, both UCR and NCVS crime rates are socially constructed and susceptible to political influence, we should not be surprised when they diverge again.

APPENDIX. *Uniform Crime Reports (UCR) and National Crime Survey-National Crime Victimization Survey (NCS-NCVS) aggravated assaults by gun involvement, 1980–2001*

	UCR			NCS-NCVS		
	Total	Gun	Nongun	Total	Gun	Nongun
1980	654,957	156,535	498,422	1,706,900	452,755	1,254,145
1981	643,720	151,918	491,802	1,795,800	452,448	1,343,352
1982	650,042	145,609	504,433	1,754,300	473,243	1,281,057
1983	639,532	135,581	503,951	1,517,310	337,935	1,179,375
1984	685,349	144,609	540,740	1,727,300	422,666	1,304,634
1985	723,246	154,051	569,195	1,605,170	463,262	1,141,908
1986	834,322	177,711	656,611	1,542,870	390,522	1,152,348
1987	855,088	182,989	672,099	1,587,460	537,850	1,049,610
1988	910,092	192,029	718,063	1,741,380	485,124	1,256,256
1989	951,707	204,617	747,090	1,664,710	444,056	1,220,654
1990	1,054,863	243673	811,190	1,600,670	432,008	1,168,662
1991	1,092,739	256794	835,945	1,608,580	481,049	1,127,531
1992	1,126,974	278,363	848,611	1,680,182	557,723	1,122,459
1993	1,135,099	284,910	850,189	2,532,303	827,486	1,704,817
1994	1,119,950	268,788	851,162	2,526,588	876,894	1,649,694
1995	1,099,179	251,712	847,467	2,049,831	683,131	1,366,700
1996	1,029,814	226,559	803,255	1,910,368	627,378	1,282,990
1997	1,022,492	204,498	817,994	1,883,111	552,028	1,331,083
1998	974,402	183,188	791,214	1,673,641	475,425	1,198,216
1999	916,383	164,949	751,434	1,503,277	362,098	1,141,179
2000	910,744	164,845	745,899	1,292,512	339,869	952,643
2001	907,219	166,021	741,198	1,222,163	321,305	900,858

Sources: Uniform Crime Reports (http://www.fbi.gov/ucr/ucr.htm#cius), 1995–2001; Federal Bureau of Investigation (annual), 1980–1994; National Crime Victimization Survey http://www.ojp.usdoj.gov/bjs/cvict.htm), 1993–2001; Bureau of Justice Statistics (annual) 1980–1992.

References

Biderman, A. D., & Lynch, J. P. (1991). *Understanding crime incidence statistics: Why the UCR diverges from the NCS.* New York: Springer.

Blumstein, A. (1998). "Violence certainly is the problem – and especially with hand guns." *University of Colorado Law Review* 69:945–965.

Blumstein, A., Cohen, J., & Rosenfeld, R. (1991). "Trend and deviation in crime rates: A comparison of UCR and NCS data for burglary and robbery." *Criminology* 29:237–263.

Blumstein, A., Cohen, J., & Rosenfeld, R. (1992). "The UCR-NCS relationship revisited: A reply to Menard." *Criminology* 30:115–124.

Blumstein, A., & Wallman, J. (2000). *The crime drop in America.* New York: Cambridge University Press.

Bureau of Justice Statistics. (Annual). *Criminal victimization in the United States.* Washington, DC: U.S. Department of Justice.

Federal Bureau of Investigation. (Annual). *Crime in the United States.* Washington, DC: U.S. Government Printing Office.

Jencks, C. (1991). "Is violent crime increasing?" *American Prospect* (winter):98–109.

Kindermann, C., Lynch, J., & Cantor, D. (1997). *Effects of the redesign on victimization estimates.* Washington, DC: U.S. Department of Justice.

Lanza-Kaduce, L., Greenleaf, R. G., & Armstrong, M. (1995). "Trickle-up report writing: The impact of a proarrest policy for domestic disturbances." *Justice Quarterly* 12:525–542.

Lauritsen, J. L. (2005). "Social and scientific influences on the measurement of criminal victimization." *Journal of Quantitative Criminology* 21:245–266.

Menard, S., & Covey, H. C. (1988). "UCR and NCS: Comparisons over space and time." *Journal of Criminal Justice* 16:371–384.

Messner, S. F. (1984). "The 'dark figure' and composite indices of crime: Some empirical explorations of alternative data sources." *Journal of Criminal Justice* 12:435–444.

O'Brien, R. M. (1985). *Crime and victimization data.* Beverly Hills, CA: Sage.

O'Brien, R. M. (1990). "Comparing detrended UCR and NCS crime rates over time: 1973–1986." *Journal of Criminal Justice* 18:229–238.

O'Brien, R. M. (1996). "Police productivity and crime rates: 1973–1992." *Criminology* 34:183–207.

Rennison, C. M., & Rand, M. R. (2003). *Criminal victimization, 2002.* Washington, DC: U.S. Department of Justice.

Rosenfeld, R. (2004). "The case of the unsolved crime decline." *Scientific American* (February):82–89.

Walker, S. (1985). *Sense and nonsense about crime: A policy guide.* Belmont, CA: Wadsworth.

Walker, S. (1999). *The police in America* (3rd ed.). Boston: McGraw-Hill.

CHAPTER TEN

Missing UCR Data and Divergence of the NCVS and UCR Trends

Michael D. Maltz

INTRODUCTION

The National Crime Survey (NCS, now the National Crime Victimization Survey, or NCVS) was originally designed to provide a check against the crime statistics voluntarily provided to the FBI's Uniform Crime Reporting (UCR) Program by police departments (President's Commission, 1967, p. 21). Pilot surveys (Biderman et al., 1967; Ennis, 1967) had confirmed the widespread belief that many crimes are not reported to the police, the so-called "dark figure" of crime, so a survey would provide information about the nature and extent of unreported crime. Because the survey – which gathers data directly from household residents concerning victimizations they may have experienced over the past six months – provides a more direct check on the true amount of crime, it is considered superior to the UCR for this purpose.

There are also reasons that the UCR may be considered superior to the NCVS. After all, the UCR is a *complete count* of crimes reported to the police, whereas the NCVS is based on a *sample of crimes* recalled by citizens aged 12 years and older, in 45,000 randomly selected households, which occurred within the past 6 months. A complete count has no sampling error, whereas the sampling error for the NCVS exists – and is growing as financial considerations dictate reductions in sample size.[1] Moreover, the detailed nature of UCR reporting makes it

---

[1] The budget for the NCVS has been static for some time, whereas the cost per interview has grown steadily. The Bureau of Justice Statistics (BJS) has been exploring ways of reducing the per-interview cost to maintain a sample size that would provide a sufficiently large sample for statistical significance.

possible to look at specific time patterns (hour of day, day of week or month) and places where crime is occurring, a specificity that is not available using the NCVS.

The UCR has its own set of problems, however. Some police departments may "cook the books" by underreporting the number of crimes reported to them by victims – that is, crimes reported to them by citizens may not be recorded as crimes or may be recorded as less serious crimes. For the most part, the FBI cannot determine when this occurs, so these errors are usually hidden from the FBI's view – and from public scrutiny – except when newspapers uncover them.[2]

Aside from this, for various reasons, a great many police departments are unable to report *all* of their crime statistics to the FBI, sometimes omitting occasional months, sometimes whole years. To put it bluntly, there are large gaps in the UCR data for some agencies and states (Maltz, 1999).

Nor does the FBI keep this a secret; in fact, in *Crime in the United States*, which reports annually on the amount of crime reported by the police, the FBI describes the methodology and the estimation procedures they use to deal with missing data.[3] It has had to make estimates because reporting crime data to the UCR program is largely voluntary.[4] Despite this, researchers, policy makers, and journalists regularly use the UCR data to evaluate programs, policies, and agency efforts. They implicitly assume (implicitly, because few of them even acknowledge that there are any gaps) that the FBI's estimation procedures are adequate for their purposes. But these procedures are not adequate for all purposes; they can and do produce significant errors.

[2] In some cases in the past, the FBI has specifically excluded suspiciously low reports from some agencies.
[3] For example, the 2002 issue of *Crime in the United States* (FBI, 2003, p. 444) states: "Because not all law enforcement agencies provide data for complete reporting periods, the UCR Program includes estimated crime counts in these presentations.... Using the known crime experiences of similar areas within a state, then national Program computes estimates by assigning the same proportional crime volumes to nonreporting agencies." In addition, a lengthy table following this explanation describes problems with the data of entire states that necessitated estimation of their crime totals.
[4] A number of states now require police departments to report crime data to state agencies, which then check the data for consistency and forward the compiled data to the FBI (Maltz, 1999, p. 45). We know of no agency that has received sanctions for not complying with reporting requirements, however.

To summarize, the error structure of the NCVS is well-known and due to issues of sample size and structure, whereas the error structure of the UCR has been largely ignored. Under grants from the National Institute of Justice and the American Statistical Association,[5] we have been working on documenting the errors and developing an improved estimation (or imputation) procedure for the UCR, using the monthly raw data obtained from the FBI, both directly and through the National Archive of Criminal Justice Data (NACJD). This chapter describes the nature and extent of missing data in the UCR, to help in understanding how its unreported data may affect the relationship of UCR and NCVS crime rates.[6]

I first provide some background information about the UCR, which the FBI began collecting in 1930, describing the extent of police reporting over the last few decades and the reasons for nonreporting. The procedures used in cleaning the data are then outlined, showing the different types of "missingness." I then discuss the imputation methods that will be used to compensate for the missing data. I conclude with a discussion of the impact that imputation is expected to have on the utility of the UCR and the extent to which it can be compared with the NCVS.

UCR HISTORY

The International Association of Chiefs of Police (IACP) initiated the collection of crime data in 1929 "... to disclose facts hitherto unknown such as:

1. How much crime there is
2. Its geographical distribution
3. Whether it is on the increase or decrease
4. How it varies for different types of offenses
5. The success obtained by the police in its investigation" (IACP, 1929, p. 20).

---

[5] National Institute of Justice (NIJ) grants 2001–IJ–CX–0006 to the University of Illinois at Chicago and 2004–IJ–CX–0083 to The Ohio State University, and a grant from the American Statistical Association.
[6] By the time this book is published, the complete UCR data set may be available, either through NIJ or the National Archive of Criminal Justice Data.

With the IACP's endorsement, the FBI assumed control of the collection of crime data and absorbed the IACP's UCR Program in the following year, and police departments then started sending monthly tallies of crimes to the FBI. Seven crimes were selected for the FBI's Crime Index, the indicator of how much crime the nation was experiencing: murder, rape, robbery, aggravated assault, burglary, larceny, and auto theft (IACP, 1929, p. 24). These crimes are also known as "Part I" offenses because they were sent in on Part I of Return A, the form used by the FBI to report crime data. These seven crimes were chosen for the Index because they were considered both serious and most likely to be reported to the police.[7] They were (and are) sent to the FBI on a monthly basis.

Part II crimes were considered either less serious or less likely to be reported to the police. They include other assaults, forgery, sex offenses, substance abuse, and gambling, and are not given the same play as the Part I crimes (the Crime Index), either in the media or by researchers and policy analysts.

The number of participating police departments has grown considerably over the years: there were about 700 reporting agencies in the first year (Bureau of Investigation, 1930, p. 4),[8] but they number over 17,000 today (FBI, 2003, p. 3). Even with this high number, however, there are some agencies in the United States that have never provided crime data to the FBI; the extent to which this is the case has never been investigated.[9]

For the first two years the FBI provided monthly crime reports – then quarterly from 1932 to 1941, and semiannually from 1943 to 1957. At first the reports gave crime statistics for individual agencies, but this soon changed. By 1934 the population represented in the returns amounted to 96 percent of the population in cities over 10,000 and

---

[7] "For example, arson and buying or receiving stolen property are serious offenses but so frequently concealed that the number of known offenses would be no index of their actual prevalence" (IACP, 1929, p. 182). This did not stop Congress from mandating that arson be included in the Crime Index in 1979. The FBI deals with this by publishing two figures, the Crime Index (without arson) and the Modified Crime Index (with arson), which is largely ignored.

[8] The FBI was originally known as the Bureau of Investigation; its name changed in 1935.

[9] James Lynch, personal communication, May 2005.

TABLE 10.1. *FBI population categories*

Geographic divisions	States included	Population groups	Population range
New England	ME, NH, VT, MA, RI, CT	Group I	Cities over 250,000
Middle Atlantic	NY, NJ, PA	Group II	Cities 100,000 to 250,000
East North Central	OH, IN, IL, MI, WI	Group III	Cities 50,000 to 100,000
West North Central	MN, IA, ND, SD, NE, KS	Group IV	Cities 25,000 to 50,000
South Atlantic	DE, MD, VA, WV, NC, SC, GA, FL	Group V	Cities 10,000 to 25,000
East South Central	KY, TN, AL, MS	Group VI	Cities under 10,000
West South Central	AR, LA, OK, TX	**	
Mountain	MT, ID, WY, CO, NM, AZ, UT, NV		
Pacific	WA, OR, CA*		

*Alaska and Hawaii became states in 1959.

** Group VII, now included in Group VI, consists of cities under 2,500 and universities and colleges to which no population is attributed. The following groups were added later: Group VIII consists of rural counties and state police, to which no population is attributed, and Group IX consists of suburban counties.

88 percent of the total U.S. population (FBI, 1935, p. 2), and estimates were provided of the amount of crime by geographic division and (for states with the largest number of reporters) by population group (see Table 10.1). Nonreporting was not factored into the calculations, however; the rates were based on the reported crimes and populations of the contributing agencies. In 1942 the reports began to be issued semiannually, with most attention focused on the annual report. About 15 years later, the FBI established a Consultant Committee to provide advice on improving the UCR (Lejins et al., 1958). Based on the committee's recommendations, the FBI began producing *Crime in the United States* in 1958, which made annual estimates of the crime rates for individual states, for metropolitan areas, and for the nation as a whole. To do so, however, the FBI had to deal with gaps in the UCR data due to nonreporting.

To handle the gaps, the Consultant Committee recommended a simple imputation method (Lejins et al., 1958, p. 46): "The number of reported offenses should then be proportionately increased to take care of the unreported portions, if any, of these same [Index] categories within each state." The recommendation was generally adopted, and this imputation method continues to be used to this day.

As the number of agencies providing UCR reports grew, it became more difficult for the FBI to process the monthly data from individual agencies. From 1970 on, with the encouragement of the FBI and with funding from the Bureau of Justice Statistics (BJS), states began to centralize the collection of their agencies' crime data for transmittal to the FBI. In some of these states, agencies were required to report their crime data, but in others (and in all states that have not centralized their crime data collection), reporting crime to the FBI is still voluntary.[10]

NONREPORTING BY POLICE DEPARTMENTS

There are various definitions of non-reporting or missingness that can be used in the UCR. In general, data are regarded as missing when agencies that should report crime to the UCR do not. This can be extended to include data that are reported but not at the prescribed time or for the appropriate place. Missingness under the first definition occurs when an agency that has crimes to report simply does not report them at all for those months or years. Under the second definition, data are missing when they are reported but not in the month that they occurred or not by the jurisdiction in which they occurred. Some agencies, for example, will report all of the crimes for a calendar year in December of that year rather than in the reports for the months when the crimes became known to the police. With regard to errors of

---

[10] This practice is not new. The first issue of *Uniform Crime Reports for the United States and Its Possessions* (Bureau of Investigation, 1930, p. 1) stated, "At this time the attention of contributors of crime data is invited to the practice prevailing in certain States whereby the State bureau of identification or other similar agency compiles the crime returns and transmits the reports to this bureau. Through the medium of State control, greater accuracy and comprehensiveness will be assured. This practice has been adopted by the States of Ohio and Utah and the results have been encouraging." These states subsequently terminated statewide collection of UCR data. After a long hiatus, Utah recommenced centralized reporting in 1994, and Ohio did so in 1976, only to stop in 1986.

Percent Coverage

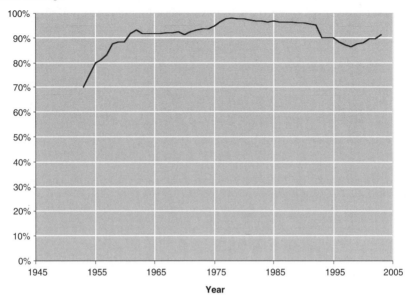

Figure 10.1. Percent of U.S. population covered by UCR.

place, some agencies do not report crimes occurring in their jurisdictions to the UCR but rely on other agencies to do so. Although these crimes are ultimately reported, they are not recorded as occurring in the appropriate location. Data missing under the first definition of missingness will affect all uses of the UCR data, whereas errors of time and place will only affect certain uses of the data. Errors of time and place can affect uses of the data that put a premium on knowing the month and jurisdiction of occurrence, but not on national estimates.

At first glance, the reporting of crime data by police departments appears to be quite good. As seen in Figure 10.1 (based on data in the annual reports, *Crime in the United States*), it seems to hover around 90 percent: from the mid-1950s to the end of the century the extent of crime reporting at first grew (in 1978 more than 98 percent of the population was policed by agencies that submitted reports to the FBI) and subsequently decreased; see Figure 10.1. More recently, it has begun to increase again: in 2003, it grew to 91 percent.

Although this statistic seems impressive, especially for a voluntary reporting program, it should be tempered with the knowledge that this is a count of the population covered by agencies that submitted *at least one monthly report* to the FBI. And some agencies submit reports for only one month – just to ensure that the agency's employee statistics will be included in the annual FBI report – so its crime data for the missing months is imputed (Maltz, 1999, p. 17). This figure, then, is an overestimate of how much actual crime reporting takes place. There is a saving grace, however: for the most part, those agencies that make it a practice of not submitting reports (or of submitting only one month's report) have little crime to report.

But there have been times when entire states have not reported their crime data to the FBI. On average, one state represents 2 percent of the total UCR data, so even the reduction of a few percent in overall reporting might mean that an entire state is missing, as has happened all too often (Figure 10.2).

There are a number of ways that reporting of crime data is not complete, and these patterns of missing data have implications for the kinds of remedial action that can be taken. Missing data are often classified as missing completely at random (MCAR), missing at random (MAR), and not missing at random (MNAR) (Little and Rubin, 1987). Data are missing completely at random when the probability of being missing is unrelated to crime and unrelated to any other factors. To be missing at random (as opposed to completely at random), the probability of being missing is correlated with crime in the bivariate case but unrelated to crime when other factors in the data set are held constant. When data are not missing at random, then the probability of being missing is related to crime, and this relationship persists even when other factors in the data are taken into account. When data are MCAR, they can easily be imputed, just by assuming that the statistics of these missing data are similar to the actual data. When data are missing at random, then models for imputing missing data can be developed. Data that are MNAR cannot be imputed in the customary ways. It is appears to be the case that the missing data rarely are MAR, let alone MCAR. This means that different imputation schemes have to be devised to account for the different kinds of missingness. The primary reasons for missing data follow, according to whether they are more likely to be MCAR, MAR, or MNAR.

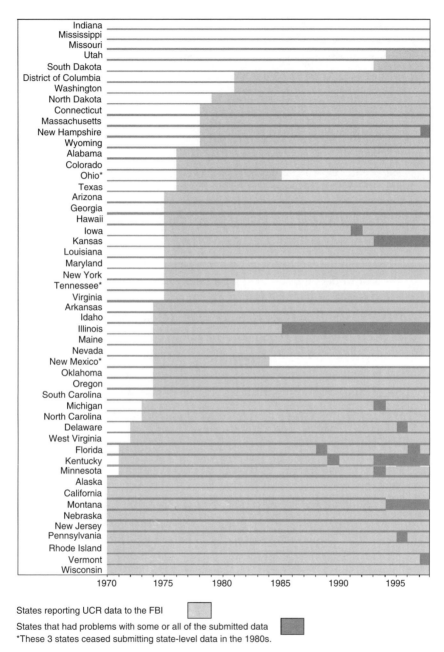

States reporting UCR data to the FBI

States that had problems with some or all of the submitted data
*These 3 states ceased submitting state-level data in the 1980s.

Figure 10.2. State crime reporting history.

Missing Completely at Random (MCAR)

1. Natural Disaster. While it is not a common occurrence, natural disasters can affect agency reporting. The State of Kentucky was unable to report four years of crime data due to a flood that damaged its computers.

Missing at Random (MAR)

1. Computer Problems. In the early 1980s the FBI studied the feasibility of replacing the UCR with a more complete reporting system, one that would marry the increased need for specificity in crime data with the increased ability of computers to store and analyze complex data. The result of their investigation was a report (Poggio et al., 1985) that recommended the development of incident-based reporting. The National Incident-Based Reporting System (NIBRS) was soon adopted by the FBI to become the next generation of crime reporting and is currently used by agencies policing about 20 percent (and growing) of the U.S. population (see Chapter 3, this volume).

NIBRS is much more comprehensive in its collection of data. Right now an agency's monthly report of Part I crime is on one sheet of paper: x murders, y rapes, . . . ; z unfounded murders, q unfounded rapes, . . . and so on. But NIBRS reports the details of each crime. That is, each crime may have six record types associated with it (Akiyama and Nolan, 1999). There is an administrative record and separate records to describe each victim, each offender, each offense, each element of property associated with the crime (cars, drugs, stolen items), and each arrestee.

The architecture of the software to handle NIBRS is complicated. Software companies looking to tap the police market developed products that they thought could readily handle the NIBRS system (and produce UCR summary crime reports as a simple by-product); however, most of them were overly optimistic in terms of both the ease of development and the time it would take to complete. As a consequence, many agencies and states were left high and dry with incomplete software solutions, with no means of reporting either the (summary) UCR data or the more complicated NIBRS data. The net result of this has been missing data from agencies as they converted to NIBRS.

2. Noncompliance With UCR Standards. Some agencies do not follow the UCR reporting guidelines and therefore have their crime data estimated by the FBI. This is notably true of the crime statistics in Illinois, which since 1985 has not followed UCR guidelines in reporting rape data. Specifically, by law Illinois does not distinguish in its reports from male-on-male sexual assault and male-on-female sexual assault. (Its promised conversion to NIBRS should correct this situation.)

Missing Not at Random (MNAR)

1. Undercoverage. Some agencies have never reported their crime data to the FBI. Although little specific information is known about these agencies, most of them are probably quite small.

2. Nothing to Report. Some agencies with no crime for many months omit sending those months' reports to the FBI. This is especially true of agencies in states that do not centralize FBI reporting or require reporting to state agencies.

3. Administrative Issues. Agencies may not provide crime reports for every month to the FBI for a host of administrative reasons (Maltz, 1999, p. 116). The officers assigned to deal with crime statistics may be transferred or promoted, leaving others to learn the ropes, and it may take a few months before the new personnel understand the data collection and reporting intricacies. In addition, the agency may face budgetary problems or be under pressure to return more officers to the street. In these situations, it is not uncommon for a reporting gap of a few months to occur.

4. Coding Errors. In our analysis of the raw UCR data, we found negative numbers of crimes for some months. A related issue was the discovery of impossibly large numbers of crimes for some months, as can be seen in Figure 10.3. A crime-by-crime analysis of the data showed the number of crimes to be 9,999 (see accompanying table to Figure 10.3), which is used in many statistical programs to indicate missing data. These coding errors were recorded as missing data. Because agencies differ in their data auditing ability, these errors are likely to be associated with agency size and automation.

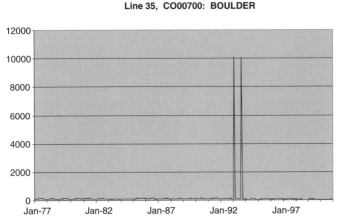

Figure 10.3. Incorrect reported crime data.

5. Unrecorded Crimes. As mentioned earlier, some police departments have pressure put on them to reduce crime by either not reporting or downgrading crimes reported to them by citizens. For example, an aggravated assault, which is one of the seven crimes included in the Crime Index, may be downgraded to simple assault, a crime category that is not included in the Index. In the early 1970s, Seidman and Couzens (1974; see also "Crime in Capital," 1972) found that many larcenies in Washington, DC, that should have been valued at over $50 – at the time "larceny $50 and over" was an Index crime – were downgraded to "larceny under $50," a crime not in the Index. As a consequence, the FBI changed the Index category "larceny" to include all larcenies.

More recently, police departments in Boca Raton, Atlanta, New York, Philadelphia, Broward County (Florida), and St. Louis have apparently been underreporting their crime data.[11] In other words, this is a continuing problem; unfortunately, it is not one that can be easily detected and accounted for statistically.

---

[11] See the *Miami Herald,* May 3, 1998, "Sugarcoating? Officer faked Boca crime statistics"; *Atlanta Journal-Constitution,* May 21, 1998, "Manipulation of crime figures alleged"; *New York Times,* August 3, 1998, "As crime falls, pressure rises to alter data"; *Philadelphia Inquirer,* November 1, 1998, "How to cut city's crime rate: Don't report it"; *Miami Herald,* April 9, 2004, "Crime stats show sudden rise"; *Miami Herald,* April 11, 2004, "Crime software putting policing in flux"; *St. Louis Post-Dispatch,* January 15, 2005, "When is a crime not really a crime?"

Summary

Missing data are often classified as missing completely at random (MCAR), missing at random (MAR), and not missing at random (MNAR) (Little and Rubin, 1987). When data are MCAR, they can easily be imputed, just by assuming that the statistics of these missing data are similar to the actual data. From a brief perusal of the reasons just listed for missing data, however, it is clear that rarely are the missing data MAR, let alone MCAR. This means that different imputation schemes have to be devised to account for the different kinds of missingness.

Thus, the fact that the UCR has no sampling error does not mean that the UCR contains no error. In fact, its errors may be considerably larger than the NCVS sampling error. Then by not incorporating the UCR's biases in their analyses, analysts using the UCR data are implicitly assuming them to be negligible or nonexistent.

Even if the UCR's errors are acknowledged and attempts are made to deal with them, very often the error structure is assumed to be similar to a "standard" error structure – for example, zero mean, normally (and identically) distributed, and independent (Lott and Whitely, 2003; Maltz and Targonski, 2002, 2003). *None of these assumptions hold for UCR data.*

- The mean of the errors is almost always negative; there are extremely few instances where a police department has overstated its crime count.
- The errors are not likely to be normally distributed; although we have not yet developed empirical estimates of the error structure, because of the previous point we do not expect a normal distribution to be the rule.
- The errors are likely to be both geographically and chronologically dependent.

Despite these problems with the UCR data, there are strong reasons for determining whether they can be made more useful. Only the UCR can be used to look at both longitudinal (across very long periods of time) and cross-sectional (across space) patterns of crime, because it contains computerized records for all (reporting) agencies from 1960 to the present. Thus, one can attempt to trace the effect of changes

TABLE 10.2. *Federal Bureau of Investigation imputation procedure*

Imputation procedure	Number of months reported, N, by agency A	
	0 to 2	3 to 11
FBI (also used by NACJD)	$C_S P_A / P_S$	$12 C_A / N$

Note. C_A, P_A = the agency's crime and population for the year in question; C_S, P_S = the crime and population count of "similar" agencies in the state, for the year in question; NACJD = National Archive of Criminal Justice Data.

in policies on crime that affected some (types of) agencies but not others; this is not possible using the NCVS.

It may well be that the NCVS is more accurate in its estimate of certain crimes and of national crime rates than the UCR. To compare the UCR and NCVS, to estimate the extent to which they coincide or diverge, one must not only recognize that the UCR has errors but also determine the effect these errors have on the crime rates they produce. That is, imputation may make it possible to account for biases in the UCR data and therefore enhance its comparison with the NCVS.

ACCOUNTING FOR MISSING UCR DATA

As discussed earlier, there are a number of types of missingness in the UCR data, each of which may have to be dealt with differently. If an occasional month is missing, it is not the same as when a string of months or whole years are missing.

To account for unreported data (but not the falsely lowered data), the FBI imputes the missing data using a simple algorithm (Maltz and Targonski, 2002). If the agency has reported three or more months of crime data in a year, then the crime rate for those months is applied to the entire year (Table 10.2).

If an agency has reported two or fewer months for a year, then the FBI scraps the agency's data and substitutes the crime rate of similar agencies for its crime rate. "Similar" agencies are considered to be those agencies with the following characteristics:

- they are in the same state,
- they are in the same FBI-designated population group (Table 10.1), and
- they have submitted 12 months of crime reports for that year.

The total crime count for these "similar" agencies is divided by their total population to develop a reference crime rate, and this value is applied to the agency's population to generate its substitute crime counts.

Although these imputation methods may be sufficient for annual state and national estimates of crime rates, they are not adequate to provide estimates of county crime rates (Maltz and Targonski, 2002) or of seasonal variation in crime. This is the case primarily because they use cross-sectional imputation to the exclusion of longitudinal imputation. That is, the history of an agency's own crime experience is not taken into account: if there is a seasonal component, it is ignored.

Cross-sectional imputation was used because the FBI's Consultant Committee recommended it. In fact, at that time this method for estimating crime rates was a major improvement over prior estimates, which was to base crime rates on reported crime. This meant that if reports were provided by a state's urban agencies, but not rural agencies, the state's crime rate was based on this imbalanced picture. Developing separate estimates for different population groups was a more accurate imputation method.

Moreover, when the FBI first computerized its UCR data collection procedures, around 1960, digital computers were in their infancy. Electronic devices we now can put in our pockets are more than a million times smaller and faster than those machines and have over a million times their capacity as well. It was a major operation for the FBI to enter and store the data for all 17,000 agencies for a single year. Longitudinal imputation would have required the FBI to deal simultaneously with data from the current year as well as previous years to determine seasonality and trend patterns, which at the time was not technologically feasible. To maintain consistency, it continues to use the same method today.

Developing a longitudinal imputation scheme at the agency level would make the UCR data more useful, and applying it to data as far back as possible would create a long and useful time series for studying policies. But first the data must be cleaned and the different types of missingness in the UCR data detailed. It is not always easy to determine when data are missing in the UCR, and it is even more

Line 35, CO00700: BOULDER

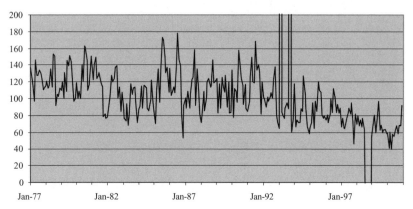

Figure 10.4. Same data as in Figure 10.3, but at a different scale.

difficult to understand why they are missing.[12] The methods to be used to accomplish these tasks are described below.

CLEANING THE DATA

The amount of data to be dealt with is considerable: it consists of crime counts for 7 crimes (and 18 crime subcategories), for 12 months, for 43 years, for more than 18,000 agencies.[13] What has made this possible is the use of visual techniques. By visually inspecting each time series (with 43×12, or 516 data points), one can determine not only where the incorrect spikes are (Figure 10.3) but also where holes exist (Figure 10.4, showing the same data but on a different scale). (When a missing datum is found, its value is set to be large and negative, hence the almost vertical lines in Figure 10.4 in the last half of 1998.) Different missing value codes are assigned to different types

[12] We used the "date updated" variable to determine whether a particular month was reported. We are also noting discrepancies, such as when no date is reported but data exist for that month. We determined that a datum was missing when we had a zero datum and no date updated. This was not always a reliable indicator, however. Determining why a datum was missing was even more difficult, but we relied on the (visual) context, as described subsequently.

[13] An initial project dealt with 24 years, from 1977 to 2000 inclusive, from which these examples are taken. The current project includes data from 1960 to 2002 inclusive.

Code	Value	Color
agency did not exist during this period	-80	blue (8)
ORI is covered by another agency	-85	blue(20)
we assign missing and record its value	-90	orange (45)
murder missing	-91	red (3)
rape missing	-92	red (3)
robbery missing	-93	red (3)
assault missing	-94	red (3)
burglary missing	-95	red (3)
larceny missing	-96	red (3)
motor vehicle theft missing	-97	red (3)
on CI page, more than 1 crime missing	-98	red (3)
no data for this month (true missing)	-99	red (3)
aggregated to February	-102	green (4)
aggregated to March	-103	green (4)
aggregated to April	-104	green (4)
aggregated to May	-105	green (4)
aggregated to June	-106	green (4)
aggregated to July	-107	green (4)
aggregated to August	-108	green (4)
aggregated to September	-109	green (4)
aggregated to October	-110	green (4)
aggregated to November	-111	green (4)
aggregated to December	-112	green (4)

Figure 10.5. Missing value codes.

of missingness; Figure 10.5 gives the codes and colors we used for the various types of missingness.

Depicting crime data is also one way to bring complex information to the general public in a way that helps them understand such characteristics as seasonality, "crime waves," how patterns in homicide may be masked (in the Crime Index) by patterns in more numerous crimes such as larceny, and, more generally, how to interpret the rise and fall of crime rates. We are in the process of developing a UCR "utility" that will permit users to see where the data exist, where there are gaps in the data, and the type of missingness that caused the gap (see footnote 6).

Figure 10.6 shows the way the data are stored in Excel files. Although the color is missing from this figure, the numerical values are given in Figure 10.5. The cells with white backgrounds are actual data points. The red cells (which appear as black in this figure) are missing data; the green cells (which appear as mid-gray) represent data points that have been aggregated, as when agencies report quarterly, semiannually, or annually. The blue cells do not represent actual missing data because

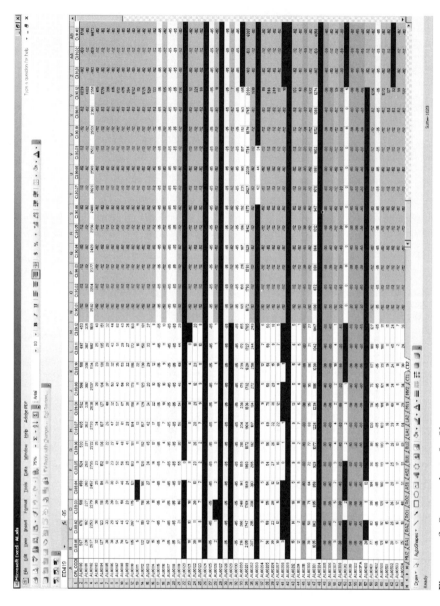

Figure 10.6. Screen shot of a file.

either the agency did not exist at the time (dark blue/dark gray) or it reported its crime through another agency (light blue/light gray). Some of the issues we are dealing with are described below.

"Covered-Bys"

Some agencies do not report their crime data directly but report them through another agency. For example, rather than have its own statistical unit, a small agency may have a larger agency (say, the county sheriff's police) send its crime data forward. In this case, the agency's crime data may *appear* to be missing but actually are not. When an agency has its crime reported through another agency, this transfer of responsibility, called a "covered-by," is indicated in the UCR data. In most cases the data are sent from a small agency to a larger one, so the effect of the transfer is not always discernible.

That this is not always the case can be seen in Figure 10.7. The Florence, Kentucky, police department did not submit its crime data to the FBI between March 1982 and December 1984, as shown by the zero crime count for this period in the figure. The Boone County Police Department's crime count clearly indicates that it submitted Florence's data during this period. The UCR data set does note that Florence is covered by Boone, but only for 1983. There was no such indication in 1981, 1982, or 1984, when it is obvious that Boone also submitted reports for Florence.

Moreover, an agency's covering status is not reported on a monthly basis, even though in this case (and doubtless others) covering does not start or end at the beginning of a year. Only by visually inspecting the data can these characteristics be found.

This "covered by" procedure will not affect estimates of crime rates at the county,[14] state, or national level because all of the crimes reported by any jurisdiction will be included in the numerator of the rate. It will, however, affect estimates at the jurisdiction level.

Aggregating Reports

Some agencies report their data annually, semiannually, or quarterly, in which case the missing months are included in subsequent months'

---

[14] Virtually all covered agencies are covered by agencies in the same county.

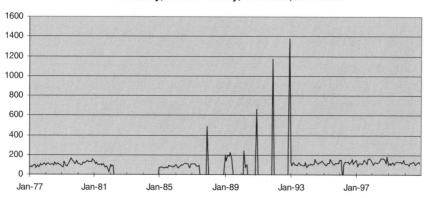

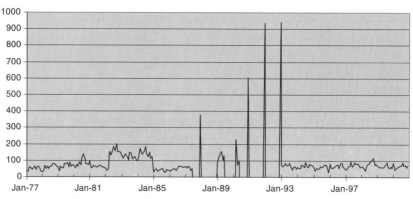

Figure 10.7. Example of a "covered-by" agency.

tallies. Moreover, in some cases when an agency misses a month, perhaps due to personnel shifts, it may report the data in the next month;
this can be seen if the agency's monthly crime tallies jump from zero
in one month to about twice the average level in the next month.

A related problem occurs when an agency actually reports its crime
annually, but divides the crime tally by 12 and allocates that number
to each month. Although the data appear to be monthly data, they
are actually annual data (see Figure 10.8). For example, Birmingham
(Alabama) and Chicago provided monthly data in 1994–1996 and
1991, respectively, but in both cases they provided the data at the end
of the year – by taking the total number of crimes and dividing them by

Alabama, Jefferson County, Birmingham, All Index

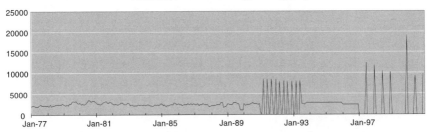

Illinois, Cook County, Chicago, All Index

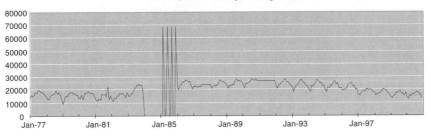

Figure 10.8. "Monthly" reporting, on an annual basis.

12 to spread them out over the year.[15] Anyone looking to study crime seasonality would be misled by this practice. It is virtually impossible to find these anomalies without inspecting the data visually.

Aggregating monthly reports across time will not affect annual estimates of crime, but they will influence temporal trends within the year.

Negative Crime Counts

Among the 40 million or so data points we dealt with, only about 5,000 were negative. A negative crime count is, of course, not possible; however, it can come about if one or two crimes are reported in a month but four or five crimes that had been reported in previous months are subsequently determined to be unfounded (or are downgraded to non-Index crimes). As can be seen from the distribution of negative numbers (Figure 10.9), most were −1 to −3, with only 142 being −4

---

[15] If the number of crimes was not divisible by 12, the remainder was distributed to some months. For example, if 62 robberies were recorded, the first 10 months would be allocated five robberies and the last two allocated six robberies.

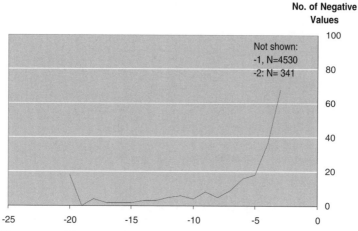

Figure 10.9. Negative values in 1977–2000 UCR data.

or below. We conjectured that an agency with four or more unfounds would need to have a substantial crime rate for this many crimes to be unfounded in a single month, so it probably was a coding error. In other words, we considered it possible for an agency to have up to three more unfounded crimes than founded crimes but unlikely for more than this.

"Zero-Population" Agencies

Some police departments overlap geographically with police departments in other jurisdictions. Examples include university police, interagency enforcement units, park and transit police, and (in some cases) state and county police agencies.[16] These agencies are termed "zero-population" (or "zero-pop") agencies by the FBI, because the populations under their jurisdictions have already been counted as assigned to their respective primary policing agencies.

When these agencies have gaps in their crime reporting, the FBI does not impute the amount of crime that might be missing from its tally. It is likely that the amounts of crime thus not counted are

---

[16] State and county police departments can also be the primary policing agencies in some areas. This is true in rural areas, where no other agencies police the populations.

relatively small, but this supposition has never been empirically put to the test.

Moreover, even when a zero-pop agency reports fully, its crime count may not be properly allocated. For example, in its county-level crime data sets (NACJD, 2005), the NACJD allocates state zero-pop agency crime to counties by prorating the crimes to counties according to their populations. However, the Connecticut State Police have major law enforcement responsibilities in the more rural (eastern and northern) counties, which have lower populations, and they have relatively light responsibilities in the more heavily populated southwestern counties. By allocating the Connecticut State Police's reported crime according to population, the NACJD allocates relatively little crime to the areas where they *do* have crime control responsibilities and most of the crime to the areas where they *do not* have these responsibilities.

CONCLUSION: ACCOUNTING FOR MISSING DATA

It is not yet possible to provide a reliable estimate of the amount of crime in the United States based on UCR data, along with a valid estimate of its associated error. While this is our goal, we are not yet there. We are currently working on two fronts to clean the data. First, as noted, we are going through the entire data set to find and categorize each missing datum, crime by crime, distinguishing between data that are truly missing and those that are accounted for in other ways (data aggregation and "covered-bys"). We intend to develop a statistical summary of the nature and extent of missingness in UCR data, so that users of this data series in the future will have a better understanding of the gaps in UCR data.

Second, we are working on the development of imputation schemes that take into account the past history of the agency as well as the seasonal characteristics of each particular crime in that state in that type of agency. We intend to compare the new schemes with those used by the FBI to use as a benchmark of their usefulness. In essence, we will simulate different kinds of missingness by creating data gaps according to the patterns we find in the data and then determine how well each imputation scheme replicates the (known) data. We also recognize that as agencies throughout the country convert to NIBRS, an understanding of the gaps in the UCR should be useful in dealing with the problems of missing data in this much more complex system. We foresee three benefits to this effort:

1. By documenting the extent of gaps in the data, those who have used analyses of the data to generate findings will now have an indication of the reliability of those findings.

2. We expect that it will become more feasible to use county-level data properly in analyzing policies. County-level data are very useful for this purpose because the sociodemographic variation among counties is much greater than the variation among states, allowing for greater discernment of policy impact in different environments. The improvements we are working on, then, should make the UCR a stronger platform for policy analysis, both of past policies and in future evaluations.

3. We anticipate that a more complete description of the UCR error structure will lead to a more cogent comparison of this data set with the other primary indicator of crime in the United States, the NCVS.

Although we cannot give a thorough accounting of missing data in the UCR at this time, we do know substantially more than we did about it, and we can make some conjectures about how missing data are likely to have affected divergence in the NCVS and UCR trends over time. Because the trends are based on national level estimates, errors in placing data in jurisdictions and in specific months will not affect these trends much. In general, over the decade of the 1990s, the amount of missing data in the UCR has increased. If no adjustments are made to the data to take account of missing data, then we would expect the estimates of the level of crime in the UCR to be progressively greater underestimates of crime and the trend to overestimate the decrease in crime. The UCR does impute missing data, but it is unclear whether these adjustments completely compensate for the effects of missing data. The effects of the UCR imputation procedures would depend on how different the agencies that did report were from those that did not and how different the months when crime was reported were from those in which crime was not reported. If imputation consistently produces more crime than actually occurred and the need for imputation increases over time, this would contribute to the divergence of the two trends by making the decline in the UCR trends less than the decline in the NCVS.

References

Akiyama, Y., & Nolan, J. (1999). "Methods for understanding and analyzing NIBRS data." *Journal of Quantitative Criminology* 15:225–238.

Biderman, A. D., Johnson, L. A., McIntyre, J., & Weir, A. W. (1967). *Report on a pilot study in the District of Columbia on victimization and attitudes toward law enforcement.* Field Surveys I. President's Commission on Law Enforcement and Administration of Justice. Washington, DC: U.S. Government Printing Office.

Bureau of Investigation. (1930, August). *Uniform Crime Reports for the United States and its possessions* (monthly bulletin, Vol. 1, no. 1). Washington, DC: U.S. Government Printing Office.

"Crime in Capital Is Focus of National Political Fight." (1972, September 26). *New York Times*, p. 37.

Ennis, P. (1967). *Criminal victimization in the United States: A report of a national survey.* Field Surveys II for the President's Commission on Law Enforcement and Administration of Justice. Washington, DC: U.S. Government Printing Office.

Federal Bureau of Investigation. (1935). *Uniform Crime Reports for the United States and its possessions* (fourth quarterly bulletin, Vol. V, No. 4). Washington, DC: U.S. Government Printing Office.

Federal Bureau of Investigation. (2003). *Crime in the United States, 2002.* Washington, DC: U.S. Government Printing Office.

International Association of Chiefs of Police, Committee on Uniform Crime Records. (1929). *Uniform Crime Reporting: A complete manual for police.* New York: International Association of Chiefs of Police.

Lejins, P. P., Chute, C. F., & Schrotel, S. R. (1958). *Uniform Crime Reporting: Report of the consultant committee.* Washington, DC: Federal Bureau of Investigation.

Little, R. J. A., & Rubin, D. B. (2002). *Statistical analysis with missing data* (2nd ed.). New York: Wiley.

Lott, J. R., Jr., & Whitley, J. (2003). "Measurement error in county-level data." *Journal of Quantitative Criminology* 19:185–198.

Maltz, M. D. (1999). *Bridging gaps in police crime data: A discussion paper from the BJS Fellows Program.* Report No. NCJ-1176365, Bureau of Justice Statistics, Office of Justice Programs, U.S. Department of Justice, Washington,

DC, September, 1999, 72 pp. Available at http://www.ojp.usdoj.gov/bjs/pub/pdf/bgpcd.pdf.

Maltz, M. D., & Targonski, J. (2002). "A note on the use of county-level crime data." *Journal of Quantitative Criminology* 18:297–318.

Maltz, M. D., & Targonski, J. (2003). "Measurement and other errors in county-level UCR data: A reply to Lott and Whitley." *Journal of Quantitative Criminology* 19:199–206.

National Archive of Criminal Justice Data. (2005). *County-level UCR data.* Retrieved February 17, 2005, from http://www.icpsr.umich.edu/NACJD/ucr.html#desc_cl.

Poggio, E. C., Kennedy, S. D., Chaiken, J. M., & Carlson, K. E. (1985). *Blueprint for the future of the Uniform Crime Reporting Program. Final report of the UCR Study* (NCJ 98348). Washington, DC: Bureau of Justice Statistics, U.S. Department of Justice.

President's Commission on Law Enforcement and Administration of Justice. (1967). *The challenge of crime in a free society.* Washington, DC: U.S. Government Printing Office.

Seidman, D., & Couzens, M. (1974). "Getting the crime rate down: Political pressure and crime reporting." *Law and Society Review* 8:457–493.

CONCLUSION

CHAPTER ELEVEN

Conclusion

James P. Lynch and Lynn A. Addington

One goal of *Understanding Crime Statistics* is to encourage and facilitate the appropriate use of crime statistics through a discussion of the divergence of the Uniform Crime Reports (UCR) and the National Crime Victimization Survey (NCVS). We also seek to build on the idea of complementarity, which originated from the work of Biderman and Lynch (1991). Specifically, Biderman and Lynch's work makes two important points concerning crime statistics. One is that all statistical systems will distort to some degree the data produced and the important lesson for researchers is to understand how this occurs so that appropriate adjustments can be made. The second point is that it is virtually impossible to get statistical systems that are organized as differently as the NCVS and the UCR to tell the same story across the board. Given these two points, Biderman and Lynch concluded that energy and resources were better invested in discovering ways to use these data systems in complementary rather than competing ways.

Although the principle of complementarity seems to be widely accepted today, this acceptance may be fickle. Complementarity has not received a real test because of the coincidence that the two series have tracked reasonably well for more than a decade. When the two series diverge, and history tells us that they will, ready explanations for this divergence must be available as well as examples of very specific ways in which the two systems (even in a divergent state) can be used jointly to shed new light on the crime problem. In the absence of these explanations and examples, criminologists may be once again plunged into an unproductive debate over which indicator is accurate and which is not. In this volume, we have sought to describe

how these systems can be used in a more appropriate and complementary way and to suggest how they might be changed to enhance
complementarity.

This concluding chapter summarizes the work of the many distinguished contributors to this volume and draws from it implications
for the appropriate use of these two statistical systems. To do so, this
conclusion is divided into four sections. In the first section, we return
to the issue of divergence in the two series and the role it should play
in assessing the validity and reliability of crime statistics. The second
section identifies certain shortcomings in each system that should be
corrected so that each system measures better that which it purports to
measure. Our emphasis on complementarity tends to avoid more abso-
lutist judgments about error in either series. It is important, however,
to identify aspects of these data collections that make the counting
of crime inaccurate and to correct them if at all possible. The third
section suggests ways the current systems could be used in more complementary ways; and the final section advocates a systemic approach
to collecting crime data that would further complementary uses of
these data and illumination of the crime problem.

Although all four sections of this conclusion include suggestions to
utilize the NCVS and UCR more effectively, the final section raises
some fundamental questions about the future of these data series and
how they should interrelate. Regarding the future of the NCVS and
UCR, we raise the question of whether a systemic approach to crime
statistics should replace the current coexisting series in which little
coordination exists between them. If this is done, then we could de-
emphasize the demand that the NCVS and UCR be parallel systems
with as similar as possible crime scope, population coverage, periodicity, and the like and begin to make the systems more complementary.
Regarding the relationship between the two series, we raise the question of what principles should determine how they interrelate. Traditionally, the victim survey served as a check on police administrative
records, since the survey was a source of information independent of
the police. With the changes in police administrative record data and
the increased knowledge of and familiarity with victim surveys, it may
be time to de-emphasize this monitoring function and to increase the
importance of complementary uses of the data series to increase our

understanding of the crime problem. An underlying issue in answering both of these questions is that if we embrace complementarity as an important guiding principle for the two series, then we must give content to this principle by specifying exactly how the systems could complement each other.

PUTTING DIVERGENCE IN ITS PLACE

It is difficult to recommend completely abandoning convergence as a gauge of the validity of any two measures of the same concept, and indicators of crime are no exception. As much as we talk about complementarity and its broad acceptance, criminologists have a certain comfort level in using convergence to evaluate the NCVS and UCR. This comfort is evidenced by the volume of research generated in this area. McDowall and Loftin (Chapter 4) provide an excellent review of the divergence and convergence literature as well as of the various ways that criminologists and others have attempted to establish convergence. Their review highlights the tension between the rigor of the standards for establishing convergence and the usefulness of convergence as a standard of validity. The more rigorous the standard of convergence, the less able the series are to achieve convergence. When the standard for convergence is exactly the same rates of crime every year in both series, the two series do not converge. When the standard is convergence over a long-term trend, the series meet this standard. The problem is that the less rigorous standards (which may be more reasonable) might not be satisfying to certain audiences for crime statistics. Citizens and policy makers (and some criminologists) who focus on annual change might not be reassured by the fact that the series are "cointegrated" when they see different crime rates reported by the NCVS and UCR for a given year.

McDowall and Loftin find that the standard of convergence with adjustment may be the most reasonable compromise between rigor and interpretability. They conclude that if one is to use the convergence standard for validity, it should not be done naïvely but with a full appreciation of the differences in definition and procedures in each of the systems, and whenever possible adjustments should be made in each series to take account of these differences. Biderman and Lynch (1991) reached a similar conclusion in finding that they simply did not know enough to make all the adjustments necessary to assess convergence accurately.

Unfortunately, substantial gaps still remain in our ability to identify common elements in the two systems. Changes in the systems such as the conversion to the National Incident-Based Reporting System (NIBRS) have the potential to provide greater information because of the incident-based data collection (Addington, Chapter 8). Although our gaps in knowledge may be reduced as NIBRS matures, at this point in time, it is uncertain when NIBRS will have sufficient coverage to serve that purpose more fully. Moreover, simply adjusting for these differences in procedures may not be enough. Rosenfeld's contribution (Chapter 9) suggests that many of the forces acting on both systems, but especially the UCR, are external shocks and not things under the control of the agencies collecting the data. Changes in the sensitivity of the police industry to the treatment of domestic violence, for example, have come from women's groups and legislation as well as general changes in the cultural definition of domestic violence. It is difficult to factor these general changes in society and their effects on crime statistics into assessments of convergence in any rigorous way.[1] So, while McDowall and Loftin are more favorably disposed toward the standard of convergence with adjustment because it is both reasonable and interpretable, they are concerned about its practicality, specifically the ability to make all of the necessary adjustments to the series.

A consistent theme throughout this volume is that the measurement of crime by statistical systems is complicated by the complexity and ambiguity of major crime classes. A clear example arises with assaults. Assaults often occur in social contexts that impede identification of the behavior necessary for determining whether a crime occurred as well as the severity of the offense. Fights among siblings or those motivated by retaliation can make problematic the determination of intent, consent, or provocation. Rosenfeld's chapter clearly illustrates this problem by showing how the series track much better for

---

[1] It becomes even more complex as these forces acting on the series change over time. Rosenfeld suggests that the increases in the recording of domestic violence observed in the 1990s will not continue in the next decade.

events in which these determinations are less problematic. The same conclusion can be drawn from Cohen and Lynch's (Chapter 7) comparison of the National Hospital Ambulatory Care Survey (NHAMCS) and the NCVS. Estimates from the two surveys diverge much more for visits to emergency departments for assault injuries due to minor incidents than for serious incidents. Catalano's (Chapter 5) analysis also finds that the influence of methodological changes in the NCVS affect the trend more for aggravated assaults as compared with robberies. McDowall and Loftin note that the evidence for convergence is more compelling for clearly defined crimes like robbery or motor vehicle theft than for more ambiguously defined crimes such as assault. A sizable component of the crimes that we are most interested in – violent crimes – is inherently ambiguous. Our counting of these crimes is substantially affected both by differences in definitions and procedures across the systems that we can identify and account for as well as a multitude of factors that we cannot readily assess. For these reasons, we (along with McDowall and Loftin) advocate de-emphasizing the importance of convergence as a standard for establishing the validity of the two series and emphasizing a complementarity approach to using the NCVS and UCR.

We realize that abandoning the convergence standard for assessing validity is difficult. As such, if researchers are insistent on using the convergence standard, we recommend two particular standards and we also recommend that convergence be used only when examining change as opposed to level estimates of crime. The preferred convergence standard is that of "explainable divergence." It is unlikely that we will be able to account of all the instances of noncomparability in the two systems, not so much because we do not know what they are but because the information necessary to adjust for them is not available. Consequently, it may be more realistic to say that divergence between the UCR and NCVS is acceptable if it can be readily explained by differences in definitions, procedures, and other factors known to affect the series. Such a practice is commonly seen in economics where, for example, differences in indicators of the health of the economy are explained by a one-time event or some more major shift in the economy that would affect one economic indicator differently from the rest (Henderson, 2005). Accepting this standard for crime statistics, of course, means that we must continue to increase our knowledge of the peculiarities of these statistical systems so that we can plausibly explain why they diverge.

A distant second choice of convergence standards would be to identify the most stereotypic components of both statistical systems and use them to assess convergence and divergence. This would permit the most adequate application of the standard of "convergence with adjustment" because the sources of noncomparability are most readily identified and estimated for these crimes. The stereotypic crime is a violent crime that occurs in a public place among strangers. Currently this would be the robbery trends with commercial robberies omitted and appropriately similar units of counts used. One of the problems with this approach, as Addington's chapter makes clear, is the imprecision with which the UCR summary system can identify commercial crimes, even commercial robberies. This source of noncomparability has been much less distorting in the recent past than the ambiguity of other types of crime, such as aggravated assault, and the willingness of respondents in the survey and the police in recording crimes to use substantial discretion in determining when those types of crime have occurred. This judgment regarding the relative magnitude of sources of divergence is supported by the relatively high correlations between robbery trends (as opposed to assault) in the work cited in McDowall and Loftin's chapter as well as by the effects of the NCVS redesign. The extensive changes in instrumentation and procedures made in the survey during the redesign had much greater effects for assaults than for robbery (Cantor and Lynch, 2005; Kinderman et al., 1997).

On the property side, the likely candidate would be the burglary trends largely because evidence of forcible entry will be less ambiguous than larcenies in which theft is often confused with simply misplacing something. Moreover, burglaries are reported to the police at a much higher rate than thefts. The comparability of the burglary trends would be enhanced by removing attempts from the NCVS and commercial burglaries from the UCR. Here again, the imprecision of our ability to completely identify commercial burglaries as well as the treatment of forcible car entries as burglaries in some jurisdictions will threaten the use of this particular trend to establish convergence. Motor vehicle theft could be an alternative to burglary for these purposes because it is serious and well reported to the police thanks to insurance requirements. Moreover, Addington's work suggests the commercial component of vehicle theft is more completely identified than it is in other types of property crime.

Finally, any discussion of convergence or divergence in the two series should emphasize change estimates and not level estimates. It is much more difficult to obtain comparable level estimates from the two series than it is to get arguably similar change estimates. If we assume that nonuniformities in measurement in each series are fairly constant over time, then change estimates will not be affected. The chapters by Barnett-Ryan as well as Rennison and Rand describe systems that are changing continuously in small and some not so small ways. The analysis in Catalano's chapter indicates that many of the changes in NCVS procedures are not consequential for trends. Even the substantial effects in UCR trends observed in Rosenfeld's chapter occurred over a long period of time. The effects of these factors on annual change estimates will not be large in any given two years. In contrast, any difference between the systems can contribute to differences in level estimates.

This view is also consistent with the purpose of both the NCVS and UCR. Almost every design decision in the NCVS is made with an eye toward preserving the quality of change estimates. For example, there are a number of nonuniformities in interviewing procedures in the NCVS that are known to affect level estimates (for example, computer-assisted telephone interviewing [CATI] and unbounded interviews), but the Census ignores these nonuniformities because they are relatively stable over time and will not affect change estimates.[2] Similarly, memory decay is unavoidable in any conceivable retrospective survey, so the NCVS will not provide an exhaustive accounting of crimes within the scope of the survey and this will affect comparisons of levels across the two series. Similarly with the UCR, the UCR consistently underestimates the level of crime, since it includes only crimes reported to the police. For all of these reasons, the level estimates

---

[2] Catalano finds that the proportion of CATI interviews in the survey does affect divergence, but her analysis included the 1992 redesign when CATI was introduced into the survey in large numbers. Since that time, the proportion of CATI interviews has remained relatively stable at about 30 percent.

from both the NCVS and the UCR will underestimate the volume of crime occurring in the nation at any point in time. Any comparisons of the two series should emphasize change estimates rather than level estimates.

REMOVING THE NOISE IN THE NCVS AND UCR

Both the NCVS and the UCR have procedures that distort their description of the crime problem. Some of these procedures distort the crime problem because they make that series incomplete in its coverage of crime. Other procedures distort the crime problem because they make that series inaccurate in describing the crimes that it purports to cover. In the case of the former, it is sufficient to be aware of them. In the case of the latter, they should be eliminated or reduced if at all possible. Both the NCVS and UCR suffer from noise, so identifying this noise is not intended to discredit either system. Instead, identifying this noise assists researchers in using these data more responsibly. The NCVS by its design provides more information about the amount and nature of the noise as compared to the UCR. As such, the NCVS is addressed first in this section.

Noise in the NCVS comes from four main sources: types of interviewing procedures, failure to include series victimizations, nonresponse, and requisite adjustments to the data. Researchers using the NCVS data need to account for how these sources of noise could affect their results. NCVS estimates should be standardized for changes in interview procedures. Principal among these changes in interview procedures is the use of CATI. Split sample tests of this methodology indicate that it can have substantial effects on reporting (Hubble and Wilder, 1988). Catalano's analysis in this volume also suggests that changes in the percent of respondents interviewed by CATI have affected the NCVS trends for specific crimes. To the extent that CATI interviewing remains stable over time, it will not affect estimates of change in the survey, but if the proportion of CATI interviews increases (as is planned), the trends will be affected. Other nonuniformities in interviewing may not be that important for trends in the NCVS. Specifically, changes in the proportion of unbounded interviews included in the estimates as well as the proportion of the sample that are household respondents may not be as important for the NCVS trends as Biderman and Lynch (1991) originally believed. Although the difference in reporting for bounded and unbounded interviews is substantial in the cross-section (Biderman and Cantor, 1984; but see Addington, 2005), Catalano demonstrates that the proportion unbounded in a given year has not varied a great deal over the life of the survey, and it does not seem to affect the NCVS trends very much. The same is the case for household respondent status, which has less of an effect on reporting in the cross-section (Biderman et al., 1982).

The Bureau of Justice Statistics (BJS) should also take a more reasonable position on the inclusion of series incidents in crime rate estimation, as Planty's contribution (Chapter 6) demonstrates. Although it is clear that these counts of crimes should not be taken at face value, it is also clear that they should not be ignored either. Treating these crimes as a single event also does not seem appropriate; by definition they involve multiple events. Some reasonable compromise should be worked out that includes series incidents in annual estimates in a fashion that acknowledges the fact that they are multiple events but does not give undue weight to reports of uncertain quality. This could be as simple as imposing a cap on the number of incidents in a series that would be counted or a more complex method to model the number of events to count in a specific series.

Cohen and Lynch's chapter highlights the importance of nonresponse in the NCVS, especially for the enumeration of violent crimes. Although the general level of nonresponse in the NCVS is quite low, the level of nonresponse in groups with marginal and fluid relationships to households is higher. Under plausible assumptions about the difference in victimization between the mainstream population and these more marginal groups, this level of nonresponse can pose a problem for accurately estimating the volume of violent crime for these groups. Catalano's work supports Cohen and Lynch's assertion that the overall response rate is related to the overall level of crime reported in the NCVS. The higher the response rate, the higher the amount of crime reported. This suggests that the problem of nonresponse concentrated in more marginal groups may be large enough to affect overall rates. This should be explored further by looking at the trends in nonresponse and victimization separately for marginal and nonmarginal populations. A nonresponse study may be necessary to test the assumption on which weighting adjustments for nonresponse are based, specifically that the victimization rate of persons typically interviewed in the survey is the same as those who do not respond.

Most of these proposed changes to NCVS estimation put Census in the unenviable position of adjusting data. This is problematic, as we saw in the debates about adjusting the decennial census for the known undercounting of certain populations (Prewitt, 2003) or the dynamic scoring debates with regard to the economic statistics (Mankewi and Weinzeirl, 2004). Any adjustments are based on assumptions, and people can make various assumptions, some of which can be reasonable and others can be arbitrary. Because it is often difficult to agree upon what is reasonable and what is not, the temptation is to categorically refuse to adjust estimates for known sources of error. Census has espoused this principle, but it has also routinely made adjustments to the NCVS data. Specifically, Census adjusts sample weights to compensate for undercoverage and nonresponse. Since the principle of adjusting the NCVS data for known sources of error has been accepted in practice, we would urge that BJS consider expanding this practice to some of the sources of nonuniformity in measurement discussed earlier in this chapter. It would seem preferable to make reasonable adjustments rather than rely on data that are known to be flawed. Adjusted and unadjusted estimates could be made available and the consumer could decide.

We know considerably less about the amount and nature of the noise in the UCR. Three known sources of noise in the UCR are: missing data, decay of the intercensal population estimates, and changes in support for police data collection. One known problem that Maltz describes concerns missing data, and this problem is one that is growing over time (Maltz, this volume, 1999). Although missing data may pose greater consequences for some users of the data than others (e.g., persons doing county-level analyses), it has the potential to affect every use of the UCR (Lynch and Jarvis, 1995). The Federal Bureau of Investigation (FBI) does impute data when it is missing, but this is only done for annual rates at the national level and not for subnational jurisdictions such as states or counties. More sophisticated imputation procedures could be developed at every jurisdiction level: local, state, and national, as Maltz's work demonstrates.

In addition to missing data, the decay of intercensal estimates over the decade is a second known contributor of noise and should be factored into annual estimates of level and change. As of the early 1960s, the UCR has used the Bureau of the Census' estimates of the population in computing crime rates. These estimates are based on the decennial census and updated throughout the decade with data on migration and immigration. Over the course of the decade, however, these estimates become increasingly greater underestimates of the actual population (Biderman and Lynch, 1991). By the end of the decade, UCR crime rates overstate the actual crime rate by about 4 percent for this reason alone. Once the new decennial census figures are released, the UCR should publish adjusted figures that are not affected by errors introduced by the misestimation of the intercensal population.

A third known source of noise in the UCR comes from efforts to improve that data collection system. Innovations such as the rise and fall of state UCR programs or the institution of state mandatory reporting law can affect the UCR trends just the way that changes in NCVS interviewing procedures can influence the trends in the survey data (Biderman and Lynch, 1991; Lynch, 2003). Specific aspects of this source of noise in the UCR need to be identified and their effects on the trends assessed.

More research is needed to identify noise in the UCR. Although much needed, this research will be difficult because the UCR system is voluntary and rides on the back of a service provision system. Little is known about the discretionary judgments made by members of local police agencies regarding the recording of crimes and the reporting of these crimes to the UCR. Rosenfeld's chapter suggests that a change in the police industry regarding the treatment of domestic violence in the delivery of police service affected the recording and reporting of these events in the UCR. Biderman and Lynch (1991) argued that increases in bureaucratic nature of policing and especially improvements in record keeping and the demise of the full-service police department resulted in an artificial increases in the reporting of burglary in the UCR. These changes in the delivery of police service have repercussions for the crime statistics they generate, and we must begin to identify these changes and assess their impact on UCR trends. Because we know so little about how data are collected in individual police agencies and about changes in the provision of police services, we must infer effects from patterns in the data and their correlation with changes in the police industry. As Rosenfeld notes, this is difficult to do, and it is made more complex because we do not have a measure of "true crime" against which to assess the accuracy with which the police record data on crime and report it to the UCR.[3] Moreover, once these sources of noise are identified, the estimates of their effect are not so precise as to allow for adjustments to the series. They serve as a flag for fragile estimates and not as a basis for adjusting the trends, but certainly highlighting weaknesses in the data is preferable to ignoring them.

If we have truly embraced the notion of noise being inherent in these systems, uncovering this noise can inform us about how to best use these trends to describe crime. Rosenfeld's work, for example, tells us to be wary of trends in aggravated assault because of the noise introduced by changes in the police handling of domestic assault and by changes in respondents' view of the crime. Identifying this limitation does not discredit either system. It simply tells us how to use these data responsibly.

USING THE NCVS AND UCR IN COMPLEMENTARY WAYS IN THE SHORT RUN

There are a number of steps that could be taken immediately to enhance the complementary use of the NCVS and the UCR. These steps would involve relatively minor changes in the use of the series and not fundamental changes in the way that the data are collected. Complementary use of the NCVS and the UCR can take one of two forms: differential illumination of the same component of the crime problem and illumination of different components of that problem.

---

[3] If the Generic Area Reporting Program described later in this chapter is developed successfully, we might be able to explore this issue with an indicator of the UCR and the NCVS for the same types of places.

An example of the former would be when the UCR addresses trends in robbery and the NCVS is used to examine trends in subclasses of robbery that cannot be identified in the UCR data. The latter can be illustrated by using the UCR to describe trends in commercial robbery and the NCVS to describe trends in vandalism. The NCVS cannot be used to speak to commercial burglary, but the UCR can, just as the UCR can tell us little about vandalism but the crime survey can.[4] Specific illustration of both of these types of complementary uses of the NCVS and UCR are now described, with a discussion of the importance of crime classification as a means of establishing complementarity.

Differential Illumination of the Same Aspect of the Crime Problem
One of the rationales for developing the NCVS was its ability to do what police record systems could not. Although the principal reason for the survey was the illumination of the "dark figure of crime," the two data systems were complementary in other ways as well. The UCR is a highly aggregated system, whereas the NCS (and later the NCVS) can be disaggregated both in terms of the collection unit (individuals and households) and the information collected about that unit. When the NCS was instituted, the types of crime it included corresponded to those of the UCR Program because some envisioned that the UCR categories of crime could be disaggregated using the survey data to provide enlightenment about what was contributing to increases or decreases in these crime classes.

This utility can be illustrated by the following example. In their volume examining explanations for the crime drop, Blumstein and Wallman (2000) argue that much of the reduction of crime is due to the routinization of the drug trade and the resulting de-escalation of violence in inner-city neighborhoods. Their argument was that as the drug trade became less violent, the need for violence in those neighborhoods more generally decreased as residents had less need to take self-protective actions, such as arming themselves or affiliating with gangs. To support this point, Blumstein relied on homicide data because these data are the only component of the summary UCR

---

4   The UCR summary system only contains vandalism arrests, which is arguably a better
     measure of police activity than a measure of the incidence of vandalism. NIBRS
     includes vandalism offenses reported to the police.

system that contains information on victims and offenders and that can be disaggregated. Unfortunately, homicide is a rare event and dissimilar in many ways from lesser forms of violence. Moreover, the Supplementary Homicide Reports (SHR) had little information on many of the processes that Blumstein and Wallman claimed caused the decline in violence.

Here is an instance in which the NCVS can be used to test the generalizability of Blumstein's hypothesis because it contains much more information on nonlethal violence. Lynch (2002) examined characteristics of youth crime during the period using information on offenders from the NCVS. They found that nonlethal violence dropped much more for Black youths than White; that violence with weapons decreased much faster than violence without weapons; and that group offending decreased more than single person offending. All of these characteristics of the crime drop are supportive of Blumstein's contention. The drop occurred more in populations involved in or in proximity to the drug trade, for example, Black male adolescents. It involved reductions in the use of weapons and reductions in group affiliation for protection. This is an instance in which using the relatively aggregated UCR data in conjunction with the highly disaggregated NCVS data for the same type of crime furthers our understanding of the trends in crime. The different capabilities of each system should be exploited more fully to increase complementarity and to enhance our understanding of the crime problem. The NCVS data should be used in concert with the UCR data to disaggregate crime trends in a direct way, with references made to both series in joint reports released by both BJS and the FBI. There was a move in this direction in the mid-1990s, but it has not grown more robust over time.

The UCR and the NCVS can also be used in a complementary way in terms of their geographic coverage. The UCR is almost a census of places in the United States, whereas the NCVS is based on a sample of households in a sample of areas. The fact that the NCVS does not include and does not identify the data from specific subnational jurisdictions leaves the impression that the survey has nothing to say about these areas. This may not be the case if the increased coverage of the UCR can be used to leverage information in the NCVS to say something about areas not included in the survey. With some work, the two systems can be used jointly to describe crime in specific types of subnational jurisdictions or a subset of specific jurisdictions.

Currently both the UCR and the NCVS have little useful information on subnational jurisdictions. The NCVS tells us whether the respondent resides in a place of a particular size and whether this place is part of a Standard Metropolitan Statistical Area (SMSA). The UCR indicates the size of the place and some information about the state in which it is located and whether the place is a city or not. The UCR, however, has the distinct advantage of identifying the jurisdiction from which the data come while the NCVS does not. Although this benefit allows the assessment of individual jurisdictions and their crime rates, it does not inform regarding comparable jurisdictions or differences across jurisdictions. Such comparisons would be informative to policy makers, police officials, and citizens. These comparisons could be made if one were able to exploit what these systems together could tell us about crime in subnational units. If both the UCR and the NCVS expanded the information on subnational units that they include, they would tell us a great deal more about crime in these units than each one on its own does now. If the two systems included the same information on these subnational units, they could be linked by type of jurisdiction and both be used to talk about the crime problem in that type of jurisdiction. The UCR data can be linked to Census data at the jurisdiction level, and these data can tell us much more about the variation in crime across places than the simple size of place distinctions currently made in the UCR. In addition, efforts could be made to link the NCVS and UCR data geographically.

The key to achieving this type of joint reporting on subnational units requires the use of generic rather than actual areas. The term *generic area* does not refer to a specific area but to a composite of areas that share some common attributes. The generic area approach permits the joint use of census (UCR) and sample data (NCVS) to say something about types of areas. So estimates in the UCR could be produced for cities with populations over 250,000 in the Northeast by combining the crime rates from all of the cities of this type. The NCVS, in turn, would not have enough sample size to make reliable estimates for a given city of over 250,000 in the Northeast, but when it combines the sample from all of these areas, then its precision is greatly improved and statistically meaningful statements can be made about these areas. By defining and generating estimates for common sets of generic areas, the two systems will tell us a lot more about the distribution of crime across subnational jurisdictions. The major utility of these generic areas may not be the parallel estimates of crime per se but the ability to disaggregate the crime trends with NCVS data in specific types of areas for which the UCR can produce trends.

The joint development of a Generic Area Reporting Program (GARP) by the UCR and the NCVS may be of some use in increasing the ability of the two series to speak to each other. This would require the classification of all places in the United States into types of places on the basis of important characteristics of those areas. Marketing firms such as Claritas and others do this routinely (Claritas, 2005). They create catchy titles like "Country-Squire Suburb" to identify types of places and then discuss their socioeconomic status and buying habits. These names and types of places could be easily changed to reflect the issues of crime, such as "medium-sized industrial city in the Midwest." The British Crime Survey (BCS) has used this type of generic area typology for many years to report neighborhood-level estimates of victimization. A Classification of Residential Neighborhoods (ACORN) classifies neighborhoods into 54 types by the attributes of their populations. This classification includes such neighborhood types as "Affluent Grays," "Wealthy Achievers," and "Prosperous Pensioners" (Simmons and Dodd, 2003). Once this classification is developed, it can be applied to the NCVS sample to see whether the sample available in these types of areas is sufficient to provide reliable estimates of important crime classes and demographic subgroups. There is no guarantee that this approach to providing estimates for subnational areas will work. It may not be possible to identify useful and recognizable generic areas, or there may not be enough NCVS sample in these places to make reliable estimates. It is, however, worth doing some of this development work to have both administrative records and survey-based statistics on crime from the same types of places.

Developing a GARP system would allow for additional crime classifications by area and assessment of risk by location. In the United
States, people buy safety with their homes, and residential segregation
by class, race and ethnicity is pronounced. The difference in crime risk
across residential areas is also huge, but the NCVS only provides information on residential locations in gross population size categories or
by whether the house is in a central city of a metropolitan area. If the
development work described earlier for the GARP can be done, this
would not only be an important opportunity for the NCVS and UCR to
inform the same crime question but would also be a good way for the
NCVS to present its data on victimization regardless of whether those
data are combined with UCR data. Having residential areas identified
in a typology that combines class, race, and location in a metropolitan area (e.g., outer suburb) would make things meaningful for
citizens.

A source of subnational data is currently available in a limited
form that has the potential to aid in the development of GARP and
other approaches to the provision of estimates for subnational areas
with the NCVS. Through the efforts of BJS, the National Consortium on Violence Research, and others, Census has made available
"area-identified" NCVS public-use files. Area-identified refers to files
in which the location of respondents' residence is identified by primary sampling unit, place, census tract, block, and other units of
geography.[5] The usefulness of these data has not been fully explored,
mostly because of restricted access due to Census confidentiality concerns. Initial studies that have been conducted used the area-identified
NCVS data to examine victimization risk as well as to make assessments
regarding the capability of these data to provide subnational crime
estimates (Langan and DuRose, 2004; Lauritsen, 2001; Lauritsen and
Shaum, 2005). This exploratory work indicates that although subnational crime estimates can be made for a handful of the largest SMSAs,
the standard errors are large and may restrict the utility of the survey
for simple estimates of rates in these areas (Lauritsen and Schaum,
2005; Wiersema et al., 2000). A more promising use of these data

---

[5] The authors thank Richard Rosenfeld for pointing out the importance of the area-
identified data to the development of useful subnational estimates with NCVS data.

has yet to be explored. No studies have exploited the ability of the area-identified NCVS data to be linked with other Census data for the purpose of creating generic areas and estimates for those areas, such as those referred to in GARP. These generic areas could avoid the limitations encountered by researchers attempting to generate actually subnational crime estimates.

The NCVS also has the ability, in a limited way, to link people across incidents, whereas the UCR does not. This is potentially important because much of crime, and especially violent crime, is best understood as part of an ongoing relationship rather than as a point-in-time event. An assault on a given day may seem random when it is actually retribution for a victimization that occurred the day before. Similarly, an increase in crime can come from an increase in incidence or prevalence, and one source will have different implications from the other. The NCVS is an imperfect instrument for moving away from the point-in-time logic that underlies our crime statistics because it is not a true longitudinal design and even the longitudinal capabilities that the survey has are not fully exploited. Nonetheless, the NCVS can say something about the longitudinal nature of crime that the UCR cannot, and this should be used more in conjunction with the UCR to help us understand the crime problem. The UCR trends in aggravated assault could be presented, for example, and the NCVS could be used to disaggregate the trend into that component that is due to the prevalence as opposed to the incidence of victimization. If the crime drop, for instance, is due more to a decrease in incidence than prevalence, then we might more clearly understand why levels of fear among the public might remain high.

The NCVS also has the limited capability to link people within events, whereas the UCR cannot. The UCR arrest data, for example, cannot associate persons within the same crime event. Group offending is an important part of the crime problem, but the UCR cannot identify instances in which multiple offenders attack single victims or when groups confront groups. It would be useful to see NCVS data on offenders published routinely with the UCR data on arrested persons. Although the two indicators will differ considerably for many reasons, these differences can be informative. In such a report, the component of offending that is single versus group offending would be very interesting as would be data on the composition of these offending groups.

Illumination of Different Aspects of the Crime Problem
As many of the foregoing chapters indicated, the two systems cover very different aspects of the crime problem and include different populations. The UCR includes commercial crime, whereas the NCVS excludes it by design. The NCVS includes simple assault and vandalism in its crime counts, whereas the UCR does not.[6] The UCR includes crime against children under age 12 and sojourning foreigners, and the NCVS includes only the noninstitutionalized population over age 12. To the extent that these crimes and populations are identifiable in each data source, they should be isolated for specific attention.

Our statistical systems on crime do not capture crimes against commercial entities very well. The discontinuation of the commercial victimization surveys noted in Rennison and Rand's chapter left the UCR as the only source of data on common law crimes against commercial enterprises. The identification of commercial crimes is haphazard in the UCR, with commercial victims clearly and exhaustively identified for some classes of crime but not for others. NIBRS, as Addington demonstrates, does a better job of identifying crime with commercial victims, but its coverage is far from complete. Although the available data on commercial crime is not as good as we would want it to be, it is the only source that we have nationally. It would be informative if these data were separated out from the Index crimes and identified as a commercial crime index. At minimum, it would be useful to know what proportions of all common law crimes recorded in the UCR were crimes against commercial entities. It would be preferred to have a broader treatment of commercial crimes that included data from the UCR's summary system and NIBRS.

Another example of where the two series can be used in this type of complementary way is to provide information on lower-level "nuisance crimes." In the UCR, with a few notable exceptions, the emphasis of crime statistics systems has been on serious crimes and that is reflected

---

[6] The UCR does collect counts of simple assaults in the UCR, but the FBI does not publish them (see Barnett-Ryan, this volume).

in the International Association of Chiefs of Police's (IACP) desire to capture crimes that are "serious" and "well reported to the police." The "prevalence" of crime was implicitly in a secondary position. More recently, however, greater attention has been given to "nuisance" crimes that do not cause great injury or loss to individuals but have consequences for communities, schools, and other groups. "Broken windows" and "zero tolerance" strategies of crime control have given minor crimes new salience as leading indicators of more serious things to come and as actual facilitating factors in the generation of these more serious crimes (Kelling and Wilson, 1982; Taylor, 2001). BJS should recognize the new found importance of nuisance crimes such as vandalism and minor assaults and threats and feature these crime classes more prominently in their reporting, especially when these crimes occur within the respondent's neighborhood.

Crime Classification Is the Key

In more fully exploiting the different capabilities of the two series, changes in crime classification is key. Because there is no natural metric to crime as there is to something like income, the creation of crime classifications is extremely important. In doing so, we emphasize certain aspects of crime and cause others virtually to disappear. The UCR Crime Index is no longer sufficient by itself to serve as our major indicator of the crime problem. Indeed, there is good reason to say that it should no longer be the principal crime classification used for social indicator purposes. The Crime Index elevates the legal aspects of the offense and virtually excludes other attributes of the crime events such as the relationship between the victim and offender or the social context of the crime. Moreover, the legal attributes chosen for the Index were driven by the limits of police data systems at the time. What was "serious, prevalent and well reported to the police" in 1929 are not necessarily the same today. Recent steps to downplay the Index and to use its components are useful but still fail to exploit the richness of the data that we have available in the UCR and the NCVS (see Chapter 3). The Index crimes will certainly be inadequate when NIBRS coverage of the nation improves. Moreover, emphasizing the Index crimes in the NCVS invites discussions of divergence rather than complementarity.

The substantive and technological justifications for the Index crimes never applied to the survey and are no longer valid for police administrative data.

The summary UCR system lacks the flexibility to implement much change, so the focus must be on the NCVS and NIBRS. The NCVS has a great deal of underutilized information, as does the NIBRS. Using all of the information in NIBRS simply to recreate the Index Crime Classification (ICC) is a lost opportunity to learn more about crime. Now is the time to reconsider crime classifications suitable for use with modern information systems. The NCVS and NIBRS provide the necessary information to experiment with alternative crime classifications, and we should do so. Moreover, in that experimentation, we should not be bound by the stricture that any useful crime classification should be able to be estimated in both the survey- and police-based data collection systems. Rather each series should develop crime classifications that can tell us something important about crime and that can be reasonably estimated within each system.

Even within the current summary system, the UCR type of crime classification could be altered to shed more light on the crime problem. The Commercial Crime Index (CCI) mentioned earlier would be a useful highlighting of a class of crime that is not readily apparent in the current UCR. It would take a diligent soul to scour *Crime in the United States* to assemble crimes against commercial establishments. The CCI would make this class of crime more prominent for consumers of crime statistics, and this is currently only something that the UCR (and NIBRS) can do. Addington's analyses of NIBRS suggests that the UCR may underreport commercial crimes even among those classes of crime that it is designed to include, but if emphasis is placed on change estimates and not level estimates, the effect of underreporting may not be so bad.

The problem with thinking of new crime classifications for use with the NCVS and NIBRS is that there is so much flexibility and so much information that it is difficult to sort out which of the possible crime classes is best to use. Unlike the police chiefs in 1929, we are not bound by the limitations of police record systems; like the police chiefs, however, we must balance what we want in a crime indicator with what the social organization of the data collection system can deliver. One important goal of any crime statistics system is to convey a sense of the risk that crime poses to residents and others and to do it in a way that can inform public, and perhaps private, efforts to control risk of criminal victimization.

Effectively conveying the sense of risk to the public requires defining crime classes to which people can readily relate. In practice, this would require crime classes that can be portrayed by the media or otherwise disseminated to the public as rates in which readers can see themselves in the denominator of that rate. A crude crime rate that puts crimes over the residential population, although broadly useful, says little about risk to particular citizens or groups of citizens. A crime rate based on a class of crime that is unique to a population, an activity, or a location says something tangible to the reader. Crime classifications should be changed to emphasize populations and activities with which citizens can relate as much as these classifications emphasize the nature of the criminal acts.

Principal among these classifications would be the distinction between crimes involving intimates and acquaintances and those involving strangers. The stereotypic crime event is one that occurs in public places among strangers, and it is important that we distinguish between crimes that conform to that stereotype and those that do not. Stereotypic crime is what we are afraid of and what we demand that our police address, whereas crimes among person who know each other are more complex and require different responses. A crime classification that makes this distinction plain would be useful in communicating risk to the public.[7]

A second useful distinction that should be emphasized in crime classification is that between crimes occurring in public as opposed to private places. Traditionally the police are seen as unambiguously in control of and responsible for public places, although this responsibility is less clearly delineated in private places. Hence a street-crime rate and a non-street-crime rate should be figured as prominently in descriptions of the crime problem as the UCR Index crimes.

---

[7] Michael Rand made an attempt to use the NCVS in this manner with his 1982 BJS Bulletin, *Violent Crime by Strangers*.

A third useful crime classification would feature crime by activity at the time of victimization.[8] The NCVS asks questions about the activity of the victim at the time of the incident, and responses to these questions can be loosely grouped into four activity domains – home, school, work, and leisure. These domains encompass much of the activity in which people engage during an average day, and it would be informative to know which of these activities is most dangerous. Moreover, the responsibility for social control varies across these domains, with public and private organizations having the principal responsibility at school and at work, citizens at home, and the police in the leisure domain. If the growth in crime is concentrated in one of these domains, then we have a much better idea of what our response to that problem should be. With current crime classifications, all of this is invisible.

The activity-based crime classification poses a denominator problem because not all people are engaged in each activity. Rate estimation will require making this distinction. The NCVS does identify persons who are in the labor force and persons who attend school. One can assume that everyone is home at some point during the 24-hour day and also has some involvement in leisure. At minimum, then, one can identify who is in the numerator of the activity-specific victimization rates. Unfortunately, comparison of rates across activity domains requires taking account of time in that activity domain and not just participation. Time-budget studies are routinely done to assess the amount of time residents spend in various activities (Robinson, 1997). These data can be combined with NCVS data to get rates based on person hours in the activity. If this is not feasible or desirable, then time-budget questions could be built into the NCVS.

Although each of these crime classification systems has a different principal-defining dimension (e.g., relationship between victim and offender or activity), they all include some distinction regarding the nature of the criminal act. At minimum, the subclassifications would distinguish violent crime from property crime. Some distinctions as to the seriousness of injuries and the amount of property loss would also

---

[8] BJS has published reports on crime at work or crime at school, but it has yet to juxtapose crime rates by activity domain in any routine reports.

be made, but these would clearly be secondary to the major dimensions just noted.

Arguably, some of the information imparted by these proposed alternative crime classifications could be obtained by taking traditional crime class, like the Index crimes, and examining the distributions of these crime classes across population subgroups. The limitation with such a strategy would be that it still elevates criminal behavior over other aspects of crime events, however. The purpose of our proposed alternative crime classifications is to highlight features of crime events that are neglected in traditional crime classification. As long as the ICC has preeminence, it will overshadow more useful and enlightening ways to look at crime. As the technological limitations that drove the Index are removed, we should begin to wean ourselves from this antiquated typology and phase in other classifications to take advantage of current data collection advances and to serve more sophisticated data needs.

Whenever changes are proposed in major statistical systems such as a change in the major event classification scheme, the issue of series continuity is raised. The NCVS and especially the UCR have long time series in which many of the definitions and procedures used in each system have remained reasonably constant over time. This continuity permits the analysis of these data over long periods of time and gives us the ability to examine the effects on crime of gradual but extensive changes in major social institutions (Baumer et al., 2003). Any change to crime classifications runs the risk of disrupting the series and limiting our ability to conduct these long-term analyses. This risk can be minimized if the phasing in of new indicators is done appropriately. Certain classes of crime currently included in the Index could be retained going forward so that continuity is maintained, but they could be featured much less prominently than they are in the existing reporting program.

The very different capabilities of each series that often complicate the study of divergence can be sources of complementarity. The fact that the NCVS can be disaggregated in many ways complements the highly aggregated UCR. The availability of the UCR to provide information on small units of geography complements the largely national focus of the sample-based NCVS. We can improve our understanding of the crime problem by celebrating the differences between the two systems rather than disguising them. Alternative crime classifications that are different yet complementary across the system will announce this change in strategy. The steps we have outlined in this section are easily accomplished within the confines of the existing systems. In the next section, we suggest some more substantial changes in the collection of crime statistics that would improve the system and enhance the complementarity of its component parts.

CHANGING THE NCVS AND UCR TO ENHANCE COMPLEMENTARITY IN THE LONG RUN

The foregoing section outlined some steps that could be taken immediately to foster the idea of complementary uses of the NCVS and the UCR. These steps could be taken immediately and without major changes to the nature and organization of either system. Here we suggest actions that would involve more fundamental shifts in the goals and organization of these series.

When the major role of victimization surveys was to monitor the assessment of crime provided by police statistics, it was acceptable – and even desirable – for the NCVS and the UCR to function independently. This independence will always be the case to some extent. But as police statistical systems improve, as police perceptions of collecting statistics change, as researchers learn more about the victim survey method, and as the public perceptions of surveys change, the relationship between the NCVS and the UCR should be reassessed. Specifically, we may want to consider creating a system of crime statistics rather than simply having two statistical series dealing with crime. The difference between a systemic approach and a parallel structure approach concerns the level of cooperation and coordination between the two statistical series. A statistical system would clearly articulate a set of goals, identify a set of routine and episodic indicators, and allocate the task of collecting the required information to the range of available collection vehicles. To design and implement properly a system of crime statistics would take a great deal of careful thought as well as substantial research and development work. In this section, our goal is much more modest. Here we simply identify some of the

lessons learned from the contributions to this volume and how they
might guide the development of a system of crime statistics.

Possible Goals and Indicators

A system of crime statistics should provide a picture of crime that
is useful for identifying the volume of the crime problem, how it is
changing over time, and how it is distributed across space and the
population. This information will enable the public and policy makers
to see if some places or groups are in need of assistance relative to some
standard. Such a standard could be another area, the same area over
time, a theoretically or normatively derived standard, or even another
social problem such as accidents. A standard allows statistics to have
immediate meaning and context. For example, comparing the crime
rates of Washington, D.C., to a comparable city like Boston or even to
itself the year before allows researchers, policy makers, and the public
to understanding whether the crime problem is improving or not. The
periodicity of this information can vary as well but, because budgeting
and other matters are done on an annual cycle, annual estimates would
be the most desirable unit of time on which to present this information,
but this could vary for different components of the crime problem. The
geographic or jurisdictional unit for which estimates are made can also
vary, but national estimates would be given priority followed by local
estimates.

The scope of crime covered in a crime statistics system should be
determined by normative judgments about which violations of the law
are most significant as well as whether the collection vehicles available
can provide high-quality data on these crime types. As the foregoing
discussion of crime classification indicated, the ICC can no longer be
the only or even the preeminent social indicator of the crime problem.
New crime classes must be developed that are more informative about
the nature and change in nature of the crime problem. Without going
into the specifics of these crime classes, it seems clear that they should
go beyond those classes of crime that are serious in terms of their
durable harms to individuals and give more attention to the social
harm resulting from certain criminal acts. For example, hate crime,
domestic violence, or even public order crimes may have more import
than an aggravated assault because of their effect on collectivities that

are important for social control. High-volume acts with relatively little individual harm that undermine communities and families may have more impact than the typical theft or burglary. This idea is consistent with order maintenance policing and other more recent trends in criminal justice.

Some decisions should also be made regarding the treatment of commercial crime. Crimes against commercial entities could be treated as a private matter that need not be included in publicly funded indicators of crime. Alternatively, a statistical system could be used to expand our interest in commercial entities as offenders as in the case of fraud. Currently we have little information on these classes of crime involving fraud and commercial entities, and what we do have is inconsistently collected.

The earlier discussion of the interrelationship of the NCVS and the UCR suggests an evolution in the division of labor between the two systems from one that emphasizes the parallel nature of the two series exclusively to one that gives more weight to their complementarity. *Parallel systems* refers to making the two series as similar as possible in scope, definitions, and procedures so that they can be compared. This is advantageous if the principal purpose of the statistical series is to monitor police service. If the two systems are truly parallel, then any differences between the two systems must come from the citizens reporting crime to the police and police recording of crimes reported to them. Systems designed to be complementary could be different in scope, procedure, and definition as long as each illuminated some part of the crime problem in a way that the other did not. This emphasis is useful, if the principal purpose of the statistics is to enhance our understanding of crime trends rather than monitor police service. Both goals are important, but the relative emphasis given one or the other goal will influence the choices made regarding the adequacy of current statistical systems and their evolution over time.

Our discussion in this last chapter assumes that the goals of monitoring and enlightenment are coequal, while the assumption during the formative stages of the NCVS emphasized monitoring and, therefore, parallelism. This emphasis may have been appropriate when the victim survey method was new. At that time, the "dark figure" was in dispute and police and their statistics were regarded with suspicion. It is not clear that this situation, especially concerning police administrative data, is currently the case. As Rosenfeld and others have shown, police recording of reported crime has improved steadily over the past 30 years. The reporting of crimes to the police has increased somewhat but stayed relatively stable. Although the definition of the crime problem should never be left entirely in the hands of the police, it may be time to reduce the monitoring function of the survey and place even more emphasis on ways to make the two series complementary than was proposed in the previous section.

Allocating Information Collection Tasks to Vehicles
Once the goals of this crime statistics system are in place with an increased emphasis on enlightenment and, therefore, complementarity, the responsibility for collecting the requisite information must be assigned to various organizations and collection vehicles. This allocation should be made with an eye toward using the vehicle or vehicles that would provide the most accurate and useful information on the crime of interest. Allocation should also be performed in a manner that would provide maximum complementarity not only in collecting all of the requisite information but also in doing so in an efficient manner.

An illustration of this concept can be seen in the BJS correctional statistics that were developed largely by Allen Beck. These statistics suggest what a "systemic" approach to a statistical system would look like with respect to collection efficiency. The system is composed of four data collections: (1) National Prisoners Statistics (NPS), which provide facility-level counts of prisoners on a given day every year; (2) the National Corrections Reporting Program (NCRP), which provides transaction- and inmate-level data for admissions and releases each year; (3) the Census of State Adult Correctional Facilities (CSACF), which collects data on all correctional facilities on populations and policies every five years; and (4) the Survey of Inmates of State and Federal Institutions (SISFCI), which asks a sample of inmates in correctional facilities about their crime, the conditions of confinement, and other matters of interest. These data collections are interrelated in that each has a set of functions that are different from but complementary of the others, and, taken as a whole, they provide a much richer picture of the correctional population than would be possible without one of the other of these collections. The NPS provides aggregate counts of prisoners by a few important characteristics that allow BJS to make statements annually about the size of the stock of prisoners and its change over time. The NCRP permits annual estimates of the flow of prisoners in and out of state correctional facilities on an annual basis. The CSACF provides detailed aggregate information on inmate populations and agency policies and problems every five years. The CSACF also serves as the sampling frame for the SISFCF that is conducted at approximately five-year intervals a year or so after the CSACF. The SISFCF collects detailed information on the stock of prisoners that is highly disaggregatable and can be used to provide a large number of reports describing the inmate population and its change over time. Together these data collections offer a picture of the stock and the flows in the prison population on an aggregate basis annually and in highly disaggregate form every five years; the data relate to the entire population for some reports and on samples for others when the level of detail is too great for collection in every correctional facility. They truly are a statistical system.

In an earlier section of this chapter, we argued that statistical series can complement each other if each series offers different views of the same crime or if each series offers a view of different crimes. This framework is still useful for organizing long-term efforts at building a crime statistics system. There are a number of areas in which the NCVS and the UCR (and perhaps other statistical series) should be used jointly to describe a specific component of the crime problem. There are other areas in which one of the series should shoulder the burden of providing statistics for a particular type of crime and the other series should not.

Different Views of the Same Crime
As we noted earlier, one of the functions of victim surveys is to monitor police recording and response to crime. Researchers and policy makers will still want to know how much of matters regarded as crime by the public are not reported to the police and, of those that are reported, how many are not recorded as such by the police. Victim surveys are one of the few ways that we can monitor the police. To

that end, a systemic approach to crime data would continue to devote a certain proportion of the NCVS to producing estimates of crimes using definitions and procedures as comparable as possible to those of police record systems. Crimes such as burglary and robbery can be accurately and similarly measured in both series.

A systemic approach to crime data could also build on the idea of complementarity and use one series to supplement the other when there are known difficulties in measurement in both series. Several of the chapters in this volume have shown that nonstereotypic assault is simply difficult to measure. Certain events or certain populations are left out, are overrepresented in one series and not in the other, or are underrepresented in both. In these instances, it would be useful to consider some form of dual frame or composite estimator to merge data from each series to produce a single estimation of the level of change in level in crime. Dual-frame estimation is useful to remedy undercoverage by a particular sampling frame (Curvian and Roe, 2004). For example, dual frames are employed when empanelling juries, where both motor vehicle registration lists and voter rolls are used to identify persons eligible for jury duty. Although each frame omits some eligible jurors, the overlap in undercoverage is minimal. The resulting estimates using both sources are much more representative of the eligible juror population. Composite estimators are calculated using data from two or more sources. Projections of voting behavior often use composite estimators in which the estimate of the percent of the vote for a given candidate is a combination of exit poll data and administrative records data on the voting history of the precinct (Edison Media Research and Mitofsky International, 2004). Dual-frame and composite estimation would require a high degree of coordination among the two series, but they do offer the possibility of better estimates of the crime problem.

Sources of data for dual frame or composition estimation need not be restricted to the NCVS and the UCR.[9] As several of the foregoing

9 Another resource is NIBRS. When NIBRS achieves greater coverage of the U.S. population, it could be used in conjunction with the NCVS to provide estimates of relatively rare crime events; these estimates would be more reliable than those produced by either series alone. The ability to disaggregate both police administrative data and survey data by type of crime and attributes of victims and social contexts offers greater opportunity for joint estimation.

chapters show, counting assaults, and especially assaults that do not involve weapons and do not conform to crime stereotypes, is not easy. Respondents and recorders employ very different definitions of these crimes, and these definitions are in flux. We know from the growing literature on violence against women that many of these events are not considered crimes by the victims and so they are not reported to the crime survey or the police (Koss, 1986; Tjaden, 2000). Asking respondents to recall these events in the context of a "crime" survey may complicate eliciting mentions of these incidents. It may be more useful to attempt to enumerate these crimes in an omnibus "harms" survey where one begins with identifying "harms" of any sort and then attempts to determine the origin or source of the harm, including intentional harm as a result of criminal victimization. This would reduce underreporting of crimes because respondents will not eliminate nonstereotypic crime events from their memory search and would not require that these crimes be reported and recorded by the police. The estimate of rape and sexual assault could be an amalgam of the NCVS estimate and that from the harms survey.

Providing Views of Different Crimes

A systemic approach to crime data also could provide an opportunity to obtain information on crimes not currently captured in the existing parallel structure. Dividing the labor between the two series is difficult in part because of the legacy of the monitoring goals of the series and the resulting need for parallel designs. It is also complicated by the need for new crime classifications. Assigning responsibility for specific types of crime is difficult when the range of crime types has not been articulated. For our purposes, we assume that the ICC or some form of this crime classification will persist and suggest ways of allocating these crimes to different collection vehicles. With respect to new crime classes, we have suggested some directions that crime classification might take, and we use these suggestions to shape our discussion of who might be responsible for collecting the information necessary to define these crime classes.

Allocating Responsibility for the ICC. There has been a willingness to depart from the principle of parallelism with respect to the NCVS and the UCR in the case of homicide. The UCR has responsibility for collecting data on homicides and the NCVS does not because of the difficulty of collecting these data in self-report surveys. The idea of allocating responsibility to each series according to its ability to collect high-quality data on that crime is not new, and we expand on this logic. As demonstrated in this volume, crimes that are serious and well reported to the police are well captured in police administrative records and should be the responsibility of the UCR. Crimes that are not well reported to the police but are reasonably well captured in self-report surveys should be the responsibility of the NCVS. Using these principles, we would argue that the UCR should be responsible for motor vehicle theft, and that NCVS should be responsible for theft other than motor vehicles.

Motor vehicle theft is well reported to the police and could easily be dropped from the ongoing NCVS without affecting knowledge of this component of the crime problem. Theft (other than motor vehicle theft) is not particularly well reported to the police. It is a large and heterogeneous class of events that respondents are willing to report to interviewers. Non–motor vehicle theft is an ideal candidate for collection in a sample survey. Moreover, surveys can easily capture contextual information on these theft events that can be useful in separating the important events from those that are less consequential. Although theft is a high-volume crime, it is not clear how important it is in the allocation of police resources. With the demise of full-service departments, much of police attention to thefts involves certification of the occurrence of the event for insurance reimbursement purposes. This is often done by mailing forms rather than sending units to the scene. Given these changes in police priorities, it is not clear how assiduous the police are in collecting accurate information on these events and whether police administrative data should be the principal vehicle for collecting data on this type of crime.

In comparison, the collection of data on serious nonlethal violence (i.e., rape, robbery, and aggravated assault) as well as burglary should be shared. Serious nonlethal violence should be shared, in part, because of the importance of these classes of crime for public perceptions of safety as well as for crime-specific reasons. Robbery is captured reasonably well in both systems and is, therefore, important for monitoring purposes. Aggravated assault and rape are not captured well in either system, so multiplicity – not just with these two series but possibly others – is required to get good estimates of these crimes. Responsibility for burglary would also be shared between the systems because of the importance of this crime for the monitoring function.

Allocating Responsibility for New Classes of Crime. The suggestions made for new classes of crime involve giving greater importance in the definition of crime classes to attributes of the crime event other than the behavior that constitutes the criminal act. Given the aggregate nature of the UCR and the absence of information on the attributes of victims, offender, and the crime event, the UCR summary system will have almost no role in the collection of data for new classes of crime. NIBRS, on the other hand, could figure prominently in the collection of information necessary to define new classes of crime.

We have suggested a commercial crime index or classification to feature more prominently crimes against commercial establishments. NIBRS should be used to produce this indicator because the self-report survey method has been shown to be not particularly well suited to collecting this information. As Rennison and Rand note (Chapter 2), in the early 1970s, the Justice Department fielded victim surveys of commercial establishment to estimate the volume of crimes against businesses. For a variety of reasons including the difficulty of getting and maintaining a good sampling frame and the effects of respondent selection in an establishment survey, these surveys were discontinued (Penick and Owens, 1978). Although the BJS has conducted a more recent pilot survey of commercial establishments, it is unclear that conditions have changed to make these surveys more viable. For this reason, a fully implemented NIBRS should be the vehicle of choice to collect information for this type of crime.

Crime could also be classified according to the activity of the victim at the time of the incident. If such a classification of crime were adopted, it would seem to be more suited to a survey vehicle than police administrative records, largely because certain activity domains are semiprivate, with the result that a large proportion of the crimes occurring in these domains are not reported to the police. In schools, for example, there are procedures for dealing with minor crimes such that these events are reported to school officials rather than the police. The same is true in workplaces. In addition, surveys can easily ask questions about whether respondents participate in activity domains and about the intensity of their participation and thereby provide denominators for the activity-specific rates. Denominators for these rates would need to be generated elsewhere, if administrative records were used to estimate these rates. For example, the police could identify crimes that occurred in workplaces in their jurisdictions but another organization would need to provide the counts of persons in workplaces in that jurisdiction in order to compute a rate for crime at work.

The responsibility for estimating rates of crime among strangers and intimates as a separate crime classification may also be open to differential allocation across the two series, but this is less clear than for activity domain classification. The common wisdom is that crimes among intimates are often viewed as private matters and not reported to the police, but this has been shown to be an oversimplification. Consequently this responsibility may best be shared between the two series.

One additional feature of a system of crime statistics worthy of note in allocating tasks to vehicles is the issue of keeping current with the changing nature of crime. Earlier in this chapter, we lamented the fact that there have been so few revisions of the statistical series on crime. Other statistical series, such as those in the economic area, are updated more routinely to keep pace with a changing economy. Occupation classifications, for example, must be revised as new industries are created and old ones disappear. The same is true for the "shopping basket" that is used to measure inflation in the Consumer Price Index (CPI). New products are added routinely. Keeping our statistical series on crime up-to-date is complicated by the need to maintain series continuity and preserve the integrity of year-to-year change estimates. Any changes in series run the risk of introducing error into these change estimates. To date, the emphasis has disproportionately been on maintaining series continuity, but it may be time for change in this priority.

The responsibility of keeping current on crime problems by including new types of crime would seem to fall largely to the NCVS. We argue this because the NCVS can be changed more quickly than the either the UCR summary system or the NIBRS. Supplements to the NCVS can be fielded in about 18 months whereas changes in the UCR summary system (such as converting to NIBRS) occur in geological time. One of the reasons that the UCR has been so resistant to change is the difficulty of making these changes. Recall that the UCR is a census and largely a voluntary system; both of these circumstances make change exceedingly slow. There are limits in what can be done with the NCVS. Changes of content in the survey must be done in ways that minimize the disruption to the ongoing statistical series. This is not always easy or possible. The NCVS has implemented a number of supplements without apparent ill effect on annual estimates, so this supplement format seems like a reasonable way to stay current while minimizing series disruption.

This discussion of ways to transform the NCVS and UCR into a true system of crime statistics is intended not to be a comprehensive road map for change but to draw attention to what we consider the imperatives for moving crime statistics in the United States to a new level. Our examination of divergence between the NCVS and the UCR has made apparent the tendency to view the series as separate entities and not part of a larger whole. This parallel structure may have been useful at one time, but it does not seem appropriate today. The concept of complementarity naturally leads to thinking about how the NCVS and the UCR should coordinate their efforts in a more systematic way. Our discussion is offered as a way to provoke more careful and comprehensive consideration of these issues.

CONCLUSION

Rethinking our system of crime statistics is warranted at this time because our statistical series on crime are under attack and need to be defended. This attack comes not from clearly identified "enemies" but from general indifference. Almost two decades of dropping crime has lessened the salience of crime as an issue and the attention to statistical series that deal with crime. This indifference is coupled with a general decay in government statistical systems. The interaction of these forces is having a devastating effect on our crime statistics.

As the authors in this volume have pointed out, many festering problems exist in our two statistical series on crime. The UCR has undergone a number of changes, including the implementation of NIBRS and the rise and fall of state programs. The result has been substantial increases of missing data over time and unknown effects on the quality of the data. The NCVS, in turn, has been buffeted by cost increases from the Census Bureau without commensurate increases in BJS's budget. This resource depletion has led to deep sample cuts such that in 2004 change estimates could only be made for two-year averages rather than on an annual basis. Rennison and Rand (this volume) identify other cuts in the survey that affect the quality of the data. This instability in both systems needs an infusion of funds to stop it. BJS's budget for the NCVS should increase as the costs from Census increase. The FBI is a voluntary system that has relied on the largesse of local police agencies for its data for decades, and it may be time for the FBI to shoulder some of these costs to stem the tide of nonparticipation.

Although these problems have been more than a decade in the making, few are paying attention, and no one appears motivated to ameliorate the situation. As researchers dependent on accurate and ongoing crime data, it behooves us at this time to take stock of our statistical series to understand the crisis facing the UCR and NCVS and the necessity to do something about it. At some point, the current decline in crime will end, and crime policy will once more return to center stage. Without careful tending to the existing crime data sources, researchers and policy makers will reach out for information on the crime problem only to find that none is there or that what is available is of such poor quality as to be useless.

References

Addington, L. A. (2005). "Disentangling the effects of bounding and mobility on reports of criminal victimization." *Journal of Quantitative Criminology* 21:321–343.

Baumer, E., Felson, R., & Messner, S. (2003). "Changes in police notification for rape." *Criminology* 41:841–872.

Biderman, A. D., & Cantor, D. (1984, August). "A longitudinal analysis of bounding, respondent conditioning and mobility as a source of panel bias in the National Crime Survey." Presented at the American Statistical Association, Social Statistics Section, Philadelphia.

Biderman, A. D., Cantor, D., & Reiss, A. J. (1982). "A quasi-experimental analysis of personal victimization in the National Crime Survey." *Proceedings of the American Statistical Association, Section on Survey Methods* (pp. 516–521). Washington, DC: American Statistical Association.

Biderman, A. D., & Lynch, J. P. (1991). *Understanding crime incidence statistics: Why the UCR diverges from the NCS.* New York: Springer-Verlag.

Blumstein, A., & Wallman, J. (2005). *The crime drop in America.* New York: Cambridge University Press.

Cantor, D., & Lynch, J. P. (2005). "Exploring the effects of changes in design on the analytical uses of the NCVS data." *Journal of Quantitative Criminology* 21:293–319.

Claritas, Inc. (2005). *American Red Cross: Customer segmentation pumps new life into blood donation efforts.* San Diego, CA: Author.

Currivan, D. B., & Roe, D. J. (2004, May). *Using a dual frame sampling design increase the efficiency of reaching population subgroups in a telephone survey.* Paper presented at the Annual Meetings of the American Association of Public Opinion Researchers, Phoenix, AZ.

Edison Media Research and Mitofsky International. (2004). *Evaluation of Edison-Mitofsky Election System 2004.* Washington, DC.

Henderson, N. (2005, October 8). "Storms took toll on jobs in September: Unemployment rate up to 5.1%." *Washington Post*, p. D01.

Hubble, D., & Wilder, B. E. (1988). "Preliminary results from the NCVS CATI experiment." *American Statistical Association Proceedings of the Survey Research Section.* Washington, DC: American Statistical Association.

Kelling, G., & Wilson, J. Q. (1982, March). "Broken windows: The police and public safety." *Atlantic Monthly*, pp. 1–10.

Kinderman, C., Lynch, J. P., & Cantor, D. (1997). *The effects of the redesign on victimization estimates: Data brief.* Washington, DC: Bureau of Justice Statistics.

Koss, M. (1996). "The measurement of rape victimization in crime surveys." *Criminal Justice and Behavior* 23:55–69.

Langan, P., & Durose, M. (2004, December). *The remarkable drop in crime in New York.* Paper presented at the meeting of Italy's National Institute of Statistics.

Lauritsen, J. (2001). "The social ecology of violent victimization: Individual and contextual effects." *Journal of Quantitative Criminology* 17:3–32.

Lauritsen, J., & Schaum, R. J. (2005). *Crime and victimization in the three largest metropolitan areas, 1980–1998.* Washington, DC: Bureau of Justice Statistics.

Lynch, J. P. (2002). *Trends in juvenile offending: An analysis of victim survey data.* Washington, DC: Office of Juvenile Justice Delinquency Prevention.

Lynch, J., & Jarvis, J. P. (2003, November). *Exploring the sources of non-response in the Uniform Crime Reports.* Paper presented at the Annual Meetings of the American Society of Criminology, Denver, CO.

Lynch, J., & Jarvis, J. P. (2005). Towards an error profile of the Uniform Crime Reports: Assessing the magnitude of missing data and the effects of imputation. Unpublished manuscript, John Jay College, New York.

Maltz, M. (1999). *Bridging the gaps: Estimating crime rates from police data.* Washington, DC: Bureau of Justice Statistics.

Mankewi, N. G., & Matthew W. (2004). *Dynamic scoring: A back of the envelope guide* (Working Paper 11000). Cambridge, MA: National Bureau of Economic Research.

McCleary, R., Nienstedt, B. C., & Erven, J. M. (1982). Uniform Crime Reports as organizational outcomes: Three time series experiments. *Social Problems* 29:361–372.

Penick, B., & Owens, M. (1976). *Surveying crime.* Washington, DC: National Academy Press.

Prewitt, K. (2003). *Politics and science in census taking.* Washington, DC: Population Research Bureau.

Robinson, J. P. (1997). *Time for life: The surprising way that Americans use their time.* College Park: Pennsylvania State University Press.

Simmons, J., & Dodd, T. (2003). *Crime statistics England and Wales, 2002/2003.* London: Home Office.

Taylor, R. B. (2001). *Breaking away from broken windows: Baltimore neighborhoods and the nationwide fight against crime, grime, fear, and decline.* Boulder, CO: Westview Press.

Tjaden, P., & Thoennes, N. (1998). *Prevalence, incidence and consequences of violence against women: Findings from the National Survey of Violence Against Women.* Washington, DC: National Institute of Justice.

Wiersema, B., McDowall, D., & Loftin, C. (August, 2000). *Comparing metropolitan area estimates of crime from the NCVS and UCR.* Paper presented at the Joint Statistical Meetings, American Statistical Association, Indianapolis, Indiana.

Index

Other books in the series *(continued from page iii)*